D0983323

Subversion and

Social Change in Colombia

INSTITUTE OF LATIN AMERICAN STUDIES
COLUMBIA UNIVERSITY

Subversion and Social Change in Colombia

ORLANDO FALS BORDA

Translated by
JACQUELINE D. SKILES

ST. FRANCIS SEMINARY
SALZMANN
LIBRARY
Milwaukee, Wis. 53207

NEW YORK AND LONDON
COLUMBIA UNIVERSITY PRESS
1969

This book, a translation of the first Spanish edition,
published in 1967, has been revised by the author on the
basis of the 1968 Spanish edition.

Copyright © 1969 Columbia University Press
Library of Congress Catalog Card Number: 69-19458
Printed in the United States of America

To Camilo Torres Restrepo

The Institute of Latin American Studies of Columbia University was established in 1961 in response to a national, public, and educational need for a better understanding of the nations of Latin America and a more knowledgeable basis for inter-American relations. The major objectives of the Institute are to prepare a limited number of North Americans for scholarly and professorial careers in the field of Latin American studies, to advance our knowledge of Latin America through an active program of research by faculty, by graduate students, and by visiting scholars, and to improve public knowledge through publication of a series of books on Latin America. Some of these studies are the result of research by the faculty and by graduate students. It was also decided to include in this series translations from Portuguese and Spanish of important contemporary books in the social sciences and humanities.

Subversion and Social Change in Colombia by Orlando Fals Borda is one of these translations; it was published in 1967 in Colombia (Ediciones Tercer Mundo) with the title *La Subversión en Colombia; El Cambio Social en la Historia*. This book, however, is something more than a mere translation. It was written during the academic year of 1966–1967 when Dr. Fals Borda, Professor of Sociology at the National University of Colombia, was Visiting Professor of Sociology in the Institute of Latin American Studies at Columbia University. This book is thus a translation from Spanish of an important contemporary book by a well-known Latin American sociologist, but it is also, at least in part, a product of the on-going research program of the Institute of Latin American Studies. We are grateful to Mrs. Jacqueline Skiles for her skillful translation of this important book. The publication program of the Institute of Latin American Studies is made possible by financial assistance from the Ford Foundation.

Preface

I HAD primarily one concern in writing this book, the future of Colombia. Although it is in many ways a privileged country that was at one time capable of self-development and was outstanding for its progressive and heroic people, during this century Colombia has undergone a melancholy change. Through a series of collective frustrations, "Colombia the beautiful" found itself caught in a web of spiritual, economic, and political deformations. A disaster of this sort commands our attention and ought to engender concern not only among the ruling classes whose decisions are responsible for the change, but also among those social scientists whose mission it is to fathom the meaning of past events as well as of those that are to come.

The dilemma is of such complexity that there is no solution other than to examine the situation with new objectivity, derived from the application of the scientific method to problematic and conflicting expressions of reality. As a general rule, objectivity has until now been linked to the study of "middle-range" problems in which techniques of cross-sectional analysis have been used to determine functional situations in social systems. In the case at hand, owing to the acuteness and pressing nature of the conflict, the problem that the social scientist has formulated for himself carries within it a certain tendency to seek solutions, to suggest alternatives, and even to admonish and call to action, as do indeed occur in this book in the sections referring to the present situation and its alternatives. Knowledge is coveted not as an end in itself but for the purpose of projecting for the future a better society than the one we have now.

Colombia needs to be studied from this new perspective because it must be able to move toward the future with clear objectives and at the lowest social cost. The country has paid very dearly in human lives and material resources for earlier attempts that resulted in collective frustrations, economic stagnation, and technological lag. We intellectuals and men of science of Colombia should at least sense the urgency to commit ourselves to this great task of the century—planning and supervising the building of a new society among us, a society capable of fully developing the resources of the earth and fulfilling the aspirations of those who inhabit it and work it, with special regard for the members of the poorer classes. This is the basic commitment to which it is hoped this book will lead. I have written it not only as a sociological study but also as a way of clarifying some of the historical processes that impinge upon present realities, with an eye to formulating a strategy useful for assuring the advent of that superior society to which we all aspire.

I admit, therefore, to being biased toward what Lester Ward would call "social telesis," that is, toward the acknowledgment of *purpose* inherent in social phenomena. In admitting this, I also acknowledge two concommitant elements: (1) that conflict is implicit in all strategic endeavors for collective self-improvement; and (2) that the model that emerges from the analysis of national historic processes is that of social disequilibrium. The use of this model, along with the perspective of telesis, leads to recommendation of the projective method that has been favored in works by those sociologists most genuinely interested in situations of "progress" and conflict. (See Appendix C.)

Adopting the disequilibrium model does not, of course, imply rejection of the alternative bias, that of the functionalists who follow the equilibrium model; the latter can be useful in analyzing relatively stable sectors of human society. In practice, as several authors have shown, it is fruitful to combine study of the synchronous aspects with analysis of diachronic ones. In this book an attempt has been made to follow these guide lines and to indicate the directions to be taken for carrying out similar future endeavors. Those theoretical incongruencies that occur when the same concepts are transferred literally from one framework to the other are noted only in passing.

In addition to acknowledging the technical difficulties of the task that I have set for myself, I wish to suggest that the application of the projective method within the framework of conflict and disequilibrium may call forth the ire of groups whose interests are found to be affected by the study of social change, once the mechanisms they have been employing consciously or unconsciously to dominate the rest of society are revealed.

Domination by traditional religious, political, and economic groups has been based particularly on the passive ignorance of the people. Since this is sooner or later broken down by serious sociological investigation, sociology is seen by dominant groups as a "subversive science" (for example, as was political science at the time of Bolivar's dictatorship or economics during the 1940s).

This may be the trial by fire for the social sciences in emerging countries: their effectiveness as such may be measured by their capacity to understand what is meant by the term "subversion." A sociology that is committed in this way through those who practice it may provide more contributions of consequence to society and science than the sterile or pseudo-science that is taught in some universities of Colombia under the guise of sociology. True (scientific) sociology rightly confronts the vital problems of the collectivity and does not disguise them with verbalisms. When sociology avoids the commitment that leads to situations of action and passion for fear that attacks may be directed its way by groups with vested interests, it does not even arrive at the heart of the causal explanation of historical changes. At this very point its *raison d'être* as a positive science and a true factor in the progress of nations is destroyed.

It is not superfluous, finally, to stress that the other purpose of this socio-historical outline is to better understand the nature of the intense change that is occurring today in Colombia and, by possible analogy, in other countries of the "third world." Even though this task is being carried out here within a relatively different framework, no conceptual innovations are made for their own sake nor is there any intention to proffer a new theory of social change. It is hoped, however, that the book will be read and considered as a whole because it has been systematically conceived as such and it would be a serious ethical error to cite any of its parts or to comment on them out of context. Perhaps some hypotheses of interest may be derived from the preliminary and experimental use of the integrative framework proffered in this book that will stimulate scholars to examine them more closely. This would be extremely useful because it would serve, among other things, to discard whatever in this endeavor should be left aside.

Since Latin America seems to be approaching the historical moment of its universal affirmation, we can do no less than pay strict attention to the characteristics of the present situation. In Colombia, furthermore, it is necessary to advance the alternatives that will facilitate the solution of the problems inherent to this situation, for the task of achieving the valued goals that have been set by certain leaders as well as the people themselves since 1925 is not yet completed. These are goals that have been dramatically reiterated in our times, goals that make for basic changes in a social order that continues to be unjust. This endeavor ought to shape the transcendental creative impulse that would lead to the transfiguration of Colombia.

Writing a book is not a mere act of will. This one is the result of many years of sociological and historical research combined with practical applications of hypotheses in actual situations of social change. As may be presumed, the thought herein does not derive from merely one source or school, nor is it conditioned by only one set of contacts. It reflects the stimulus that I have received from aforementioned experiences and from personal contact and discussion with colleagues from Colombia and other parts of the world. I would like to mention especially these persons in order to manifest my personal recognition of their contribution, without thus implying that they are responsible for the contents of this book.

I should mention first my companions in the university struggle and that academic and scientific creative endeavor which culminated in the founding of the former Faculty of Sociology, now a department of the Faculty of Human Sciences of the National University of Colombia. Outstanding in this group is the late Father Camilo Torres Restrepo, symbol of the "generation of *La Violencia*," whose ideological vision and consistency of character are increasingly recognized. The futile silence that has been decreed in the country concerning his life and his work on behalf of the cause of social renewal is being abundantly compensated for not only by the loyalty of the various national groups that keep his memory alive but also by the international repercussion of his life since his death in February, 1966. His principles and the story of his life have appeared along with commentaries in publications all over the world and are included in the agenda of ecclesiastical and secular meetings. These are acts of recognition that will be multiplied as time goes by. The intellectual and personal influence of Father Torres has been and will continue to be important. He was a moral subversive, the kind that blazes new paths. For this reason, dedication of this book to him is not merely an act of friendship but one of just recognition of his contribution to the understanding of the meaning of the times in which we live.

Other colleagues of the Faculty of Sociology, both Colombian and foreign, made essential contributions to the preparation of this book, especially in their criticisms of the first draft or through comments made on diverse occasions. They are María Cristina Salazar, Gerardo Molina, Jorge Garciarena, Darío Mesa, Eduardo Umaña Luna, Carlos Castillo, Cecilia Muñoz de Castillo, Rodrigo Parra, Federico Nebbia, Guillermo Briones, Tomás Ducay, Luis Ratinoff, Humberto Rojas, Alvaro Camacho, Magdalena León Gómez, and Fernando Uricoechea.

I should give equal recognition of help to Professors T. Lynn Smith (University of Florida), José A. Silva Michelena (Central University of Venezuela), Frank Bonilla (Massachusetts Institute of Technology), Celso Furtado (University of Paris), Bryce Ryan (University of Miami), Wilbert E. Moore (Russell Sage Foundation), Charles Wagley, Lewis Hanke, and Amitai Etzioni (all of Columbia University), Arthur Vidich (New School for Social Research), Kalman Silvert (Dartmouth College), A. Eugene Havens

(University of Wisconsin), Florestan Fernandes (University of São Paulo), Luis A. Costa Pinto (United Nations Institute for Training and Research), Andrew Pearse (Institute for Training and Research in Agrarian Reform, Chile), José Matos Mar (University of San Marcos, Peru), and Pablo González Casanova (Autonomous National University of Mexico). I also express my gratitude for the assistance received from the Reverends Gonzalo Castillo Cárdenas, Juan A. Mackay, and François Houtart.

Of no less importance has been the critical influence of my students at the National University of Colombia, the University of Wisconsin, and Columbia University during 1966, to whom I presented the outline formulated for this book. I was extraordinarily stimulated also during my visit to Cambridge, Massachusetts, in January, 1967 where, after my exposition of the re-evaluated concept of subversion, very helpful comments were made by, among others, Professors Gino Germani and Albert O. Hirschman (Harvard University), Everett E. Hagen (Massachusetts Institute of Technology), and Glaucio A. Dillon Soares (Latin American Faculty of Social Science, Chile).

Among my companions of intellectual debate whose ideas I have used on more than one occasion in this book, Otto Morales Benítez is outstanding. His studies on the colonization of the Quindian region, *caudillos*, and other themes of interest concerning Colombia are endeavors that we Colombians shall come to appreciate more and more.

I received important institutional support from the Land Tenure Center and the Department of Rural Sociology of the University of Wisconsin and the Institute of Latin American Studies and the Department of Sociology of Columbia University. I express my cordial thanks to the respective directors of these entities: Peter Dorner, Douglas C. Marshall, Charles Wagley, and Herbert H. Hyman.

I give my most sincere thanks also to my family and personal friends who encouraged me in this task, and no less to the dedicated secretarial helpers who patiently prepared the text for the press.

April, 1967   *Orlando Fals Borda*

Contents

Subversion and

Social Change in Colombia

INSTITUTE OF LATIN AMERICAN STUDIES
COLUMBIA UNIVERSITY

CHAPTER ONE

Subversion and Historical Purpose

ALTHOUGH the theme of the relation between order and violence is as old as civilization, the seventeenth-century scholar Thomas Hobbes is its best-known exponent. The opposite poles of the violent, primary "natural state" and the ordered "social state" are presented with dramatic force in the pages of his *Leviathan* (1651) for the purpose of expounding the reasons of community living. According to Hobbes, the community came into being in order to control the violence that would otherwise prevail among men owing to the scarcity of resources available for their survival. But the control of violence does not mean that society has been immunized against it. In fact, an order that is brought into being by means of social coercion already embodies elements sufficient to make it problematic: it is an order based on tensions and contradictions.

It is logical to expect that such a precarious social order would suffer periods of alternately greater and lesser significance, and world history confirms this. Illustrious scholars from Heraclitus to Toynbee have written about rise and decline; thesis, antithesis, and synthesis; the Yin and the Yang; light and darkness; the terrestrial world and the New Jerusalem. Human societies experience rhythms that lead from relative stability to intense change in order to arrive at another period of relative stability. The main fluctuations appear as waves arising from collective endeavors to transform society according to certain idealistic, religious, or political precepts.

In order to understand Colombian history, particularly in terms of its great fluctuations, it is necessary to describe sociologically and analyze the collective endeavors that have developed periodically for the purpose of transforming society.

Such endeavors are social movements. As such they embody their own dynamics along with the necessary mechanisms for achieving the goals that have been set. These are the goals which define the purpose of society in a given period. Thus these movements seem really to be teleological struggles that are manifested as social phenomena.

A socio-historical analysis conceived in these terms makes it possible to sharpen the study of the current general situation of conflict that characterizes life in certain regions of Colombia. It also links these situations to significant events of the historical past and leads to an anticipatory or projective concept of the phenomena studied, thus establishing the possibilities for an adequate method of prediction. This occurs because there is an implicit recognition of the *telos* or purpose of society, without which, if we are to believe Hobbes, human life cannot be understood and social organization is impossible (cf. Hegel, 1896 edition; Ward 1883).

Telos and Utopia

Unlike the processes of the organic world, those of the social world embody a fundamental *telos*. This has been a classic thesis of sociology since the days of Comte, Spencer, and Ward. Comte accepts "development" as inherent to society, leading man through successive stages toward the positivist world (Comte 1851–1854). Spencer establishes a "law of progress" that leads to liberty, security, and wealth by means of successive group differentiations (Spencer 1857). Ward speaks of a "law of aggregation" to explain the transition of the universe from a cosmogeny to a sociogeny; in the second stage man would be able to control society in order to achieve the supreme good and happiness (Ward 1883).

When these theories are divested of the mysticism that prevented their serious consideration, their basic soundness can be verified through historical events. In each of the great, periodic movements or collective endeavors that are studied in this book, for example, the goals toward which the societies have moved are readily discernible. In great part these goals have been utopian: stimulating ideals that foster action to achieve a "promised land." But the ideals are ultimately conditioned by the realities of the environment, leaving in history residues marked by the resulting tensions.

For the sociological analysis of Colombian history the concept of utopia may prove useful. Utopian ideas are found at the beginning of each of the great periods of transition studied. Once the conflicts among elements of society resulting from the introduction of a utopia have been resolved, the utopia has been conditioned and only its historical residue is left; a new and relatively stable social order appears. Yet this new order too has implicit tensions and incongruities.

Use has been made here of the theories of the sociologists of conflict (especially those of the nineteenth century, whose circumstances were similar to those of observers in today's developing countries), and theoretical support for this book has been sought from two apparently contradictory works which actually complement each other in terms of the sociology of knowledge and in the projective interpretation of history: *Ideology and Utopia* by Karl Mannheim (1941) and *Die Revolution* by the German anarchist, Gustav Landauer (1919).

Mannheim conceives of "utopia" as a complex of ideas that tend to determine actions which have as their object the modification of the prevailing social order. They are "orientations transcending reality which, when they pass over into conduct, tend to shatter . . . the order of things prevailing at the time" (1941, 169). As such, it is the opposite of "ideology," which is the complex of ideas that seek to maintain the established order or a particular social situation. *Ex hypothesi*, utopia ("nowhere") cannot be fulfilled and this leads Mannheim to postulate the existence of absolute and relative utopias. The latter are those that are partially achieved, conditioned by realities from which a portion of ideology is derived. There is a certain process of loss or *decantation* in the transition between the utopia and the realization, so that no utopia is ever fully realized. Rather, the partial realization of a utopia leaves exposed the inconsistencies, contradictions, and "hypocrisies" of human societies.

The nature of the prevailing social order is the object of Landauer's critical study. He calls such a system *die Topie*, or "topia," and establishes its characteristics as stability and authority, shaped by the traditional institutions of a particular period of time (1919, 12). The relative stability of the topia gradually disappears until disequilibrium is reached; at this point the utopia emerges to foster forms of collective action and popular ferment. However, this activity does not achieve the utopia but leads instead to a new topia, owing to the internal process of contradiction that is implicit in all human society. And thus the rhythm flows. Nevertheless, there appears a historical period during which the old topia no longer exists and the new one has not been achieved. This period of conflict and anomie is called "revolution" and leads from the relative stability of the first topia to the relative stability of the second.

Mannheim as much as Landauer is in agreement, then, that utopias are only partially fulfilled, leaving their residues in the social orders, or producing decanted relative utopias. This implies not only an evolutionary historical process but also a dialectical one, for the prevailing order permits the development of "ideas and values that contain . . . the unrealized tendencies representing the needs of each era . . . capable of destroying the prevailing order" (Mannheim 1941, 175).

While both these scholars postulated the role of a subversive minority in the inception of a utopia, neither was able to indicate which other social elements intervene in the "revolutionary" period. That is, neither discussed the elements of the process of decantation of the absolute utopia. This is a vacuum that very much deserves to be filled; Colombia, among other nations, is now in one of these periods of transition between social orders—it is desired that a four-hundred-year-old topia be discarded in order to found a new society.

A search of the literature for a specific, sociological description of this class was rather without results. Scholars tend to jump from one stage of historical development to another, pointing out that there is an acute period of transition, but without giving systematic information concerning its nature. The principal authors describe general or partial aspects of the phenomenon. Thus, for example, Marx in his analysis of the French revolution (1928 edition) and Engels in his studies of Germany and Austria (1933 edition) establish the connections between ideologies and economic groups for fostering or frustrating social movements; Ogburn describes the situations of cultural lag in the material and non-material components of a social order (1950 edition); Toynbee underscores the role of schism in the social body, the creative and dominant minorities, and the internal and external proletariat—that is, he shows the importance of social organization in the rise and decline of civilizations (1947); Sorokin points out the importance of values and ideas in social change in order to carry a society from an ideational stage to an idealistic or sensate one (1957). Surely with the work of such authors as a starting point it should be possible to derive an integrative sociological framework for ordering and systematizing observations regarding the content of transition. Similar expectations may be derived from reading the works of modern exponents of the sociology of conflict: Simmel (1908; 1955 edition), Coser (1956; 1961 edition), Munch (1956), and Dahrendorf (1958, 1959).

Ultimately, what is needed to understand the social rhythms of Colombian history is a master theory similar to that of "revolution" of Landauer. This theory should describe and analyze satisfactorily the *condition* or *situation* of the specific transition, or the configuration of the changing order during a critical period, and not merely the *processes* of change (differentiation, revolution, conflict, assimilation, acculturation, accumulation, adoption, and so forth) as currently defined, or their consequences. There is need for a "model" or mental abstraction to make possible analysis of the components of the social order as seen in a very dynamic and contradictory moment, a model that also manages to adequately systematize observations. It is necessary to "take a snapshot" of the transitional process in the sense of Bergson (1930, 327), not only to see its synchronous elements and factors but also to facilitate the understanding of the dynamic phenomenon. This would establish its cause and effect relations in the context of historical time. Such an attempt to harmonize the structural with the dynamic for the purpose of understanding a situation of change could contribute to the analysis of the society that is at hand today in Colombia, a society that tends to elude scientific analysis.

Thus if the critical period of transition is conceived as the temporal expression of an entity, a social fact in itself, the elements that lead from one social order to another may be isolated. It is important to recognize the possibilities afforded by conceiving this entity as a type of transitional society with its own form of integration, distinct from the relatively stable society from which it develops at a given historical moment. Typology of this variety has not been neglected in sociological literature, but it does not go very far; it only demonstrates the expected—namely, that rapidly changing societies reveal acute internal contradictions (see Appendix A).

On the other hand, the study of the *direction* of the transformation (which is another way of speaking of *telos*) may lead to the understanding of the problem of change in social orders in a more defined manner. The aforementioned sociologists agree that social change in moments of intense development has an inherent direction and that it has expressed collective goals. These goals determine the direction of the process, subject to the conditioning by technological, economic, or demographic elements. They form a value factor that moves society in a specific direction, leaving a mark on history.

The teleological explanation, which has had such distinguished exponents in sociology, appears to be pertinent here. It leads to the thesis of topia and utopia; for there can be no utopia or society with conscious social movements without prior goals. Specifically, it can be seen in the case of Colombia that at least three occasions have arisen producing acute, difficult transitions: (1) the missional transition whose ideology motivated the conquistadors and *doctrina* priests to change the form of local Indian life and to construct a new society through an alliance of the cross with the sword; (2) the liberal-democratic transition that was in part a reaction against the prior topia, against the "bugles and bells" (Sarmiento 1883), and that was responsible for the partial discarding for the first time of the colonial heritage; and (3) the socialist transition whose ideology appeared in Colombia after 1925 in response to the modern movements of proletariat redemption through discovery of the mechanisms of control of the means of production.

As we shall see, these three utopias ultimately underwent the process of decantation. They left behind residues in the form of social orders conditioned by collective goals or purposes that were the objectives of these utopias. A fourth period of transition seems to be taking shape in our time as the social and economic conditions of the moment combine with a more authentically American reiteration of the socialist utopia. Thus, in the present as in the past, the *telos* stands out clearly; and the endeavor to follow certain models or to achieve certain goals has led or leads to periods of acute social conflicts in which ideologies, groups, institutions, and techniques fulfill certain functions.

It is hypothesized that these periods are temporal expressions of what is considered social phenomenon in itself (Landauer's "revolution"). They serve as bridges between the realities that are residues of the decanted utopia on one hand, and that which is unrewardingly sought on the other. In other words, it is the bridge between the current social order, and that which has not yet been achieved. It is this specific structure that will receive central attention in this book, conceived of in sociological terms for the purpose of analysis. It is the social condition that is called *subversion*.

Subversion as a Moral Concept

Subversion is a condition traditionally viewed as a threat to society because it seeks to destroy society. It has been seen in this way since the time of the Romans: Caius Salustius spoke of "*subvertere leges ac libertatem*" in referring to Catalina. The idea expressed in Latin was carried over to the Romance languages (and others) whose dictionaries define "to subvert" as "to upset, ruin, disturb, overturn, destroy . . . in the moral sense, such as to subvert the social order" (Royal Spanish Academy). Thus a negative meaning for the word, connoting something evil or immoral, is preserved in all orthodox dictionaries and texts. It is used, for example, in McCarthy-type literature, anti-Communist symposia and conferences, and in general by persons who belong to the established social order and fear the action of rebellious groups. This meaning of the word has prevailed historically. It has been forgotten that those who gave origin to the word were citizens satisfied with the status quo who benefited from the existing order, albeit sometimes, like Caius Salustius, aberrant.

The orthodox definition of subversion has been formulated in such a way that it has become an element in the justification of the prevailing social order of a given historical moment. He who subverts is anti-social. Similar is the idea of heresy and heretics—whose destiny is the pyre. Thus institutions and their representatives, no less than dictionaries and academies, become the guardians of the established order with little regard for the necessity of change. They maintain the fiction of its vitality. In genuine cases of subversion and heresy it is often forgotten that many subversives and heretics have in time become the heroes of a new society and the saints of a revitalized Church. Their attitudes and beliefs have not been accepted in their own time because these threatened vested interests. With historical perspective, the anti-social elements are seen to be others: those who defend an unjust social order, believing it to be just only because it is traditional.

In reality, subversives desire to destroy only that which they consider inconsistent with their ideals and rather seek to reconstruct society according to new norms and precepts. The first rebel of this type was probably Moses, rallying his people against the tyranny of the Pharaohs. According to the Scriptures, God was the source of the legitimacy of Moses' rebellion and showed Himself in great plagues sent against the oppressors defending the existing social order. The prophetic voices of social protest in the Old Testament called attention to these subversive origins of the Jewish nation (Castillo 1967). Colombian rebel groups of 1850 and 1922 may be considered in the same light, fighting for ideals they regarded as just. They had a sincere desire to build a new society. In their own time they were seen as evil, dangerous, and even traitorous elements. Today many of their ideas are accepted, and it is recognized that the rebels were justified in holding them.

The persistence of the idea of subversion as something immoral in the face of historical evidence showing that subversion can be moral presents a problem for epistemology. A concept that loses its meaning after a certain number of years is useless or incomplete because it does not correspond to reality. This in turn reminds us that the subversive not only wants to destroy what he believes to be inconsistent with his ideals but also wishes to reconstruct society according to new moral precepts. Thus he is not a common criminal, nor does he seem so by the consensus of modern times, which tends to re-evaluate the traditional bases of all societies.

In the case of Colombia, the sociological interpretation of subversion should provide the possibility for analyzing the real situations and conditions of social conflict and the transition from one general life pattern to another, recognizing that in those patterns there may exist autonomous normative and moral complexes that are relatively accepted. To eliminate from the idea of subversion its traditional immoral ingredient is to provide a scientifically productive concept.

CHAPTER TWO

The Refraction of the Social Order

ANALYSIS of Colombian history suggests that all subversion, by its mere incidence, produces a phenomenon of break-up and redirection analogous to that of the refraction of the sun's rays passing through a prism. This refraction of the social order causes it to break up and redirect its exposed elements, thus disintegrating into its component parts and forming a different texture or structure. In order to understand the importance of this process, it is indispensable to have a clear idea of what is meant by "social order." It is also important to clarify the meaning of certain concepts that shall be employed throughout the text, such as change, development, and revolution, relating them to the central concept of subversion. Furthermore, it is advisable to establish the rules of procedure used for the study of historical periods.

The Conception of the Social Order

There are many ways of conceiving the social order and therein originates the confusion concerning it. The persistence with which the term appears, in works of the past century as well as of the present, shows that it has attributes corresponding to reality, and indicates that it may be useful as a general concept for referring to distinct patterns of life and behavior in a given region.

In the most general terms, the social order is that complex of ongoing life patterns manifested in a society during a given historical period through mechanisms formed by socio-cultural elements. This definition is too broad to be useful in sociological research; those mechanisms must be specified whose interaction in time makes it possible to perceive the existence and sense the rhythm of the social order. Concrete expressions of such mechanisms are certainly found in complexes such as agriculture, in institutions such as the church, or in groups as those of kinship. An overall examination of them may reveal a certain formal congruence from which a sense of integrity of social order may be derived. Thus, agricultural practices, the ecclesiastical institution, and the family group may be seen as social phenomena that mutually support each other. Nevertheless, within this formal congruence, unharmonious counterpoints and disruptive tendencies may be observed (Bateson 1958, 171–97).

One way of better understanding these mechanisms of formal congruence and latent disruption is to systematically objectify (or "operationalize") them, grouping them in "components" of similar mechanisms and elements. Thus, still reflecting both congruence and disharmony, the social order may be defined as those components that provide the inhabitants of a particular region with both a social self-image and an image of the world, and a style of acting, perceiving, and valuing with sufficient temporal durability to be transmitted from one generation to another (cf. Mannheim 1941, 170; Gellner 1965, 60–61). Such components are: (1) social values; (2) social norms; (3) social organization; and (4) techniques.

It should not be surprising that these components are based on the best-known and oldest concepts of sociology. Their importance is such that without them it is impossible to formulate even a simple socio-historical explanation. (Consult Appendix B for pertinent definitions.) Through various combinations of these components the sociologists of yesterday and today have been able to describe and codify the principal phenomena of community life. This ample framework is considered indispensable because it serves as a point of departure for specific theoretical developments and for working hypotheses on social change. This framework especially underscores the relativity and internal contradiction of the components of the social order; these should be conceived of and understood in the context of a specific situation. In effect, the values, norms, social organization, and techniques, as well as the concrete elements that differ from or contradict them, are historically and sociologically determined.

However, there is a certain advantage in viewing these components as basically congruent, not only because they are always found together in reality but also because they make it possible to carry out diachronic studies, using cross-sectional "flashes." Thus the components may be hierarchically ordered according to their importance in the integration of the social order. At the same time values and dominant ideas tend to saturate the other components (cf. Smelser 1962, 25–33).[1] This does not mean that the other components have no effects on the social order, especially as causes for changes in it. Particularly noticeable is the impact that the autonomous accumulation in technology may have at a given moment in stimulating reactions of a demographic or economic origin. Nevertheless, these reactions themselves must obtain the support of values and become embodied in institutions for their effect to have any permanence.

For these reasons it is advisable to avoid partial concepts of the social order, such as the idea of a "moral order" (Cooley 1902; Redfield 1957), or of the "myth of authority" (MacIver 1947, 42), or of the "rules of conduct" (Goodenough 1963, 100), as these recognize only values or norms. Nor is it satisfactory to say that the social order is a constellation of systems with relatively autonomous subsystems, because apart from duplicating the current definition of society as a larger social system, one falls into the error of *definitio ab definiendum* (Moore 1963, 15).

Subversion as a Sociological Category

According to Mannheim, under appropriate conditions, the absolute utopian statements concerning new social goals are affected by the environmental reality and produce relative utopias with their own portion of ideology. This utopia leads to the discovery and specification of the latent incongruities in the components by which the social order is articulated. Thus the utopia becomes a set of ideas and values that tends to dominate the direction that social change should take. It seeks expression in the norms and finds support in the existing social organization.

But then other phenomena emerge that lead to significant change. Conditions for change are fostered by the latent inequalities and disruptions, regional differences, crises or necessities in the economic and political institutions, by the relations of domination and dependence among nations, and even by the internal autonomous exchange between components of the social order. Furthermore, it may occur that accumulation in the technological complex produces important secondary effects.

These phenomena, in isolation or in accumulation, have consequences for the social order, and tend to cause a breakdown among its internal elements upon reaching an adequate critical point.

The impact of the conflict unleashed by the utopias has the virtue of illuminating the incongruities in the present patterns of living. Furthermore, by means of the inherent dialectical process, this impact makes it possible for a series of values, norms, institutions, and groups, along with their supporting technological elements, to maintain their rhythm and direction and to polarize around the condition or natural situation of tradition.

But owing to the internal wear-and-tear on the established order, or the defeat of its society, and to the effect of the unrealized tendencies representing the necessities and urgent demands of the era, the contrary elements, which until this time had been latent, are refracted. These elements now openly manifest themselves to challenge traditional elements. These counter-elements, which are dialectical responses to the elements of the condition of tradition, are (1) counter-values, (2) counter-norms, (3) rebel organizations, or "disorgans," and (4) technical innovations (see Appendix B).[2] They are in turn integrated and polarized among themselves, constituting a competitive condition within the body of the same society, which is called subversion.

Subversion is thus defined as that condition reflecting the internal incongruities of the social order discovered by its members during a given historical period in the light of new, valued goals. The period of subversion can be said to last from the articulation of incongruities of the prevailing order (after the impact of utopian thought in a given situation) to the emergence of the new social order (which will reflect at least partially goals of the formerly rebellious group).

The conflict that occurs under subversive conditions reveals not only regional variations but also historical types. In general, two types of subversion can be distinguished: (*a*) that produced by military-ideological conquest; and (*b*) that of mainly local or national origin. In both cases radical change in the patterns of living of a people is sought or imposed, verified within a determined period of time, having similar mechanisms and factors (see below).

Subversion has a transcendental aspect: its appearance implies contradictions of a significant enough nature to bring about the complete transformation of the social order in which they are experienced. For this reason, subversion should not be confused with simple social change. It is an index of inconsistencies and discordances of significance, going from the larger aggregations of the society to local groups and to the personality itself.

When the élan leads subversion to the appropriate point, organisms, techniques, and attitudes conducive to change are developed, producing acute perplexity, anomie, or insecurity in the patterns of social interaction. This occurs through the employment of three *mechanisms of compulsion:* political hegemony (through conquest or rebellion), leadership ability, and social diffusion from saturation by the new and dispersion of the rebel elements (further elaborated in Chapter Four). These mechanisms impose direction on social change. They are managed in turn both by traditional groups and by subversives who seek to impose their respective viewpoints and valued goals on the society.

Naturally, a sense of perplexity springs from the confrontation with values and norms. This indecision may last a long time. Nevertheless, permanent indecision is impossible because this is not a goal pursued by either subversion or tradition. The process thus leads to an anti-climax, which is a sign that the groups are seeking reconciliation. The ability with which they carry out cooptation of opponents, and the strategy employed at crucial moments in so doing, may be sufficient for imposing their respective points of view. The duration of the acute period and the anti-climax of the conflict will also depend on the vigor and persistence of the subversive elements or their opposites.

A master process of *adjustment* then begins between the condition of tradition and the condition of subversion which seeks relative stabilization in the new social order. For this purpose, not only are the compulsion mechanisms that attempt to maintain the direction of change employed, but also the *stabilizing factors* that put down roots in order that the future tradition may grow up and the survival of the transformed elements be guaranteed. The main stabilizing factors are: the socialization of development, the legitimation of coercion, ideological persistence, and technological support (see Chapter Four). Taken into account are the following: (1) the incompatibilities of the elements in conflict, their inability to impose or seek substitution, compromise, mutual tolerance, or accomodation; (2) the compatibilites of the elements to produce assimilation, amalgamation, addition, or accumulation; and (3) the capacity for diffusion, saturation, and control of the new elements at the basic levels of social integration.

During this period of adjustment, with the compulsion that accompanies it, the new topia emerges, along with the residues left by the confrontation. Then the new social order is formed. This order, transformed into a new tradition, will carry implicit within it the contradictory residues for the emergence of an eventual subversion, and the process is repeated (cf. Hegel 1896). Figure 1 shows the disintegrative impact of conflict, the utopia with its conditioners, the refraction of the social order, and the adjustment-compulsion of tradition and subversion that leads to the new social order.

The use of this theoretical scheme does not imply a tendency in Colombian history toward the periodic repetition of a cycle of change in identical sequences and without reversals. Rather, the scheme is used to try to establish the mechanisms and factors common to the four cases of intense change studied in this book since all four appear to belong to the same conceptual category of "subversion" as defined herein. But the cultural differences of each period and the different roles played by ideas and economic and social conditions in the causal chains of these changes are also acknowledged. The scheme is therefore an open one.

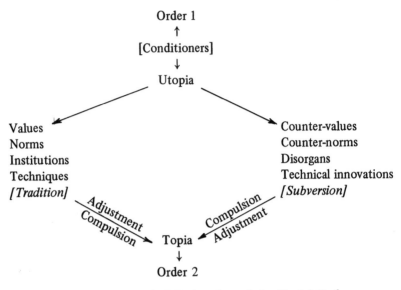

FIGURE 1. Dialectical Refraction of the Social Order

Transition and Incongruity

Not all patterns of tradition are lost during periods of subversion with their stages of destruction and reconstruction of the social order. On the contrary, even when vanquished militarily, the social order tends to endure, acquiring immunity to change and engendering *ad hoc* mechanisms that resist attempts to impose change. But this conflict itself weakens the old order, leading to more serious incongruities.

During times of subversion, the feeling grows that the norms learned during childhood do not provide a firm basis for behavior or a stable reference in cases of doubt. Traditional norms are no longer a clear answer to the questions that social processes begin relentlessly to raise for people. The incongruities appear in many guises, from breakdowns in the material culture to dislocations in the most sacred recesses of personal beliefs.

As a consequence, life becomes paradoxical and contradictory. Life in Colombia today, as in past epochs, is fraught with difficulties for rational interpretation. Even so, its contrasts have a peculiar enchantment. They provide the stimulus of the unexpected, or the spur of danger, at a time when the strong, old flavor of traditional patterns is beginning to lose its attractiveness. It is a dynamic life of very rapid change in which the old, the present, and even something of the future are mixed and in which every norm seems to have its counter-norm.

Regarding the most recent period of transition, it is merely necessary to cast a rapid look at the country's profile to discover that it is no longer shaped by the same instrument that molded the stable colonial society, even though the latter persists in many forms. So many attitudes and loyalties have been uprooted, and so many schisms have occurred in apparently monolithic institutions, erosions and collapses of personal and collective myths, that the substance of the colonial tradition stands exposed to the elements, losing what had been for four hundred years an impressive vitality. Even so, characteristics of some of these customs are still recognizable, and the roots of tradition continue to support even change.

These schisms and incongruities are observed at all levels, from national society to community and other local groups. Furthermore, great struggles develop on the level of ideas, many of which have their origins in latent divergencies or in revolutionary and utopian formulations (those of Mannheim, for example) that favor the progress of Colombian society, especially of the working classes. Professors, university students, and often the laborers and rural workers themselves, discover the inherent but hidden economic inequalities and the moral inconsistencies in the prevailing order, translate their instinctive response into action, and declare themselves in revolt. They bolt into the streets and fields in a daring gesture to dramatize their viewpoint and accelerate change, seeking the advantages of political power to enact their ideals. However, groups and individuals dedicated to the continuation of the prevailing order rush into the breach, disposed to throw themselves deeply into the struggle and to counteract the effects of subversive groups.

The incongruities become more acute when new groups and parties of revolutionary stamp appear, and at the same time the opposite, oligarchical movement, *La Mano Negra* (the Black Hand), arises. Guerrilla groups and brigades are organized to strike; but well-financed and well-equipped counter-insurgency groups also appear. Propaganda departments and committees for community action are established, and magazines and pamphlets are published for the purpose of awakening the people—only in order that they be sabotaged, subtly coopted by the other side. Or the attempts meet silence and are ended through economic pressures brought to bear against them by champions and agents of the status quo. The Christian rebellion of priests committed to "aggiornamento" occurs; and then comes the respective reaction of the local ecclesiastical institution, leveling thundering anathemas at the attackers. Both liberal and conservative vanguard intellectuals lift their voices in an opportune effort to reform the platforms of their respective parties, only to have the hierarchy respond with the silent blow of the usual maneuvers by the political machines of yesteryear.

For this reason there is talk now of a "moral crisis" and the experiencing of an acute sense of perplexity in this period of heroic anomies. There is no satisfactory answer. Furthermore, the intensity of internal conflict increases. The indices of criminal behavior go up everywhere; personal insecurity becomes more intense in both cities and rural areas; the rates of suicide, hijacking, robbery, and pilfering increase. Young people ignore the counsel of their parents, and the lack of understanding mounts inside and outside the family. Churches lose their followers, political parties their electorate, and press columnists their readers. Businessmen fight against their workers who wish to prevent the closing of factories. And as if this Hobbesian picture were not enough, the nation itself undergoes an eclipse in hemisphere affairs and is marginal in making important decisions pertaining to universal technology and culture.

Meanwhile, at the basic community and family levels, battles are also waged for and against the tradition of the social order. In many places this conflict becomes evident to the researcher with the least effort on his part: signs, for example, placed at intersections of main roads may announce such important innovations as agricultural cooperatives, and invite trucks carrying food products and manufactures from cities to rural areas to stop there. And these establishments, with their impersonal rules of operation, are located near old beer taverns, where rural quoits players, clad in ponchos, gather in old-fashioned camaraderie as did their fathers and grandfathers before them.

A short distance from the highway may be found experimental plots where government agencies, with the approval of the landowners, are making advances in their attempts to plant improved seed. Nevertheless, these same landowners, apparently so receptive to change, have other plots a short distance away where they reverently bow to tradition and continue to sow as though they were unacquainted with any technical agency.

If the visitor were invited to sleep in one of the peasant homes— some of which have both the traditional straw roof and the durable asbestos tile manufactured in the city—he would be surprised to find on the wall, beside the sacred effigies, the carefully framed university diploma, witness to the course on community development attended by the eldest son. On a night table is an unusual interloper, the transistor radio. At the break of day as the family prepares to get up to resume its daily work, an irreverent mixture can be heard: the rhythmic prayer of the awakening grandmother contrasting with a Mexican ballad blaring from the radio turned on by the young grandson who stretches in the dim light.

This typical young man may be the victim of internal incongruities and conflicts of which he is hardly aware. For example, although he accepts the mechanical reality of the radio, he will continue to sprinkle with salt the water that has just gushed into a new well, thinking that this act will magically guarantee that the water will continue to come forth. He hopes to become a chauffeur or a mechanic and to see the world; but he is also influenced by his desire not to lose the security of his niche in the community. He takes with him attitudes of the rural man that are no longer efficacious. While laughing at the phantoms that the electric light dispels, he continues to believe in the river spirits, which he now conceives of as black locomotives and not as gigantic animals of gold in which he believed before.

In short, it is easy to see that such incongruities may be observed in family relationships (especially in the conflicts of generations), in the interpretation of natural phenomena, in the differences in agricultural techniques, and even in individual personalities. Of course the examples given are partial ones; they do not stress sufficiently that in the same places persist values which are related to traditional economic, political, religious, and educational institutions which reduce the speed of change. However, it is important to register not only the saturating tendency of change for all institutions but also the often discordant acceptance of the new within the old. Beliefs and deeds that in past decades would have evoked strong protest are today accepted as part of the nature of things. People seek the accomodation that will enable them to continue the routine of life within the new and unstable cultural patterns. Some achieve a certain measure of accommodation; others experience psychological or social tensions.

Incongruity, discordance, inconsistency, anomie, and moral crisis are thus the attributes of the situation of conflict which many people of Colombia are experiencing. It is a process of disintegration of the established order and creation of a new society in which all are voluntarily or involuntarily involved, those in the forefront and the laggards, the distrustful and the daring, the old and the young. It is a process that often cannot be understood or even felt because of one's own involvement in the rhythm of its encompassing dynamic. But it leaves its mark on almost all customs and beliefs.

Change, Development, and Revolution

The ideas of change, development, and revolution mentioned on previous pages will also be used later, and so merit a brief treatment for the purpose of relating them to the conceptual framework that has been adopted.

Social change, the generic category under examination here, is immanent in society by virtue of its existence (Sorokin 1957, Chaps. 38 and 39). It may be endogenous or exogenous, according to the unit to which it is attributed; and according to the degree of intentionality it is spontaneous (unanticipated) or guided (planned) (Moore 1963, 29–30). Change follows "normal" courses with latent and unconscious effects while a social order prevails and is capable of reaching evolutionary stages of great import (Sahlins and Service 1960). Only when change accelerates or modifies its usual course does it become in part a conscious act and begin to acquire a definite meaning. The quality of guided change is not even necessarily subversive; it may be promoted within appropriate limits by agencies or institutions interested in controlling it in order to maintain the status quo. Change becomes subversive only when it is fostered by rebel groups committed to the transition from one social order to another.

In contrast, if one accepts the fact that all subversion has an expressed historical purpose, the effort to achieve these subversive goals gives a special character to the process of change and transforms it into socio-economic development, a type of social movement. Therefore the telic element of subversion becomes an intrinsic part of the definition of socio-economic development. Furtado and Fernandes, among others, consider it to be such. As a matter of fact, Furtado (1961) establishes the technical bases for determining the differences between a developed country and an underdeveloped one by using classical concepts of economic science (the model of the capitalist nation) and its tools—the indices of productivity and the rate of capital accumulation, the growth of income and gross national product, and the diversification of services. He takes a second step (1965, 1966) in order to acknowledge the role of ruling groups in the promotion of the development process, the incidence of political factors, and the importance of ideologies, and by doing so he completes the circle of economic-social causality. Fernandes explains development in the following manner: "Social development is the literal translation of the historical manner by which men struggle socially on behalf of the destiny of the world in which they live with the corresponding ideals of the organization of human life and the active and increasing dominion over the factors of disequilibrium of the class society" (Fernandes 1960, 223).

Viewed in this way, socio-economic development should be the process that leads from one social order to another. Development is achieved when the transition from one social order to the next is completed; that is, when the corresponding subversion is created, resolved, and surpassed.

Scientists have established indicators to decide whether a country is moving in this direction or not, especially in the contemporary sense of attempting to achieve modernization and industrialization. Nevertheless, the concept of development as such cannot be considered applicable only to modern situations; if it were, it would be of no great importance. The term itself is not new; it had already appeared in articles of the "Economiste français" in 1895 ("countries in the process of development"). The phenomenon has therefore had historical periodicity. It may be said that there was development when the original inhabitants of America adopted the colonial order even though they had lost many values that were superior to those of the Iberians. There was also development when new economic groups were created in Colombia between 1848 and 1867.

The differences between those processes and that which is generally designated "modernization" are more of content than of form: (1) in the greater emphasis given today to rational planning and technical control as a result of scientific accumulation; (2) in the nature of the key groups that play roles in the industrial transition; (3) in the nature of the values and norms transmitted in the situations of contact and transition; and (4) in relatively new phenomena such as "international stratification" and the patterns of domination and dependence in economic and political relations between modern nations (Horowitz 1966). Development in Colombia occurred even during the bloody and difficult stage of socialist subversion in the present century, seen not only in the economic and demographic indices of the period, but also in the basic change in attitudes and values experienced by the peasantry, giving origin to a new social order.

It may be said that this extends the concept of development too far. However, it would be worse to reduce development to a synonym of modernization. In this case it should be discarded as useless because, as was said earlier, the idea of modernization itself (as that of traditionalism) is relative and must have specific references in time and place for its meaning to be thoroughly understood. Otherwise it could be equivalent to a servile imitation of countries that are considered modern today, a solution whose terms should be carefully studied in underdeveloped countries because it may be historically and socially inapplicable therein. Not even the idea of planning is peculiar to modernization (in present times); many ancient societies achieved in their own way the same kind of controlled activity or guided social change. In many ways the Spanish colonization endeavor was planned, to a degree and with such effectiveness that its results can still be seen.

For this reason, if the concept of development is going to be kept at all, its recurrent bases in the past should be sought and its telic quality, or that of a social movement in determined historical circumstances, should be recognized.[3]

Viewed from another perspective, development also becomes the process by which an order disintegrates and an absolute utopia is frustrated. If a society is to move from one social order to another, development will preserve many elements of the prior order and will move toward adjustments and compromises that are often frustrating. From this derives the empirical possibility of measuring the effect of development after a certain period of time in order to determine the degree to which it has departed from the original goals stipulated by the utopia, and whether or not there has been significant progress. One of the fundamental criteria that may be used for this purpose is that of "social cost." By means of the "cost" it may be established in which areas there has been advancement and at the expense of which traditional or subversive elements (Horowitz 1966, 65–69 and Silva Michelena 1967).

This empirical possibility is especially attractive as part of the predictive method that is designed to anticipate the results of change according to institutions or sectors and which is derived from the formulations presented earlier. Obviously, it would be useful to cast light on how to reduce the cost of making a social transition. This would also make it possible to evaluate processes of development that have already ended, especially those in which there were unexpected outcomes such as the stagnation and decadence of some sectors.

Finally, regarding the inclusion of the concept of revolution within this framework, it is important to note the difference between social change that is achieved through force and that which is achieved through political adjustments and maneuvers during the period of subversion (in this way it differs from Landauer's broader concept of "revolution"). Both types of change may cause a society to advance toward the goals of a utopia. In fact, there have been cases in which the situation of subversion has been overcome without an appeal to total violence in order to gain a new social order, such as occurred in Japan in 1871. Nevertheless, the moment may occur when the use of violence becomes indispensable to avoid frustration of the subversive élan. Violence is then imposed as the predominant strategy for achieving the valued goals through accession to political power, especially if the rebel groups have already made advances and consider themselves in danger of losing what has been achieved (Brinton 1952, 277–85). Then the "precipitators" (MacIver 1942, 163–64) or "accelerators" of subversion (Johnson 1966, 98–99) make their appearance. The use of force and of circumstance (either as precipitators or accelerators of conflict) at this moment transforms development into revolution.

It may be observed that circumstances propitious for revolution emerge from the subversive period prior to the revolutionary coup. Revolution is prepared directly or indirectly at the initial stages of subversion, and grows according to later needs and development. Revolutions that are attempted spontaneously or as the result of a moment of fanatic enthusiasm are not usually successful.

This process of preparation and acceleration through precipitators may easily be seen in the cases of Mexico in 1910, Russia in 1917, China in 1949, and Cuba in 1959. Once the necessary subversion has advanced, a decision is made to act strategically with violence in order to force change. From this moment on, anarchy becomes more acute, the perplexity, indecision, and insecurity of the people increase, and the patterns of expected behavior established during the prior period of socialization are broken down until the revolution is accomplished (cf. Johnson 1966, 2–14).

In Colombia there have been only two cases of revolution conceived in this manner: one between 1853 and 1854, and the other in 1948. Both were frustrated with regard to their overall goals. Nonetheless, some degree of socio-economic development was achieved, as sought by the subversion preceding the revolution. Undoubtedly, the triumphant revolution is more compelling in the direction of an absolute utopia (Hobsbawm 1959), but cannot attain it (Landauer 1919). Yet such a revolution dramatizes the social and economic transformation and opens great possibilities for social invention and experimentation.

Obviously, a revolution is not a *coup d'état*, which is the circulation or alternation of elites within a given order, or a palace war (Sorokin 1957, Part III; Mendieta y Núñez 1959). Furthermore, revolution should be seen as a reflection and consequence of that other violence, repression or coercion, that follows its course through traditional channels. If maintaining situations inconsistent with the valued goals of society by the power elite can be justified, then certainly the same procedure can be honored in the hands of those who seek the end of injustice. This is the concept of the just rebellion or "counter-violence" to which we shall return later.

The Analysis of the Refraction of Social Orders

It should be stated once again that this book is but an outline to establish some of the most evident features that come to the fore in a sociological analysis of Colombian history. The nature of the data and the circumstances of the work have encouraged a combination of two research methods: one is predominantly historical, by which certain regularities in the history of the country are established, based on a reading of primary and secondary sources; and the other is predominantly sociological, by which hypotheses have been subjected to empirical test in several contemporary communities. The study of historical events and the establishment at the same time of current evidence that may be measured or operationalized have been essential tasks in the conception of this book. Furthermore, the data obtained constitute supports for establishing chains of cause and effect. From these a more precise concept is gained of the role that certain types of groups have played and continue to play in history; and the function of philosophies, ideologies, and attitudes that have inspired and now inspire them to act at crucial moments is clarified.

Thus it is not a matter of a simple chronological history that culminates with contemporary cross-sectional studies. It is rather a matter of analysis of social entities, compared as they have existed in the past and in the present, in order to gain greater understanding of the realities that surround us and to contribute to the answer of a hackneyed question, "From whence do we come and where are we going?" The past is studied through historical events as they were registered by chroniclers, historians, and autobiographers, although there are disadvantages derived from errors of observation and systematization in their works. But there is no alternative. With regard to the present, the study proceeds through direct observation and systematic measurement of the expressions of group life in diverse regions of the country.

This book limits itself to the implications derived from historical study and presents only qualitative data and general hypotheses, some of which have been tested in various communities.[4] Other monographs will make possible the confrontation between hypothesis and present reality, with measures of that which is measurable and proposals of corrections that may be necessary.[5]

For the historical analysis as much as for the sociological measurement of the present, six rules of procedure are used for developing the frame of reference for the study of subversion:

1. The elements and factors that produce stability of the social order are isolated, as are the contradictions (hidden or manifest) that explain its implicit instability.

2. The nature of the elements, especially their cultural content, that participate in the social transformation is specified.

3. These elements are related to a specific time and place in order to avoid the relativity of such concepts as traditionalism and modernism.

4. The perspective adopted is that of the common people; that is, there is understanding of the influence that conscious mass movements may have on ruling groups or, conversely, of the effect that events directed by elites may have on local communities and on the working classes.

5. The concrete elements are grouped according to analogues or dominant features in order to permit an overall vision of the processes and to construct general concepts (such as ethos and the normative framework).

6. Key or strategic groups are determined—those that prove to

be fundamental for the functioning of society during the period in which the respective social order prevails as much as for periods of transition. Such groups are determined in order to assist in distinguishing one period from another. Determination of such groups serves to identify a social order or a subversion. This is time saving in description and discussion.

The socio-historical analysis of the crises engendered by refraction of social orders in Colombia has been aided by the valuable contribution of Professor Luis López de Mesa, who published *Escrutinio sociológico de la historia colombiana* in 1956. It is a much more systematic work than his earlier and classic study, *De cómo se ha formado la nación colombiana* (1934).[6] It merits the special attention of persons interested in social change in Colombia and serves as a starting point for the expositions that follow.

Professor López de Mesa perceives six "frustrations" in the history of Colombia, in the style of Toynbee with his thesis of challenge and response:

1. The disappearance of the San Agustín culture through the impact of the Carib invasion.

2. The "disappearance" of the Muisca or Chibcha culture owing to the Spanish conquest.

3. The leaderless condition of the colonial intellectual groups during the Spanish reconquest in the War of Independence.

4. The break up of Gran Colombia in 1830.

5. The lack of national integration toward the end of the nineteenth century, the disaster of the last civil war, and the loss of the Isthmus of Panama in 1903.

6. The political violence (*la Violencia*) of 1948 and subsequent years.

Both Professor López de Mesa's personal approach and that of this book acknowledge the crises of the Spanish conquest and those of the recent period of *la Violencia*. He differs concerning San Agustín, the effect of the war of national liberation and Gran Colombia, and the concept of the disaster of Panama.

With regard to the first point, agreement would be possible if this work had begun with the analysis of the fifth century when Agustinian culture was at its apogee (Duque Gómez 1963, 107). Nevertheless, all researchers admit that the mystery of San Agustín is still unresolved and any interpretative attempt may be risky. Even so, it is praiseworthy that Professor López de Mesa marked the beginning of Colombian history in San Agustín rather than in the founding of Santa Marta or Santa Fe de Bogotá as is the implicit suggestion of many other students of Colombian history.

The other divergencies follow as a matter of course from the development of Professor López de Mesa's central hypothesis: that the cause of frustration is the considerable disequilibrium existing between the intellectual groups and the masses in general. "The center of gravity" of the Colombian people "is very high," in the oligarchy, which makes the structure unstable (López de Mesa 1956, 274). The failures from 1816 to 1830 and those of the end of the nineteenth century are understood on this basis. It is an elitist conception of history.

Naturally, this conception does not make it possible to apprehend the other dimension—that which is gained from the perspective of the people themselves. If historical events are termed popular movements because of the common people's involvement in the processes of change, the *Comuneros'* revolt of 1781 and the crisis of subversion from 1848 to 1867 (which we shall study later) become significant; yet Professor López de Mesa omits them from his study. Within this populous-oriented conception of history the events of the dictatorship of José María Melo acquire greater importance, for example, than the *libido imperandi* of Rafael Núñez, the religious compulsion of Miguel Antonio Caro, or the skepticism of José Manuel Marroquín. The wars of independence and the fragmentation of Gran Colombia appear as no more than change-overs of the ruling classes, of little social and economic significance for the people as a whole.

Professor López de Mesa is not incorrect concerning the role that Colombian elites have played in the calamities that the country has suffered throughout its history. His well-founded accusation of the four persons responsible for *la Violencia* is a piece for anthologies. It is only necessary to complement López de Mesa's thesis with a study of related concepts, which shall be done in the following chapters.

CHAPTER THREE

The Rise and Decline of the Chibchas

It is difficult to make a study in depth of the order existing in Colombia before the arrival of the Spanish, nor is it really necessary for the purposes of this book. It is little less than impossible to analyze that history from rather demanding viewpoints. There are no documents or codices of that epoch that might illustrate this aspect, and all the available data are of archeological origin or are derived from biased chronicles written soon after the conquest. Such data make it impossible to say much about this theme or to delve into its sociological implications.

Nor will it be possible to formulate an ethnographic synthesis that would cover all the pre-Colombian cultures for they differed greatly. As an alternative, following the lead of Professor López de Mesa, the Chibchas may be taken as the main group. They inhabited an area from the savannah of Bogotá to the area occupied by the Guanes in what today is the Department of Santander.

This was the main center of the New Kingdom of Granada, where the capital of the vice royalty was established and from which the peninsular elite governed. It seemed to be the site of the most advanced pre-conquest culture (Pérez de Barradas 1950–51). The influence of the Chibchas who lived there was felt far from the territory they controlled directly through military agreements and the exchange of products. The dialects of those areas, which covered almost all of what is now Colombia, were related to the Chibcha language. Thus the culture of this central group is of great

importance for understanding the on-going patterns of life that
prevailed before the conquest. Its key group was human-ecological
in nature, formed in the rural neighborhoods called *sybyn*.[1]

The *sybyn* were of central importance for the Chibchas, judging
by the reports of chroniclers. They were similar to the better
known *ayllus* of the formative period of the Inca empire and seem
to have functioned in a similar manner. Thus the adjective *ayllic* is
derived to characterize the order now under study. This term is not
necessarily applicable to the Inca civilization (or to the Aztec) at
the time of the conquest since it had already advanced considerably
toward a very rational autocratic and centralized structure. However, it may perhaps be applicable to such less politically developed
groups as the Chibchas.[2]

We will proceed here to study the components of the ayllic order: its values, norms, social organization, and technology.

Tolerance and the Sacred

In the era of the arrival of the Spanish to the savannah of Bogotá
—which they baptized as "the valley of palaces (*alcázares*)" owing
to the multitude of walled-in areas that spread before their eyes
—the Chibchas had a very unusual civilization. On the one hand
they had gone beyond the merely tribal stage and were beginning to
envision a new type of society. On the other hand, they had not
arrived at the complexity of the Inca culture. The peoples of the
Andean savannahs were in an intermediate stage and were apparently undergoing an active change that made them receptive to
conquistador intruders.

The receptivity that saturated their values made their social order
somewhat flexible and oriented toward the future; the same seems to
have occurred as well at certain times in the history of the Mayas
(Spinden 1930). Ironically, it was not the hosts of King Aquimin-
zaque who achieved what was valued by Chibchan society. It was
instead the forces of his destroyer, the politician-general Hernán
Pérez (brother of the Spanish forces commander, Gonzalo Jiménez
de Quesada). The most illustrious prophecies of the Chibcha empire
were fulfilled by Hernán Pérez: political unity for the region was

secured. At the same time, however, the *sybyn*, or rural neighbor-hoods, for reasons unforeseen in their dynamics, declined to a point from which only complete transformation could rescue them.

The dominant values that appear are those of a group disposed toward social development and alert to the possibilities of cultural contact with the Spanish. It is an ethos of incipient tolerance in contrast to the ethos of resistance displayed by more advanced American civilizations (the Aztec and Cuzco) as well as by less developed groups (the Pijaos and the Motilones, for example). Since this ethos has two ingredients, one of a religious nature and the other arising from a tendency toward development, it might be characterized as *tolerant sacralism.* As a whole it would include mainly the following values:

1. An *animistic* orientation toward the phenomena of the universe involving a passive acceptance of the power of nature over man. This orientation is clearly seen in the fertility rites described by the chroniclers, and in the role played by certain animals such as the frog, the serpent, and the lizard (Piedrahita 1942, I, 14 ff.) The Chibchas worshiped the sun and the moon; and the rocks, mountains, and wind also shared in popular veneration (Simón 1953, II, 249–50; Piedrahita 1942, I, 40–45). A large part of the religious rites and the impressive ceremonies that they performed on the lakes had animistic roots (Zerda 1883; Triana 1951, 156–61; Zamora 1945, I, 202; Simón 1953, II, 163–70).

2. A *familial* or primary orientation in social relations. It seems that the monogamous union predominated in local groups although the *uzaques* (local chieftains) were polygamous. Matrilinealness fostered broad kinship relationships that were useful for the tasks of the fields and for war activities. Ethnocentrism manifested itself in conflicts and jealousies between different tribes, especially between the "states" of the north and the south; loyalty to diverse *uzaques* was symbolized in various ways as, for example, through the use of banners and body markings (Castellanos 1886, I, 69–72).

3. A *natural* type of activity; that is, orientation to the rhythm of the environment in which they lived. There was great respect for the forms and processes of nature, especially those connected with animistic expressions. Water was of tremendous importance owing

to the diverse forms in which it was found and utilized in the region: cataracts such as that of Tequendama, periodic flooding of the savannah, swamps from which fibrous plants were gathered for various crafts, sacred lakes, showers and fogs that had specific meaning. In general the Chibchas were at the mercy of the natural elements, especially with regard to agricultural activity.

The Chibchas also used nature in ingenious ways, as shown by their habitations and the materials used in constructing them, the manufacture of musical instruments, pots, textiles, pigments, and various decorations, the domestication of the guinea pig (*curí*) and well-developed botany.

4. A *futuristic* tendency with regard to the collective goals of the society. The Chibcha society seems to have combined socio-political élan with religious impulse. Evidence collected during the process of socio-cultural assimilation in colonial times indicates that the Chibcha religion was much stronger and more resistant to change than the budding political system. Yet local society was so receptive to change that during the first months of contact with the Spanish, the Chibchas made attempts to assimilate them as "children of the sun" (*Suagagua*), who according to legend, were expected. (Simón 1953, I, 281–82). They also made efforts to mix with the invaders racially and to adopt their tools and practices for tilling the soil. There was, indeed, the case of a *uzaque* who, the day after meeting Quesada, asked to be baptized (Castellanos 1886, I, 107; Aguado 1906, 136). It was not that he had abandoned his old deities but that he found little difficulty in assimilating the new ones brought by the conquistadors. The same cultural receptivity revealed itself later, even in the face of violent resistance provoked by the Spanish abuses, when over a period of sixty years the natives learned Spanish and almost completely forgot their own vernacular (see the next chapter).

Community and Providence

The normative framework of the Chibchas, legitimated by their sacred values, carried the goals and principles that guided behavior to more concrete levels. Even though there are natural reservations with regard to a study made in historical retrospect and using secondary sources, the following general categories of the many pertinent norms seem to appear: (1) that of *communal stability* for assuring the identity, homogeneity, and continuity of primary groups and for reinforcing the necessity of mutual aid and collective action in the tasks relating to subsistence; and (2) that of *providence* as compulsion to respect the genetic forms of utilization of the natural environment; it also involved an elemental conception of wealth and its accumulation.

Communal stability manifests itself in the way in which the Chibcha communities survived the impact of the conquest, in spite of centrifugal practices such as the labor-depleting obligations of *mita* and *minga* imposed by the Spanish. The original inhabitants managed to preserve their primary groups, the same ones that had served them in the communal work on the lands of the chieftains and priests, organization of their warrior groups, their craft work and trade, and for procreation and transmission of the traditional culture.

The idea of providence is documented through the descriptions of coarse agricultural tools used by the Chibchas. Dwellings and the techniques of healing, the customs for bartering goods, and the means of transportation also expressed the same norms. The main exception is that of the construction of agricultural terraces (Broadbent 1964b). However, the latter were never employed as extensively or as intensively as they were by similar groups in other parts of the continent.

From Neighborhood to Incipient State

As was stated before, the Chibchas were integrated on the basis of small ecological units or neighborhoods, the *sybyn*, that the Spanish identified as *parcialidades*, *partes*, or *capitanías*. The *parcialidades* were groups of families, often related to each other matrilineally, that lived together in a determined geographical area under the supervision of a captain (Broadbent 1964a, 15–22). They were the basic groups for the socialization of the inhabitants; they fostered institutions of mutual aid and the individual or collective use of land. It appears that they were identified by a toponym or, in the absence of such a name, by that of the captain in power.

At the time of the conquest, the Chibchas were moving from that neighborhood stage of social organization to one based on the convenience of a centralized state as a result of the predominance that the *zipa*, or king, of Hunza (now Funza) was beginning to exercise over the *uzaques* and tribal chiefs. There were recognized hierarchies of *uzaques* and captains. The former, like the kings, lived in stockaded villages, some of considerable size; the captains lived in scattered settlements with their respective neighbors and practiced sedentary agriculture. The Chibchas manifested incipient castes, having a few ruling families (the processes of inheritance of positions and property, for example, were still flexible and exogamy was practiced along with endogamy). Ascriptive roles predominated and the resulting action, in general terms, was prescriptive because neither the values nor the norms easily permitted deviation in personal conduct.

Furthermore, there was regional economic specialization, with sites given for markets and commercial transaction; a religion with some practices of collective pilgrimage (*correr la tierra* or "to travel over the land"); and a system of communication between the stockaded villages. The Chibchas also had groups that specialized in diverse arts and crafts.

The Hoe and Human Energy

The Chibcha group made its adaptation to the natural environment by means of digging-stick agriculture based on a wooden hoe with a stone point and periodic burnings. For this purpose, their *parcialidades* were established in scattered fashion in the dry parts of the savannahs and on the slopes of the hills where they sometimes built rudimentary terraces. Tubers (especially potatoes, and native varieties of *cubios, rubas,* and *ibias*) were their main food. Their patterns of settlement as well as the cultivation of tubers have persisted throughout the centuries (Fals Borda 1957, Chaps. Four and Nine). Furthermore the Chibchas had empirical techniques of health care, elementary knowledge of metallurgy, spinning, goldsmithing, mining, and construction; but they were unacquainted with the wheel and their astronomy was very elementary. Their weapons for attack and defense were limited to simple artifacts that depended, like the elements mentioned before, entirely on human energy.

The Chibchas confronted the material and spiritual forces of the Spanish conqueror with the socio-cultural elements that have been mentioned. The first contact, short and intense, was extremely destructive for the local society. It was the lightning strike of a group compelled by an ideology foreign to American soil. Subsequent episodes destroyed the old order and molded a new one by the action of persons and institutions that sought to turn the Chibcha neighborhoods into groups of serfs. Thus the ayllic order formally disappeared, leaving its mark only on isolated elements. A few such marks became part of the new order through the tenacity of the descendants of the Chibchas and also through the realistic tolerance shown by many conquistadors.

CHAPTER FOUR

Formation of the Seigniorial Order

It is unnecessary to reconstruct Hispanic culture of the sixteenth century (as was done with the Chibcha culture) in order to explain the social life patterns that emerged from Spanish rule in the New World. There is much information already available on this matter, and in addition it is of interest only to determine which were the special aspects of Hispanic society and culture (among the great variety manifested by the diverse subcultures of the Iberian peninsula) that were transferred to the colonies and definitely established.

The condition of conquest and subjugation led to the coerced adoption of certain aspects of the conqueror's culture, but also the vanquished who survived the shock were able to apply selective criteria that accelerated the acceptance of certain innovations and retarded that of others. This was done through the defense of values originating in the traditional ayllic order. These factors of local receptivity and resistance allow us to discover in the conquest certain mechanisms that throw light on the nature of subversive processes.

Absolute Utopia and Relative Utopia

None of the Hispanic elements transferred to America were of greater import than the political-religious system formulated soon after its discovery. The general philosophy that inspired the formulation and the theory of the state it engendered were certainly products of the age; but also represented in it were the qualities of the Spanish people and the idealistic personality of their rulers, especially Queen Isabella of Castille. She was a strong woman, a queen with deep Christian convictions developed in the battle against infidels. As a defender of the faith and sponsor of Columbus' enterprise, she could not do otherwise than attempt to translate her beliefs into acts of government. For she interpreted the victory at Granada as a confirmation of those ideas by divine will in order that they might be disseminated throughout the recently discovered world.

It was in this way that the discovery of America could be interpreted as a supernatural reward for a mystic and heroic people that had taken religion out of the cold cloisters and council lucubrations to place it on the battlefront, in the reality of violent confrontation (Ganivet 1923). This people had been triumphant. A state such as this could not be an end in itself but rather an instrument by which to enlarge the Kingdom of God on earth. The American expansion provided the opportunity for it to realize this mission. The dynamic initial impulse of the conquest derived from the intention to take maximum advantage of this opportunity to combine the sword with the cross. From this emerged the Church-state as a "historical instrument of the Catholic epic" (Ríos 1927), a new missional utopia. This development of the missional utopia affected America and Spain equally, transforming both.

The missionary idea of Queen Isabella had already appeared in the documents exchanged with the Holy See, used to produce the Papal Bull, *Inter Caeteris*, of Alexander VI on May 3, 1493. The commitment obtained by the kings of Castile was based on the twofold conviction: of the necessity to save the souls of the Indians, and of their willingness to embrace the Catholic faith. Such an opportunity could not be overlooked. In order to achieve this goal, the Pope as the Vicar of Christ on earth granted the respective patronage to the kings of Castile who were thereafter entitled "Patriarchs of the Indies."

The intention of Spain to expand the Kingdom of God into the New World was incorporated into the earliest instructions and agreements (*capitulaciones*) directed to discoverers and expeditions. It was required that there be in every group a chaplain or confessor who was to supervise the conduct of soldiers and colonists and see to it that the valued goals were encouraged. Justice must reign and salvation of the human race within the framework of Christianity must be accomplished. The Spanish conquest thus became "one of the greatest attempts the world has seen to make Christian precepts prevail in the relations between peoples" (Hanke 1949, 1).

Spain was capable of the task: at that time it was the principal power in Europe. Its kings, especially Charles I (Charles V of Germany), were careful to give orders in consideration of the Christian intent. They attempted to gain a better understanding of the nature of the new cultural contact through a series of experiments carried out in Hispaniola, Cuba, Venezuela, and Guatemala in order to learn how the Indians might not be harmed (Hanke 1935). Great debates developed during the first decades of the sixteenth century to determine the "just title" of the kings to American lands, under what circumstances a "just war" could be alleged in these territories (Solórzano 1647), and the question of the Indian's "human nature." The colonization experience in re-occupied Spain introduced a new physical pattern of settlement, the gridiron, having a rectangular plaza and straight streets, as a possibility for overseas territories that was slightly more efficient than the older patterns of Iberia (Foster 1960). The very Renaissance atmosphere of the age stimulated innovations of all types, from numerous material inventions (new kinds of ships, tools, and arms, for example) to the designation of regions and cities as "New." Even utopias based on Plato's *Republic,* echoed by Thomas More and Campanella, gave rise to important social experiments in America such as the hospital-towns of Bishop Vasco de Quiroga in Mexico (Zavala 1937). Fra Bartolomé de las Casas certainly personified this utopia and fought for it until death.

Judging by these examples, the Spanish political and intellectual elite of the era was inspired by a desire to rise to the moral challenge of the circumstances and to take advantage of the opportunity to develop a superior civilization. Thus in these circumstances religion ceased to be an esoteric or merely utopian experience in order to become the bearer of a specific ideology that was translatable to acts of social organization. A concrete, temporal *orbis christianus,* with a "colonial scholastic ethic," and rights and doctrines had to be built, such as other later groups required for their own secular ideologies

(Höffner 1957). That which was transplanted to America in order to create the new order was an ideology as much as it was a collection of rituals. It was the expected decantation of the missional utopia.

The idea of such an absolute utopia had repercussions mainly among the governmental elite of Spain and a few apostles, some of whom found their way to Roman Catholic altars. It could be translated to the American (or Spanish) context only through minor officials and representatives who were less quixotic and more opportunistic. The dazzle of the new attracted them to begin a new life or to develop a society in America that would in many ways be superior to that of Europe. But in the process they diluted the absolute utopia of the kings and popes and produced a relative utopia, with its portion of ideology, that of the agents of power who faced *in situ* the double reality of the Indians and the conquest. The absolute utopia was registered in the laws of the Indies and was symbolized by the crown of the King-Patriarch; the relative utopia was translated to the local environment in the *derecho indiano*, the customary ways of resolving issues in the Indies. The laws of the absolute utopia were obeyed; but they were not fulfilled in reality. Homage was paid to the absolute king as a distant deity who united the empire; but realistic government was accomplished through the very expedient Council of the Indies.

The conquistadors had their own ideas concerning the nature of their mission. Many came to America only with a craving for riches and power, but they justified these impulses on the basis of religion, according to the chronicles of all the countries; placing God, Santiago, or the Virgin at the service of the conquering forces in order to capture an idolatrous king and take over his treasury, for example, was very common (cf. Groot 1889, I, 23).

Nevertheless, once the earthly greed was satisfied, they returned to the colonies as settlers to reconstruct the local society in terms of the relative utopia. Thus, for example, they transformed the feudal serf system of *behetría* into the Indian trusteeship one of *encomienda;* they freed themselves of the limitations imposed by the sheep-raising interests of the Mesta and developed the *hacienda* cattle farm; they were dissatisfied with the disordered settlements of the peninsula and built towns according to a more rational plan; they collaborated with the missionaries to indoctrinate the Indians, for whom convenient positions were found in the new society; they promoted an adjustment between the indigenous society and Spanish society that would bring out the best and most useful elements of both, and destroyed that of the former which according to the utopia ought to be destroyed.

A residue of the whole idealistic intent of this era persisted in ongoing ways of life not only in the dominions but also on the peninsula. These were expressed in the imperial institutions that arose from real situations, in the new social self-image and image of the world and in an hispanic-creole way of behaving, perceiving, and valuing. That is, a new social order, the seigniorial, was created on the basis of the key group of *señores* or overlords, developing during the subversive period of the conquest.

If the absolute goal of the missional utopia was creation of the "City of God," the real goals were in the transmission and reproduction of an ideology with additions, substitutions, and adaptations; that is, of the seigniorial society that prevailed on the Iberian peninsula. Even so, this relative utopia was effective for purposes of transforming the local order. Ultimately, the Patriarch of the Indies was to govern vassals that did not wish to be angels, but men; and more than men, they wished to be *señores*. From this decantation of purposes there developed the society of the colonies.

The Christian Subversion

The transplanting of the missional utopian ideals and their realistic translation into concrete values, norms, and types of seigniorial organization produced in America the refraction of the prevailing, morally autonomous, ayllic order. This permitted disintegration and redirection, and the upsurge of a complete condition of subversion in Indian societies.

In order to clearly understand the nature of this conflict it is necessary to examine the way in which the components of the ayllic order (values, norms, social organization, and techniques) and their specific elements became polarized and integrated when this order was challenged by the Spanish. Their entrance reinforced and dramatized the natural condition of tradition. This is a general process of change to which reference is made here as the *refraction* of the social order. This refraction causes the traditional components to become better articulated and more consciously employed after the cultural confrontaton with the components of the intrusive order. Especially during its initial climax, the conflict causes these intrusive elements to be seen as daring new values, opposed to the traditional values of the Chibchas; as strange norms in relation to those employed locally; as peculiar institutions that seek to modify indigenous ones; and as unusual and even extraordinary techniques and practices that complement or supplant those developed by the local artisans and tillers of the soil. In other words, during this period of refraction, through processes of confrontation, many specific crucial values, norms, institutions, and techniques of the Christian subversion are seen as counter-elements by the American people defending their traditions. These counter-elements are dialectical responses to the existing condition and for this reason may be grouped into four broad categories that correspond to the components of tradition, those presented in Chapter Two: counter-values, counter-norms, disorgans, and technological innovations, respectively.

The refraction of the local order imposed by the conquest was effective principally in the transformation of the Chibcha political institutions, in the destruction of the native religion of Bochica, and in the local adoption of isolated social complexes such as the market, dress, language, and agricultural practices. But the refraction was not so effective with regard to other socio-cultural mechanisms such as the value content of the native religion, popular myths, legends and beliefs, music, botany, and such occupations as pottery-making, mining, and spinning. In these areas adjustments were made between the Hispanic subversive and the traditional American alternatives (see later discussion).

Evidently, the killing of the main chieftains and their successors between 1537 and 1539 caused an almost total demoralization of the Chibchas. There were groups that fled to the mountains; others committed collective suicide; yet others practiced psychic withdrawal, thus alienating themselves socially from the Spanish (Aguado 1906, 207). Epidemics of new illnesses such as venereal disease and smallpox were annihilating. For those who survived the plagues, *mitas*, and wars, and who stayed where they were, the only outlet for the anomie of the climax of subversion was in passivity and resignation.

The duration and characteristics of this period of indecision in the local order may be derived from the data concerning the adoption of Hispanic socio-cultural complexes by the Indians and the definitive accommodation of the latter in the new social order. It appears that the last important uprising promoted by the chieftains of Tundama and Sugamuxi occurred in the northern part of the Chibcha region about 1540. There is no mention of bellicose action after this and apparently the groups began to accommodate themselves to the new situation. There was also an intense struggle on the part of local peoples to defend their agricultural lands in the *sybyn*, a struggle that was partially won with the legal recognition and marking off of reservations of land (*resguardos*) toward the end of the sixteenth century (Fals Borda 1957, 72–77; 1961a, 115–16). However, this important fact was not yet a sufficient index of the absorption of the Chibcha culture by the dominant group even though the framework within which the new seigniorial order would be developed had already been delineated.

According to the tenets of the utopians, it was obvious that the religious sphere would be the essential area in which the scope of the Christian subversion of the local order would have to be measured. In fact, though merely a formal aspect, the emergence of the cult of Our Lady of Chiquinquirá was registered as significant about 1590. A regional pilgrimage, this cult might be interpreted as a syncretic substitution for the previous religious displacements to Suamoz and Guatavita (Groot 1889, I, 193–97; Triana 1951, 159). The change was more complete in other complexes, as, for example, in native dress and language, both symbolic elements of the greatest importance that furnish some pertinent clues and that can help us to determine the period in which the subversion ended.

According to available data, Chibcha dress suffered two exogenous assaults: one from the Spanish missionaries who through successive decrees forbade nudity, obliging the Indians to wear pants and shirts and also to cut their hair; and the other from the Quechua servants or guides, the group that conquistadors had brought from Peru, who introduced the *bayetón* or poncho that originated with the Mapuches-Huilliches, the garment that became the present-day *ruana*. Both counter-norms implied serious conflicts with local tradition in which hair-cutting was a form of punishment and wearing a mantle around the neck cut in *bayetón* style was defaming. By the end of the sixteenth century, however, the Indians dressed according to the new norms and even the chieftains had adopted the dress of the Spanish nobleman (Fals Borda 1953).

In like manner, by about 1598 the Chibcha language was no longer employed for carrying out activities as basic as commercial ones. The Jesuits discovered that they could make themselves understood by the natives in Spanish and discarded the use of Chibcha, which they had learned in the convent (Groot 1889, I, 211, 226). It is possible that within the family the traditional dialect might continue to be used and the survival of a few Chibcha words until today witnesses to this. But the emergence of a new generation in open and accepted contact with the Spaniards eliminated the possibility of the strong linguistic resistance found among local groups who spoke Quechua, Aymara, or Maya, for example.

These data concerning the absorption of new cultural elements such as language and dress of the Spanish-Creole subversive groups, the actual possession of land in reservations, and the appearance of the cult of Our Lady of Chiquinquirá indicate that the period of acute contradiction and pronounced incongruity of the subversion of the local order ended about the close of the sixteenth century; that is, two generations (sixty years) after the first contact in 1537. Cultural and social congruity was soon reestablished, based on the society and culture of the ruling groups, with the necessary adjustments in order to assure permanence but oriented toward the Hispanic ethos. From this there developed a monolithic society that was much more resistant to change and more "sacred" than that which the Chibcha or Spanish apparently had had before.

The Adjustment in Values

The Spaniards obviously had a complex, seasoned cultural reservoir, that of Western culture, that they could not refrain from using even though they might have endeavored to rise above it morally on behalf of the Crown. It was precisely the force of those customs and beliefs, transferred to the other side of the ocean, that made it impossible to see the perfect expression of the missional utopia in the seigniorial order. Rather, such an ideology engendered part of the manifest or latent contradictions of this order. On the other hand, values, norms, and institutions emerged that were very practical and that are summed up here as the on-going ways of life during the colonial period.

These ways of life, counter-elements of the ayllic order, not only express the decantation of the utopia but also reflect the influence of socio-cultural elements of the changing local order. It was neither possible nor necessary to effect a total imposition by force in the colony, the imposition of the conqueror on the conquered. Signs of reconciliation and understanding are found in many areas of contact. Thus a process of *adjustment* and *compulsion* developed, leading to the new social order. Assimilation, syncretism, or accommodation was sought among discordant elements through adjustment. Attempts to impose a direction on change were made through compulsion in order to soon achieve its relative stabilization (see Chapter Two).

Within the value component it is the ethos and the central or dominant values that determine the vital, affective meaning of society and that provide the existential framework for the behavior of people. At the risk of simplifying the phenomenon, the thesis might be advanced that the dominant counter-values of the "Hispanic topia" (that conditioned a good part of the adjustment by reason of the conquest) turned around two main ideas: the idea of castes as a morally justified pattern of living and the idea of urban concentration as the model of the civilized way to organize and control society. Many basic patterns of behavior in the American colonies seemed to arise from the combination of these two ideas in an ethos of *caste urbanism.*

The idea of castes as social strata in which lineages are perpetuated and mixing of certain racial groups is avoided was quite old in Spain. It went back at least to the times of the disintegration of empires when fiefs appeared. Feudalism on the Iberian Peninsula had certain characteristics that distinguished it from its northern counterpart, essentially in those relating to communal privileges (*fueros*) and rights of lords and vassals (Hinojosa 1905; Zavala 1935). Even so, its fundamental structure was based on ascriptive and hereditary positions contained in two social strata, one of *señores*, or overlords, superimposed upon one of serfs. Upon becoming a social value, such a structure received the sanction of the Church whose theologians produced arguments to justify its existence. They were the arguments wielded by the group under Juan Ginés de Sepúlveda and Bishop Juan de Quevedo, at the beginning of the sixteenth century, to reinforce the position of the *encomenderos* (those entrusted with managing, subjugating, and exploiting the Indians). Any person convinced by these arguments could not do otherwise than accept the differences between the two groups (especially the economic and racial ones) and rationalize them as facts within the divine order of the universe. The conditions under which the conquest was realized, of course, facilitated the application of these ideas and confirmed their advantages in more than one sense. They found concrete expression in the seigniorial counter-norms and in the subversive social institutions we shall study further on.

The idea of *civitas*, of which the Chibcha had very limited knowledge, had achieved some importance in Spain as a consequence of occupation by the Arabs whose urban concentrations were the foci of a great civilization. This complex implied the appearance of an administrative, political, religious, and lettered elite in a man-made environment sometimes surrounded by defense constructions. The elite depended for physical sustenance on a *peasantry* in the surrounding rural area. This peasantry was a native subculture that remained dominated by the urban power elite. Between the two groups was established a new monetary economy, an impersonal trade system, military service, and taxation (Redfield 1956). Thus a level of integration was achieved that included basic locality groups as well as their related urban groups. In the case of communities formerly of the Chibcha dominion, such urban elites functioned at first in the capitals (Santa Fe, Tunja). Later, with the growth of new Indian towns called *reducciones*, or upon their being transformed into regular parishes, such urban (white) groups appeared in them as were connected with the administration.

When the Spanish moved to America with this urban complex, they needed to transform the Indians (gradually) into peasants or farm hands similar to those of Castille for the very concrete purposes of economic manipulation and social and religious control. Consequently, one of the first tasks of the administration was to concentrate the native population in, or close to, the towns or *reducciones* where they could be civilized according to patterns established on the peninsula. Not all of the complex was duplicated, of course, and this enormous and continuous effort to civilize by means of urban concentration was a partial failure in those areas where scattered settlements already existed. The Spanish had then to accept an adjustment with the inhabitants, to leave them settled according to their customs, demanding of them only weekly assembly for purposes of indoctrination and trade in the service centers or in the *reducciones*. Nevertheless, little by little a centralized political-urban power structure was established, one that was more mature and strong than that prevailing before 1537. It was reinforced by a religious structure, also more institutionalized. This made possible intensified community relations on a much broader scale than that of the *ayllus* or *sybyn* neighborhoods while their existence continued to be respected.

The imposition of the counter-values of caste urbanism naturally led to significant consequences, and in the traditional local values. Three distinct processes of adjustment and compulsion may be discerned: (1) the assimilation of the ayllic values of animism, the family, and nature; (2) the substitution of the values of futurism for the counter-values of otherworldliness and earthly submission; and (3) the addition of new values: those of neo-Manicheism.

With regard to the adjustments of assimilation of animism, the family, and nature, it should be remembered that in these three sets of counter-values the Chibcha culture was compatible with the Hispanic one. For example, in relation to magical animism, the belief in the malignance of the winds or in the evil eye often imputed to the Indians was in reality a Spanish belief. Legends, fables, and images, especially those concerning indigenous animals such as the frog and the lizard, and produce such as corn and pineapple, were maintained and propagated along with those brought from the Iberian peninsula. Thus the popular beliefs, myths, and legends of both peoples were reinforced, creating a cultural nucleus that was perhaps more resistant, but rich and varied. It is expressed in the "American baroque" art of churches, convents, and palaces with their sculptures, engravings, and carved woodwork.

This cultural foundation was broadened by the adoption of certain Christian formalistic (sensory) stimuli. The difficulties of understanding experienced by the Americans encouraged overemphasis of the images, rituals, and liturgy as alternative forms of communication. Thus, with the tolerance of the clergy, a three-headed deity was adored as if it were the Holy Trinity; the images of Bochica were incrusted with the Crucifix; the blessed palm was burned to placate the storm (Groot 1889, I, 327, 427; Fals Borda 1961a, 280–84). The difficulties of teaching theological ideas such as those of "soul" and "worship" were insuperable (Uricoechea 1871, xlix). In short, the syncretism and formalism imposed by the adjustment to local animism left popular, peasant religion almost emptied of its original meaning (Mariátegui 1934; Rojas 1928) In this sense peasant religion harmonized very well with the variety of religion brought by the conquest as part of the decanted utopia.

Furthermore, even though the Chibchas could be polygamous, it appears that in practice monogamy predominated; thus the requirements made by the missionaries about monogamy should not have encountered much resistance. The indigenous family practices that survived for a longer period of time, and that are still observed today in various localities of the Andean region, are incest and a type of free union (*amaño*). However, these are practiced only sporadically and are subject to stringent restrictions. A large part of family socialization was turned over to the religious institution, either within the *reducciones*, where the Catholic religion was learned, or on the haciendas having *concertados*, or resident laborers. Thus it was not difficult to arrive at a synthesis of the counter-values and the traditional values of family-centeredness. They were reinforced in the colony.

The same type of assimilative adjustment was made between the values and counter-values related to nature. The Spanish, as much as the Americans, had great reverence for nature and their technology was of the adaptive type, respectful of the genetic processes of the environment. The basic activities involved were mutually reinforcing.

There were also assimilation and addition in music and recreation: the Chibchas expressed themselves by means of instruments that were essentially natural (a type of bamboo flute, *guacharacas*, conch shells) while the Spanish brought stringed instruments such as the cithern and the harp.

On the other hand, otherworldliness was one of the counter-values most emphasized by the Spanish missionaries. They achieved amazing success in imposing the rites and liturgy of the Church—elements, as was stated earlier, more easily grasped by the indigenous mentality. There is no indication whatsoever that a similar attitude had existed among the Americans before the conquest. The Chibcha took refuge in otherworldliness as an escape from subjugation, sublimating their *taedium vitae* in the visions of the other world that were presented to them by the indoctrinating priests.

Thus, a two-pronged complex was developed: (1) the fatalism and indolence among the common people (which substituted for the former more dynamic idea of the future), witnessed to by almost all observers of the colonial period; and (2) the submission and subordination to the upper castes that turned the peasants into servants of the glebe. Therein originated the attitudes of resignation that were so prevalent, and engendered expressions such as "God giveth, God taketh away," or "What's the use?" The complex also encouraged superficiality in matters of religion. All these examples were still to be observed in rural areas in 1950 (Fals Borda 1961a, 276–80).

Otherworldliness related to submission was not limited to subordinate peoples; it appeared also among dominant groups as a rule of behavior that justified, legitimated, and expected servility from sub-jugated peoples. For the new groups of the upper strata, submission was part of the moral order and, as such, the normal way of life of the seigniorial order. Basically it was a positive orientation toward the present. On the one hand the new ruling groups were guaranteed wealth, prestige, and power; and on the other, the peasants found an anchor of security in these values. This was the security of compulsive coercion: castigation, such as expulsion from the lot assigned them by *concertaje* on the hacienda; the stocks and the whip; banishment from their expected place in heaven by anathemas from any pulpit or confessional. The acceptance of passive attitudes and their inclusion in the process of socialization was so prevalent in the Andean region of the New Kingdom of Granada that a veritable *Pax Hispana* was achieved, altered only during the revolt of the *Comuneros* (see later discussion).

The counter-values of neo-Manicheism were added to the new seigniorial order as part of the Christian doctrine taught to the Americans. It implied the definition of human nature as sinful, contempt for man as a source of evil, and the pursuit of God as Paraclete and refuge of love.

The introduction of the Christian idea of sin caused confusion in simple indigenous customs and not only in anthropophagy, nudism, polygamy, and free marital liaisons or *amaño*, that could have had positive functions. Furthermore, idols were seen as personifications of the devil. But many Americans secretly persisted in their beliefs. The undercover continuation of many of these practices, valued for ages, is an element of the classic "Indian reserve" and melancholy, his hypocritical mistrustfulness, which are noticeable even today in many places.

Moreover, the emphasis on seeking God as a refuge of love tended to provide the believer with an escape from his suffering condition on earth, thus confirming his political passivity from a new angle and blessing his acquiescence to the caste order. Escape from this evil world was possible only in death. For this reason it proved to be functional to promote the idea of the tortured Christ, crucified and impotent, among the Indians. This was the Christ of the popular tradition, "born in Tangiers," that once caused Unamuno (1922) to say "This Christ of my land is earth." This Christ-centered cult of death led to attitudes of contempt for life on earth, asceticism, and passivity among believers (Mackay 1933; López de Mesa 1934, 14–15). Thus neo-Manicheism brought together a series of counter-values that reinforced the seigniorial order through fear and came to be an almost unassailable defense of the sacral tradition.

The Adjustment in Norms

A process of adjustment and compulsion similar to that related to values occurred also in the normative framework of the seigniorial order. The two general ayllic norms of communal stability and providence continued, adapting themselves to the condition of sub-version imposed by the conquest. Two sets of counter-norms were added by the Spanish: that of prescriptive rigidity and that of acritical morality.

The older norms of communal stability were mainly assimilated through the new scheme of town building (*reducciones*) combined with grants of land reservations (*resguardos*). The former as much as the latter respected the collective method of land use and the traditional indigenous organization of the *sybyn*. The chieftains maintained their positions as captains, but with new functions of authority and new roles to fulfill in relation to the conquistadors. In turn, the Spanish imposed similar conditions of dwelling and labor on individuals who wished to own land whether it was through private land grant (*merced*), sale, or occupation. These adjustments were important because they achieved the stabilization of the rural population on occupied lands; they permitted the Spanish to accommodate themselves as the upper caste in community structures without destroying already functioning systems and assuring the continuation of socio-political local groups and the payment of taxes. Only the resident-labor system of the *concertaje* disrupted the community by relocating isolated families on haciendas. But other communities were reconstructed there which also fitted into the seigniorial order.

The Spanish counter-norms regarding providence do not seem to have been very incompatible with traditional norms of the ayllic order. The Spanish as well as the Chibchas were at the mercy of nature in many respects even though the former had better tools and medicines. In any case, the Americans adopted animals and agricultural and mining techniques of the intruding order and, in turn, the Spanish assimilated elements of indigenous botany, agriculture, and alimentation. In addition, the Spanish brought a concept of trade and commerce based on money which seems to have had somewhat equivalent counterparts among the Chibchas (Aguado 1906, 266; Simón 1936, II, 273; Oviedo y Valdés 1852, II, 409). Thus it does not appear that there would have been any significant conflict in this area and the adjustment was greatly facilitated.

Prescriptive rigidity, instead, had to be added to the local tradition. It comprised the norms that perpetuated the caste structure supported by the ethos of Hispanic culture. These norms were employed to differentiate according to race, occupation, and social position, a practice that was especially prominent in education, local government, and the promotion of civil servants and clergymen. Those who belonged to the "lower castes" or whose blood was considered to be of a "bad line" or who had servile or menial occupations were hardly able to lift their heads. And on the contrary, those who belonged to the upper castes could not degrade themselves by taking on domestic occupations or doing manual work. Good lineage was the basic requirement for a distinguished life, and for political, religious, and social promotions. Such was the case in the Andean region where there developed the *chapetona* (white peninsular) caste of gentlemen, bureaucrats, and landed gentry; that of artisans and *ladinos* or mixed-bloods; and that of small peasant farmers and Indians.

Acritical morality refers to the norms of the seigniorial order that derived their compulsion exclusively from the allegiance to formal authority, especially political and religious authority (prescriptions, dogmas, and beliefs).[1] They were strengthened throughout the years. In the political sphere, consistent with the utopia, they became concentrated on the "sacred" image of the king of Spain who came to be almost deified by the Indians; in the religious sphere they were legitimated by the rule, "The sages of the Holy Mother

Church are competent enough." Acritical morality has been observed in the rural communities of yesterday and today through the
analysis of attitudes toward certain agricultural practices, such as the
care and destruction of seed, or toward the implications of innovations, such as hospitals and community development boards. The
legitimation of these norms is not found in any structure that we
would designate as "rational" today or in the ayllic order, in relation to which they were counter-norms; they can only be justified
by reference to the emergent values of the seigniorial order.

Señores and Ladinos

The diffusion of these counter-norms and counter-values was carried out by a series of institutions and groups established by the
Spanish to which the Americans responded with new forms of social
organization. The conquistadors began with their peninsular conception of caste urbanism; the Chibchas responded with groups that
were adequate for the task of disseminating the new forms among
social levels down to the neighborhood, in harmony with this ethos.
Some of these groups subverted the local society.

As was said before, one difficulty responsible for corrupting the
meaning of the absolute missional utopia of the Church-state was
that the subjects who went out to the "promised land" did not have
the prophetic vision of the idealistic elite, the kings and popes. The
attitudes and norms transmitted by those particular Christians to
local groups let the radiance of the utopia shine through only in
part. In fact, a large part of the conquistadors' motivation derived
from a very uncelestial craving for riches and power. Their ideal of
manliness was the soldier; even the cloistered clergy and mystics
became "knights of the divine." Although they talked a lot about
what was just, they revealed that they had only an abstract idea of
justice, whereas their sense for what was human was only too concrete (Mackay 1933, 17).

Therefore it should not be surprising that the gigantic efforts of
Fra Bartolomé de las Casas to organize his ill-starred agricultural
colony at Cumaná came to naught because the farmers that he took
from Spain decided to become *señores*, or lords, and to "consider

themselves gentlemen, going with the conquistadors in order to rob" (Casas 1929, Book 3, Chaps. 156–60). For this very reason Bernal Díaz declared in his *Historia verdadera* that his comrades had come to serve God, but also to get riches and power (Díaz del Castillo 1943, II, 394).

The extension of lordly dominion to the colony was automatic with the transplantation of Christianity. On one hand there was the right of occupation through war; on the other, there were compromising antecedents of the feudal-serf system of *behetrías* on the peninsula (Ots Capdequí 1946; Ballesteros y Beretta 1944, I, 689). The cooperativeness and docility of a large part of the conquered American groups had no less effect. With regard to this particular there was indeed a battle between the defenders of the missional utopia and the conquistadors who were unable to subsist without the service of the Indians. Promulgation by Charles V of the humanitarian *Nuevas Leyes* (New Laws) of 1542 (the last stand of the utopians) that terminated trusteeship of the Indians (*encomienda*) caused serious rebellion in all the Spanish colonies, especially Peru; four years later the Emperor was forced to retreat from his position. He had evidently touched upon the basic mechanism of the extension of political rule to America.

The *encomienda*, along with its subsidiary institutions such as the levy tax and the indoctrination and distribution of Indians (Zavala 1935), was established in the Andean region after 1538 and the arrival of Quesada to the savannah of Bogota. It did not imply possession of lands; it was above all an expedient of control over tax collecting and for religious instruction. It was required that the Indians be cared for and well treated and that their possessions not be taken from them. Nonetheless, the *encomienda* very soon became a full-fledged instrument of economic domination that allowed illegal confiscation of the land by the trustees.

This trend was maintained even in the face of the opposition of kings. Once the *Nuevas Leyes* were passed the strategic group of *encomenderos* (to whom the Indians had been entrusted by the crown) encouraged a system of land tenure, the hacienda system, which they had earlier developed. The hacienda soon came to prevail in the history of America with the same seigniorial elements (except tribute) and within the legal framework of the *mercedes* or land grants (Bishko 1952). The tribute came to be camouflaged in another social invention, the system of *concertaje* with the residence of landless agricultural workers in a servile condition on sections of haciendas (Fals Borda 1957, 77–81). Thus the binomial lord-servant outline prevailing on the Iberian peninsula was duplicated.

With the elements provided by these two key groups, the *encomenderos* and the *hacendados*, the social, political, and economic bases were achieved for establishing an institutional structure that was resistant to change, extremely efficient, and that reinforced the caste system. Now a higher caste was superimposed on the rudimentary one of the ayllic order, left headless with the deaths of the Chibcha kings. This was the endogamous caste of the arrogant white *señores*. The colonial administrative groups, those of military officers, and those of the ecclesiastical hierarchy also became part of it. Thus the predominance of ascriptive positions was confirmed and the values and norms of this type of society led to action that was prescriptive.

Meanwhile, the Americans were accomodated in the lower stratum of the caste society. But a uniform distribution did not result from this process of accomodation. Distinct groups appeared, placed in various positions and fulfilling certain functions which made local society complex and differentiated.

Subversion of the local order originated not only with the lordly conquistador group but also with some persons and groups of the traditional order that from an early time had shared that purpose. These groups were a social link between the two cultures during the first years of the conquest. They had to openly confront the defenders of their own traditional society. However, with the institutional backing of the señores, these subverters managed to break down the resistances. These linking groups of the Spanish-Catholic subversion or their members were called (and are still usually called) *ladinos*. Within our frame of reference, they form a type of dissident group whose values and norms are basically Spanish as opposed to being of the traditional order. Their group's influence reached as far as the elementary level of rural neighborhoods by means of a saturating process of subversive diffusion. By fostering and activating this basic process the *ladinos* became prominent key groups of the period. In great part, the adoption of the new and stability of the emerging order depended upon them.

The first and most important group of ladinos highlighted a phenomenon that is found in the three subversions studied in this book: a division occurs in the dominant traditional group, which makes way for a rebellious, iconoclastic subgroup that no longer shares the existing ways of life. In the last two subversions this rebel group emerged spontaneously, without need for external military coercion. In the case of this first subversion the change is exogenous and partially imposed. But it is in any case a confrontation of forces that splits the local traditional elite in two, creating a "counter-elite." Thus the name *counter-elite* may be given to that group of persons of prestige status that turns against the prevailing order for ideological reasons and seeks its change as well as its political power (cf. Eisenstadt 1964, 308–16; Bottomore 1964, 9; see also Appendix B).

The counter-elite of the period of the conquest in which the subversion occurred was composed of the chieftains who were nominally converted to Christianity, who had the upper Spanish caste as their reference group, and who confronted their former kings or *uzaques*. This counter-elite was distinguished in several ways: (1) by the adoption of the nobleman's dress; (2) by learning the Spanish language, for which purpose they had special schools organized by the Church; (3) by accepting positions or offices within the new social structure such as those of church porter, sacristan, governor of land reservations, or tax collector; (4) by the full ownership of haciendas after the fashion of the Spanish; (5) by the adoption of Spanish names and the title "Don"; and (6) by the formation of military alliances with Spaniards in order to combat enemy tribes (V. Restrepo 1895; Triana 1922; Grott 1889). The assimilation of seigniorial standards by former chieftains in many cases made them worse despots than before and the example of their "Christian" reference group, with its new forms of coercion and punishment, inflamed the new Indian rulers' desire for authority. Thus the missional utopia was even further decanted, and latent incongruities were produced in the seigniorial order.

Another important linking group whose influence in the new

order grew with the passage of years was the group of persons that, although belonging racially to the common Indian stock, was culturally assimilated into the dominant group. These were the ladinos who were accommodated in subordinate positions in the caste structure. Their reference groups seem to have been Spanish as well as *ladino* counter-elites. Especially important as *ladinos* were Indians who left the reservations in order to adopt a trade, work in commerce, or settle themselves permanently on haciendas as *concertado* laborers or overseers. This group included those who adopted new crafts of European type such as saddlery, leather tanning, blacksmithing, tailoring, and shoemaking. It also included the first Indians to use Spanish technology in agriculture and mining; and those who dedicated themselves to various activities of the new order, street vendors of Spanish products, for example, or the personal servants of *encomenderos* and their families. Included too were those who learned to sing the Mass and popular Spanish songs; or those who learned to play European musical instruments for whom the missionaries established special schools; and those who accommodated American crafts such as goldsmithing, pottery-making, and spinning to the subordinate position reserved for them in the new order.

Also belonging to this category of link groups were the mestizos who began to achieve positions of responsibility about 1570 and whose divided loyalty forced them in the direction of the Spanish. The fact that there had not been any white women during the first fifteen years of the conquest in this part of America produced a latent incongruity in the seigniorial order: the often unjust, marginal position of the new *ladino*-mestizos produced by precisely those circumstances. This process of racial amalgamation was essential to the adjustment of the new order and strategic for the durability of the new patterns of life. In colonial times, however, as a pariah group that could live neither on the Indian reservations nor as full-fledged citizens in white parishes, the mestizos initiated serious actions in various directions. On the one hand they directed themselves against the Indians in order to appropriate their lands; on the other they sought recognition of the Spanish in order to gain entry to prestigious institutions such as the Church. For this reason their work of subversive saturation is important. The dominance of this group increased as its size did, while the indigenous communities declined; that is, the group's importance grew to the degree that the Christian subversion was finding its resolution and adjusting its elements to the emerging social order.

Evidently, the effects of these processes of adjustment and compulsion, assimilation and social accomodation, racial amalgamation, and diffusion of subversive values and norms seem to have been more marked and rapid in Colombia than in other countries of America. From this derive many of the contemporary differences among American societies. These effects also underscore the role played by those processes in conferring a certain direction to the social change they engendered. The key groups of señores (with the clergy) and *ladinos* were in this sense fundamental to these processes. There were also other change agents who merit mention: the protectors of Indians, respected Spaniards who were effective when they maintained regular contacts with those they protected; the magistrates of Indians (*corregidores*) who had the right of residence on the reservations and who are believed to have been fundamental in the diffusion of the rudimentary plow agricultural complex; and the white farmers, poor and isolated, of the type that immigrated to Antioquia, who were called "neighbors and aggregates" (*vecinos y agregados*) and who subsequently played a role in the invasions of reservations (Fals Borda 1957, 93). It is proper to expect that more thorough analysis of these elements as reference groups seeking permanence for the new order and subversion of the old might further clarify the historical process of social adjustment we have been describing.

The Leap to Iron and the Plow

About the same time an important process of technological accumulation began with the addition to the American culture of wheeled vehicles, draft animals, iron tools, the rudimentary wooden plow, and hand broadcasting of grains. New types of weapons and techniques of defense and combat in which human force was used in combination with animal energy were also introduced. This technology was a supportive element of the Christian subversion because it broke down the resistance in hard aspects of the traditional culture which it would not have been possible to accomplish in any other way. The impact of the new technology was particularly strong on the subsistence activities.

This step, which was so gigantic in the economic development of America, has unfortunately been little studied. We know very little about the impact of these new techniques on the use of ancient tools and on the traditional practices concerning the use of land and energy.

There is some information, however, concerning the way in which peninsular technology helped to reinforce the seigniorial order. In the first place, iron instruments for working the soil were almost exclusively the property of the Spanish; they were scarce and costly and were not to be found except on the haciendas (Friede 1944). Since they were so far superior to Indian tools, this discrimination was to be expected. Nevertheless, as a result of the draft labor system (*mita*) in mining and agriculture, the local people became acquainted with the new practices and utilized the instruments of the *encomenderos* and hacienda owners, which were much more efficient than the digging sticks and wooden hooks in their own field work (Mojica Silva 1948, 19). "Borrowing" was particularly important in the application of the new tools to mining emeralds and rock salt and to growing traditional crops such as tubers and corn, where the wide iron hoe could lift the plants (and make furrows) more easily and efficiently than the hooks. Thus it is possible that there was diffusion, if not of the property of the hoe, at least of its use. But this utilization remained under the control of the *señores*. At present, as is known, the hoe is a ubiquitous tool in the Andean region and the "gancho" has been relegated to secondary functions, such as the loosening of earth, and to the harvesting of tubers in sandy soil.

A similar social discrimination seems to have occurred concerning the wheat, barley, rye, and oats complex, grains which were sown primarily by and for the Spanish in the early years (Simón 1953, III 124; Aguado 1906, 315). The control over grains and their marketing remained in the hands of the upper caste through the mills they built in white parishes and on some haciendas. The Americans, how-

ever, soon learned how to yoke the oxen, plow the earth, and broad-
cast the seed; and the teaching task fell to the magistrates as a means
of securing the tribute (Grott 1889, I, 317, 516–20). The speed and
extension of the adoption of wheat may easily be estimated through
reading the chronicles and by scanning the data concerning harvests
in the region. It was of such intensity that some observers are of the
opinion that a good part of the lands of Cundinamarca and Boyacá
that are unproductive today are so because of the planting of wheat
and excessive plowing (Smith 1948). Grains were threshed by the
hooves of the hacienda mules. Later, these grains were disseminated
to the Indian reservations where they partially displaced quinoa
from which the traditional "bread" was made.[2]

The introduction of domesticated animals also had certain differentiating effects according to caste. It seems that some animals were
accepted and became widespread among the natives more readily
than others; to some were attributed certain marks of distinction
that were not shared by other more brutish ones. These were facts
of which the Spanish "agricultural extensionists" of the time surely
made note. For example, the European chicken (there may have
been American varieties, cf. Sauer 1952, 57–60) was so popular
among the natives that in many cases it "flew" before the conquistadors, becoming spontaneously disseminated in regions where the
peninsular men had not yet arrived (Aguado 1906, 475). Sheep were
widely accepted among the peasants, creating a tradition that comes
down to us today: the sheep is the poor man's "piggy bank." On the
other hand, cattle were like the credit bank of the rich who tended
to monopolize them (Fals Borda 1961a, 97; Kubler 1946). In the
same way horses were restricted to the *señores*, hacienda owners,
and chieftains of the counter-elite because preserved in them were
the marks of aristocracy of southern Europe at the time of the
Romans.

This attitude toward the horse seems to have been important in
itself because it prevented transfer to this part of America of the
plow complex of central Europe in which the horse rather than the
ox is the principal source of energy (cf. Jovellanos 1887, 362; White
1962, Chaps. 1 and 2). The preference in Colombia for the ox
brought about the adoption of plows and techniques that were less

efficient than those employed in central and northern Europe which upon being transferred to England and the United States of America made possible the extraordinary development of improved implements at the beginning of the nineteenth century (Fussell 1952; Smith 1953). Thus the Andean region remained in the stage of the ancient rudimentary plow. And, at the same time, through the differentiated adoption of the aforementioned animals for work, meat, and transportation, the structure of the seigniorial society was formalized and reinforced.

There were other animals such as the hog and the dog (distinct from the American cur) that underwent a transformation in being accepted by native groups. Utilized during the conquest as forces of attack, the hog rooting up and devouring Indian cultivations, the bulldog mangling the Indian, they came to be almost constant companions of the Andean peasants. The details of the process are unknown, however. Moreover, the introduction of many other elements to the region was also registered, some of which, such as the cultivation of anise and the olive, have been practically forgotten today. Certain European fruits (pears, apples, plums) became acclimated and grew alongside native ones (*uchuvas*, cherries, *curubas*, berries). In many places they came to be the patrimony of the poor as well as the rich, of the American and of the Spaniard.

Nevertheless, in general terms it may be argued that the greater production resulting from all these innovations and introductions was not equitably spread among the households of the colony. The new technology served to increase the wealth and strengthen the power of the dominant castes. This phenomenon is also observed in later transitions. Technological accumulations, especially of the agricultural and pastoral type, occurred with relative speed and efficiency, always as an element of support to the seigniorial order; it never failed to reinforce. Later development did not even bring technological accumulation to the critical point at which dynamic effects are produced in values, norms, and social organization.

Only in the region of Santander, to the north of Bogotá, was the development of a limited manufacturing industry achieved in the second half of the eighteenth century which engendered certain symptoms of subversion of the seigniorial order (Nieto Arteta 1962,

46–47, 322–25). It was precisely there that the first important act of sedition occurred in the country with the uprising of the *Comuneros* in 1781. The ideological confusion reigning at the time, the division that was produced among the leaders of this movement —for the Indians it was a nativistic one, for the creoles, a purely fiscal one—and the naiveté with which they all proceeded frustrated this event that could otherwise have had great revolutionary consequences. The bloody repression of genuine subversive leaders like José Antonio Galán proved effective within the limited scope of the colony. Nonetheless it established the bases and created the antecedents for the political revolt thirty years later (Morales Benitez 1957, 82–102). The seigniorial order was not changed at this time; but technological accumulation, especially in the trades, continued, and became an important element of the liberal subversion of 1848.

The Hispanic Peace

Once the Christian subversion was resolved and its purpose was sustained through two generations by the *señores* and local insurgent groups, the seigniorial order acquired an impressive durability.

Almost all the institutions established through socio-cultural adjustment lasted several centuries, in spite of the opposition of the Spanish Crown to some of them. The *encomienda*, for example, that had been declared illegal by the kings of Spain in the sixteenth century and abolished for the last time by Phillip V in 1718, persisted for many more decades. There were still a certain number of *encomenderos* when independence from Spain was declared in 1810 (Hernández Rodríguez 1949, 232). The Indian reservations began to decline only around the middle of the eighteenth century, owing to the invasions of "aggregates" and mestizos, but did not disappear from the central region until the middle of the next century. The *concertaje* system survived in many parts until the twentieth century. Castillian speech of the sixteenth century crystallized and endured in expressions of the Andean peasants until the end of the nineteenth century (Cuervo 1914, xxiv). It persists today in archaic proper names such as "Pioquinto" referring to Pope Pius V, who reigned in the sixteenth century. Popular dances and songs like the *torbellino* and the *bambuco* probably have their origins in the music brought by the conquistadors themselves and preserved by the peasants (Fals Borda 1961a, 222–29). There are many other examples.

This extraordinary durability leads us to ask how it was accomplished; the early experience might serve as an example for future movements of social transformation. Evidently there was an initial stage of intense conflict, with a climax between 1537 and 1541, in which the destructive impact of the conquest impelled by the missional utopia was felt. In these years the existing order (which was moral for the Americans) was challenged and subverted by the Christians and a counter-elite was created. All the elements of violence, coercion, and persuasion were applied to avoid a return to the former society. The anti-climax of the subversion necessary for development followed soon after, between 1541 and 1595. During this period the counter-elite became institutionalized by means of compulsion and adjustment between the Spanish and the Americans. And finally there occurred a stage of relative stabilization, after 1595—in this case after two generations—in which the ruling seigniorial groups maintained the direction of change in the new order.

The success achieved in institutionalizing subversive change during the crucial periods of climax and anti-climax may best be understood as the result of the application of various *mechanisms of compulsion* within the general process of change. The mechanisms of compulsion that stand out are: (1) hegemonic domination; (2) leadership ability; and (3) social diffusion.

1. *Hegemonic domination* involves the formation of a governing team whose members think similarly regarding social and economic transformation and who are capable of applying straight power to achieve valued goals in the social, political, and economic spheres. It involves the constitution of rebellious reference groups within the power structure of the larger society to back up related groups acting in local communities. With this object in mind, the machinery of state and Church of the colonial epoch were coordinated to promote the Christian subversion and its development at all levels of society. The state's task at that time was to promote processes of adjustment between subversion and tradition such as cul-

tural assimilation, value substitution, racial amalgamation, religious syncretism, and technological accumulation. The efficacious alliance of state and Church provided not only the ideological fuel for the creative endeavor of the subversive groups but also the organizational and temporal apparatus to reinforce decisions relative to the course of the new society. In this way all the components of the social order were provided for and a formal harmony or congruence, sufficient to produce a veritable cultural monolith, was achieved among them.

2. *Leadership ability* demands that those who direct the subversion exercise leadership with intelligence, sagaciously anticipating the movement of adversaries, concealing weaknesses, strategically withdrawing only in order to charge anew with greater force, taking maximum advantage of available resources, attacking with determination or astuteness according to circumstances. This ability was an obvious characteristic of the conquistadors and their collaborators, the *señores*, and the clergy. The lack of it leads to frustrations and failure in transitions to new stages of development, as we shall see later on.

3. *Social diffusion* is an indispensable process for carrying development and its ideology to all levels of society, especially to local ones such as the neighborhood and the family, which are fundamental for these purposes. The fact that many *señores, ladinos,* and mestizos who were disposed to promote the subversion and the transformation of local society were scattered about the country was essential to the advent of the seigniorial order.

Of equal importance are the *stabilizing factors* that are partially applied during the period of subversion (for its being short and intense) but are more steadily applied afterwards. Their object is to maintain a determined direction in change, guarantee its goals, and avoid possible frustrations. These factors are: (1) socialization of development; (2) legitimation of coercion; (3) ideological persistence; and (4) technological support.

1. The *socialization of development* requires full control of the means of domination for a prudent length of time, at least for a generation, sufficient for the new norms and values to be transmitted from fathers to sons, to cease being viewed as immoral, and to

acquire the force and congruity of tradition. The *señores* and *ladinos*, by means of the mechanisms of adjustment and compulsion they design and apply, manage to assure that the condition of subversion is overcome, imparting to the process an impulse so that the new order will move forward autonomously.

2. The *legitimation of coercion* implies the degree of control necessary to avoid excessive normlessness, chaos, and disorder that might prejudice the achievement of the valued goals. The Spanish managed to stabilize the situation owing to the efficient political-religious machinery at their disposal.

3. *Ideological persistence* requires the unwavering loyalty of the active groups, especially of the counter-elites, to the principles of the subversive movement, even though they be only decantations of utopias or lead to successive adjustments. There were a mystique, vigor, and tenacity in the conquest and in the first decades of the colony. The goals of domination and the ideals of society were clear and the *señores* and *ladinos* were dedicated to them without varying their opinion, at least throughout the critical period of the socialization of one generation by another.

4. *Technological support* results when the elements related to the use of energy and land, industry, defense, transportation, communication, medicine, and similar activities reinforce the social order or its transformation through the efforts of a technocracy or a specialized corps, or by means of social groups with which the new techniques are practiced. Evidently, the innovations promoted by the Spanish, especially in agriculture and defense, broke down resistances in tradition and made the dominant groups even more powerful and prosperous.

Contrary to the general impression regarding the differences between the conditions of the conquest and later historical crises, sociological analysis tends to show that in one as much as in the others mechanisms and factors similar to those described here have been employed. In essence, the agents of change always seek to impose it first and maintain it afterwards. In this sense there is no reason to differentiate between the Christian subversives and the liberals, socialists, and pluralists that came later. One proof of this rests in the way that the transitional groups managed to spread Christian subversion to the level of the masses so that from then on socialization by the family became a defense of the new tradition and a source of resistance to other significant changes. This fact shows that significant development penetrates as far as the neighborhood, the extended family, and the personality, and that at these levels the real confrontation with tradition occurs. Here the triumph or failure of reformist or revolutionary movements is decided. For this reason the mechanisms of subversive change are the same in 1560 as in 1860 and 1960; this will be explained in the following chapters.

On the other hand, the efficacy of the seigniorial monolith is obvious for there has been no other modern empire that has achieved such control or influence at regional levels as well as in local structures. The missionary absolute utopia was not fulfilled with this monolithic wholeness, but it was possible to achieve a social peace almost without precedent in world history.

Nevertheless, it did not appear to be a peace that was completely productive. For one thing, it was rather artificial, taking into account the economic and cultural isolation of the colonies fostered by the Council of the Indies. For another thing, it came to be somewhat close to the "peace of a cemetery," one of the spiritual passions of Saint Ignatius of Loyola. In fact, even though the humanitarian experiments of the sixteenth century failed, Loyola's Jesuits did manage to achieve the utopia in their own fashion; the *reducciones* of Paraguay were their most dramatic triumph. But there as much as in the New Kingdom of Granada, the people who worked the land and who sanctimoniously prayed in the temples were mechanically and ritually conditioned by religion and the state to their low, servile position. They were not to begin rising from this profound incongruity, from this lethargy of the tomb, until the twentieth century.

The political monolith that resulted from the Christian subversion made possible the appearance of significant attitudes. These should be taken into account in the study of subsequent subversions, for they underscore the historical inconsistencies of the seigniorial order. They are the extremes of opulence and poverty in the country; the hunger of the peasant people who live on fertile soil; the ignorance that degrades Christian man; the hypocrisies and Pharisaism of social castes; the contradiction between the universal Church and the national seigniorial-ecclesiastical establishment. These are classical expressions of a collectivity that has not found itself and that suffers because of the failures of its leaders and the spiritual vacuum left by the rejection of utopias.

In any case, once their task of development was fulfilled, the utopian elements of the Christian subversion were decanted. Their residues were combined with the adjusted values of the ayllic order. Then they took the harmonious and manifest, the incongruent and latent forms of the new seigniorial order. In this way another self-image and another image of the world were produced: a new style of acting, perceiving, and valuing, within the general perspective of Western civilization.

CHAPTER FIVE

Subversion and Frustration in the Nineteenth Century: The Liberals

HISPANIC peace lasted three hundred years, until the beginning of the nineteenth century, without any significant subversion having arisen. The rebellion of the *Comuneros* could not be classified as such because the efforts of Galán (the only rebel leader of any vision) were stopped early, before they had made any profound impact on colonial society.

Neither could the war of independence be considered subversion except with regard to the challenge that its leaders presented to certain norms of the seigniorial order. Such a challenge is important in itself, and in a sense it prepared the way for the advent of the liberal subversive élan when not only the norms but the values as well were affected. The liberators doubtlessly nourished great ideals for the fatherland and it was Bolívar who gave greatest stress to goals that were to be achieved. But his commitment did not seem to possess the power to diffuse the new elements among the common people and to saturate society with the intensity necessary to produce a real transformation. His generals and other subordinates preserved many aspects of the seigniorial way of life. It was for this reason that a great part of Bolívar's dream was not fulfilled. The Liberator died thinking he had "plowed the sea." Significant transformation only came with the advent of liberalism in the 1840s.

The study of the liberal subversion, whose revolutionary climax occurred in Colombia between 1848 and 1854 (with its anticlimax lasting until 1867), makes it possible to observe the whole process of change that stretches from one social order to another under conditions of political autonomy. The Christian subversion had had the situation of conquest in its favor: *señores* and *ladinos* supported and fomented the subversion against the traditional Amerindian elite by means that extended from flagrant physical coercion to compromise and tolerance. In the case of the liberal subversion there early occurred a serious schism in the ruling group itself. But the dominant groups soon became united to react effectively against the revolution, promoting the necessary adjustments that would guarantee their own survival.

Profound tensions and conflicts were produced in one subversion as much as in the other. Within the historical conditions, and subject to the social and economic factors of their respective periods, both subversions were nourished by utopias that first revealed the veiled incongruities and hidden inconsistencies of the established social orders. But as usual, these utopias became decanted in the social reality experienced during the conflict. The impact of the Christian subversion lasted for two generations during which the seigniorial order, which endured for eight more, was shaped. The impact of the liberal subversion was not sustained for even a generation: its frustration was dramatic. Even so, it led to significant changes owed to the dialectical force of the utopian thought which helped break down the seigniorial order. The traditionalists had to give in somewhat and to accept certain adjustments in order to overcome the implicit dangers.

The latent contradictions of the seigniorial order as seen in the light of the humanitarian ideals of its inception stood out in relief after the middle of the eighteenth century. For example, the moral problem of slavery became acute owing to the licenses issued by the Bourbons to various companies in order to intensify and better organize the slave trade. This trade fostered the creation of new businesses that became extremely wealthy at the expense of the producers in the colonies, as was the case of the Güipuzcoana Company (Arcila Farías 1946). Paradoxically, land itself began to be scarce and this was also a serious economic and political problem. Attempts to apply solutions such as land *composiciones* (recognition of squatters' rights), the end of reservations, the sale or concession of royal lands, the recognition of entailed estates, primogeniture, and mortmain only made the situation worse. They confirmed the existence of an oligarchy of landowners and a mass of indigent sharecroppers, tenant farmers, and impoverished *vecinos* (white settlers). Moreover, taxes were increased abusively and trading was hindered, a situation which created serious tensions among the manufacturing interests of the Socorro area and stimulated the contraband trade in precious metals through the Chocó and other regions (Liévano Aguirre 1963, III, 75-98). These political and economic symptoms were a prelude to the serious outbreaks that occurred later. They also indicated a reawakening of the American conscience (as a new ideology that would open the door to sedition) for critically examining certain incongruous aspects of the seigniorial order.

Spain itself, during the reigns of Charles III and Charles IV, was going through a period of recapitulation and introspection that led to a great intellectual renaissance. It was the period of Jovellanos and the sages of the *Sociedad Economica de Madrid*. Independent of the rest of Europe—although aware of English and French thought that made the revolutions in their countries possible—these sages had made an inventory of the state of the Spanish Empire, raising doubts about ideas considered until then absolute and proposing many important political, social, and economic innovations.

It was in this atmosphere of tolerance toward the possiblities for change and under these dynamic social and economic conditions that the progressive viceroys from Manuel Guirior to Pedro Mendinueta were educated before going to Santa Fe de Bogotá to govern the New Kingdom of Granada between 1773 and 1803. In the chests of one of them, José de Ezpeleta, there arrived in the colony a book that was to add fuel to the fire of enthusiasm generated by the new utopia: that of the French Revolution with its motto of "Liberty, equality, fraternity."

The Myth of Equality

In the colonies, the Enlightenment movement of the Bourbons found expression in the educational plans devised to update the systems and the contents of traditional teaching. That movement also had repercussions in impressive endeavors of scientific investigation. For example, Viceroy Guirior promoted the reforms proposed by his agent, Francisco Antonio Moreno y Escandón (and encouraged further by his successor, Viceroy-Archbishop Antonio Caballero y Góngora), that modernized the teaching of sciences such as astronomy and medicine. In addition, José Celestino Mutis, the great teacher and botanist, arrived in Santa Fé to organize the Botanical Expedition. His work, as well as that of his students and colleagues, attracted the attention of such scholars as Humboldt, who arrived to visit the institution.

Out of that stimulating environment for the study of American natural and social realities (which in part challenged the colonial norms of acritical morality) there emerged a group of young men who became the paladins and martyrs of the war of independence fifteen years later. Beginning with simple literary activities in gatherings like those of the *Eutropélica* and the *Buen Gusto* societies, young men such as Camilo Torres, Frutos Joaquín Gutiérrez, José Fernández Madrid, José Maria Lozano, Francisco José de Caldas, José Luis Azuola, Francisco Antonio Zea, Joaquín Camacho, and Antonio Nariño began acquiring the esprit de corps of a political group (Posada and Ibañez 1903, 16, 119). This spirit was, simultaneously and significantly, an American conscience. It was from the lips of these men that the message of the new humanism was to be spoken, the message that had agitated Europe in the eighteenth century and whose echo reached the colony.

The ideal of equality among men was an outstanding characteristic of this humanism. Equality had become the war cry of intellectual and civil conflicts in Europe, especially after John Locke postulated it as a function of freedom, thus justifying ideologically the rise of the new propertied classes of England. It was also a result of the secularist reaction of the period fostered by the scientific challenge to religious dogma. It found support among the philosophers of the Enlightenment who held ideas of progress and believed in man as rationally and basically good. Of course, equality became a valued goal for the architects of the French Revolution who wanted to build a new democratic society.

It was this integral conception of the transformation of human society, with its revolutionary implications, that motivated thinkers like Rousseau to write treatises such as the *Discourse on the Source of Inequality among Men* (1775). His influence throughout Europe did not fail to have political impact. The Rousseau message arrived in the New Kingdom of Granada via Spain, paradoxically, through a book written by an enraged royalist (who soon after published the panegyric of Louis XVI and Marie Antoinette), Christophe Félix de la Touloubre (Galart) Montjoie, *The Causes and the Beginning of the Revolution.*[1] It was not a book that expressed enthusiasm for the events of the Bastille, but it contained a transcription of the "Declaration of the Rights of Man and the Citizen." An official of Viceroy Ezpeleta's guard gave this book to one of the enterprising members of the *Eutropélica* society, Don Antonio Nariño, in August of 1794 (Vergara y Vergara 1903).

Nariño translated the Declaration, printed it in his own shop, and went out to sell it in the streets. He had distributed and sold only a few copies when the government and the society declared the whole thing subversive. Impressed by this, Nariño attempted to recover the copies in circulation and burned the rest (Posada and Ibáñez 1903, 95). It was too late. He was arrested, judged, and condemned to imprisonment in Africa, banishment from America, and confiscation of property. This occasion was also taken to bear a salutary pressure on the youths involved in the literary societies. The young rebels were "idlers, libertines, and attracted by the perverse maxims of the modern, prone to subversion," according to the declaration of the Church's preceptor, Diego Terán (Posada and Ibáñez 1903, 50). With these events the impact of the new utopia of democratic liberalism began to be felt in the New Kingdom of Granada.

With Nariño temporarily removed from the scene, consolidation of the liberal-democratic utopia found a champion in his colleague, the distinguished jurist, Don Camilo Torres. In the face of the political crisis produced in Spain by the Napoleonic invasions, Torres emphasized the strategic importance of remaining loyal to the Spanish crown without intermediaries, implying that the colonies ought to begin to be treated as real provinces, such as those of the Iberian peninsula. He was protesting the discrimination of the Central Junta of Spain against the American Creoles, calling attention to the fact that they were direct descendants of the conquistadors. In his *Memorial de agravios* (Memorandum of Complaints) of November 20, 1809, he claimed for justice. He declared that the Americans did not wish to go on being "flocks of sheep at the whim of the mercenaries" and called for "Equality, the holy right of Equality!" However, perusal of the Memorandum reveals that Torres was not thinking here about Rousseauian social equality or the humanitarian goals of the French Revolution, but rather about something much more pragmatic: equality between the two white groups of the landowning upper caste, the "peninsular Spaniards" and the "Spanish Americans," that is, the Spanish-born and the native elites. This ideological decantation of the liberal utopia continued to influence successive events until the declaration of independence in 1810 (cf. Umaña Luna 1952).

However, the rebellious vision of Torres and his friends led them to avail themselves of the tenets of the French Revolution, and later of the philosophy of the North American Revolution, to involve the populace in their endeavor to overthrow the ruling peninsular elite. They began to hold that "sovereignty resides essentially in the people of the nation," a thesis that denied the divine right of kings. This counter-ideology served to support the position of the Creole elite against the interests of the peninsular group, the *chapetones*. Owing to the demagogical manipulations of the *chisperos* on July 20, 1810, Torres's position prevailed and the Spanish governing group was replaced by the local elite of distinguished Creoles. The excesses committed by the "people of the nation," stimulated by the brief orgy of the overthrow of the Viceroy, Antonio Amar y Borbon, led the new ruling group to promptly decree the withdrawal of the masses, declaring anyone who called the people together again "guilty of treason" (Henao and Arrubla 1962, 349). Thus the people became "equal" but separate. The new equality was achieved only among the members of the ruling caste.

It is in this way that the war of independence inaugurated in 1810 did not imply a radical departure from the seigniorial way of life; more than anything else, it was a formal operation with a changing of the guard, an instance of "marginal change" (see Appendix B). Accustomed to the pomp of the viceroy, the people disdained President Jorge Tadeo Lozano's simplicity of manners, a matter that was an element in his subsequent overthrow. The first congress of that "Foolhardy Nation," convened in December of 1810, gave itself the title of "Most Serene Highness;" its members were representatives of high society and the clergy favoring the changeover. They continued to interpret the liberal utopia as it suited them, decanting it even more through the creation of institutions that did not basically affect the social and economic situation.

Two of these institutions were *caudillismo* and *representative democracy*. The *caudillos* (war lords) transferred the old patterns of subordination of the seigniorial order to the "democratic" context (cf. Samper 1861): Carmona in Cartagena, González in Socorro, Reyes Patria in Tunja, also Neira, Herrán, Mosquera, and so many others. According to contemporary historian Juan Francisco Ortiz, they were "a kind of little kings supported by horsemen and some infantry quickly mustered and poorly disciplined" (1907, 121–22). Similarly, according to the authoritative chronicler of the war José Manuel Restrepo, "wherever there was an ambitious demagogue or aristocrat who wished to make his mark, there appeared independent and sovereign juntas, even in poor towns and parishes" (1858, I, 89). For this reason the *caudillos* began to foment conflicts among themselves, leading to the first civil wars in Colombia. With the disappearance of the colonial authorities, real power at the level of the rural community fell to those persons able to organize troops or cavalry and to exercise control in their respective communities. These were the hacienda owners from colonial times and the new latifundists created by the republic through land grants, as a means of compensation for services rendered. These land owners had at their disposal sharecroppers, or *concertados*, organized under bosses called gamonales who were ready for an uprising or a civil war. But the caste structure remained untouched, leaving the masses of citizens in their traditional subordinate position.

On the other hand, the adoption of institutions of representative democracy patterned after those of the United States, also produced incongruities at all levels, as Mariano Ospina Rodríguez observed in 1842 (cf. López Michelsen 1955, 136–202). The very act of writing constitutions based on foreign texts was incongruent in itself; but as a part of the democratic procedures, they had to be produced "to guarantee the public welfare," as stated by the first charter of the "Foolhardy Nation," written in 1811. The constitutionalist fad became an excuse for substituting certain elites for others through a chain of civil conflicts that lasted almost through the nineteenth century. Basically, the constitutions as well as the conflicts reflected the inconsistencies implicit in the transplanting of the liberal utopia on to the local society. Owing to the interpretive filter of the ruling groups, this utopian graft left the seigniorial order untouched and diluted the democratic ideal of equality in freedom to such a degree that it became a simple myth. There existed only a type of Athenian democracy reserved for the ruling and educated minorities.

Nonetheless, this peculiar idea of equality led the dominant groups to encourage the adoption of an individualistic and entrepreneurial ethic closely related to the Calvinist one that had also been an ingredient of the Industrial Revolution in Europe (Smelser 1959; Weber 1958). This mentality was more prevalent among members of the elite (who later formed the upper bourgeoisie) and among settlers of the province of Antioquia, from which a rural middle class emerged. In other parts, this mentality was expressed in romantic gestures such as the granting of full property rights in reservation lands to the Indians in order to make them full-fledged citizens. This rite was practiced in order to demonstrate the evolution of society to more civilized stages: communal property was a primitive idea, according to Darwinian ethnologists. Consequently, the National Congress, meeting at Cúcuta, authorized the distribution of reservation lands according to law of October 11, 1821 so that "the Indians could recover all their rights, thereby becoming equal with all other citizens," an order that began to be executed about 1839. In this way the tradition of communal land ownership that had been preserved in the colony and that had suffered adjustments from the ayllic order, was ended. The actual residence and work requirements to secure land ownership that had been imposed by the Spanish were also ended. The result was to dramatize the existing inequality, and in many cases it made the situation of the peasants worse.

However, with the political organization of the Republic and its existence guaranteed, a clear tendency to change the seigniorial order on a significant scale began to be observed among the elite as well as in popular groups (Morales Benítez 1957, 12–13). This tendency had two discernible antecedents, one that was endogenous and the other exogenous. The endogenous one was the anti-Spanish local reaction that followed the war of liberation; the exogenous one was the intensification of cultural and economic contacts with Europe. The two effects together led the dominant groups to modify the situations in order to move the country toward the democratic goals that the liberators had first outlined. This movement became articulated in the decade from 1840 to 1850 to give rise to the important phenomenon of the liberal subversion, to which an introductory reference was made at the beginning of this chapter.

Norms in Counterpoint

The endogenous anti-Spanish reaction, the natural consequence of the bloody war of liberation, led local society and its ruling groups to adopt positions and to promote policies that tended to partially negate the seigniorial legacy. The most outstanding national leaders, such as Bolívar, Santander, and Zea, attempted to modify the normative framework of colonial society, notwithstanding the opposition of important traditional institutions. However, out of respect for the latter and excessive prudence, they did not dare to challenge the values themselves. It is for this reason that their efforts redounded in only marginal results that affected more the form than the substance of the society of their times—the age of splendor of the Great Colombia (cf. Bushnell 1966; see Appendix B for marginal change).

The most evident liberal counter-norms were those that challenged the seigniorial norms of prescriptive rigidity and communal stability. The liberators eliminated primogeniture and titles of nobility, banned the use of official forms of address for magistrates (in order to address them simply as "citizens") and somewhat democratized personal titles. "Don" began to be used freely, as occurs in the documentary novel of the period, *Manuela*, by Eugenio Díaz (published in 1889), and once it had gathered sufficient momentum, its use was unrestricted. In succeeding years, "any muleteer who obtained a mule team and pasture land, acquired the title 'Don' along with them," complained the writer Miguel Samper (1898, I, 196). Another example of formal liberation from the norms of social rigidity was that concerning the title "Doctor," the use of which had previously been very restricted but began to be freer in 1848 when persons such as Don Aquileo Parra, a member of the rising bourgeoisie and future President of the Republic, agreed that they should be addressed as "Doctor" without being one, but simply as a matter of "personal distinction" (Parra 1912, 684–85).

The changes required by counter-norms that attempted to destroy the seigniorial system of education (restricted to the upper castes) were a little more daring. The government promoted public education, organized official universities, established Lancasterian schools, adopted utilitarian texts (received through Spanish liberals), and fostered the dissemination of the Bible. There is little doubt that the number of students in the schools increased prodigiously (Fals Borda 1962). But the opposition of the Catholic Church also became radicalized: its bishops preached against the "rational philosophies" of Kant and Hegel, against Bentham and the British Bible Society. And to put a stop to the matter, the bishops quoted from Saint Agathan to remind believers that "innovations are inadmissible among Catholics" (Mosquera 1858, II, 5, 174, 477 *et passim*). Bolívar, inflamed at the attempt on his life in September 1828, took it upon himself to check this counterpoint in norms by banning the utilitarian texts, placing limitations on the Bible societies, and harassing university students. In fact, for the Liberator, "the political science that has been taught to the students of the university contains many maxims that are detrimental to the tranquility of nations," for which reason it was condemnable (cited by Nieto Arteta 1962, 82). This is a posture that has been periodically repeated in the history of Colombia for identical purposes. Mariano Ospina Rodríguez delivered the final blow about 1843 with the issuance of his educational plan, considered by many to be repressive, that was Catholic and authoritarian in character.

Another attempt to break the norms of prescriptive rigidity was the organization of Masonic lodges, with which the governing elite and other selected persons became affiliated (Hoenigsberg 1940; Ortíz 1907, 164). This was another channel for vertical mobility open to the descendants of the *señores*, with new status roles, expectations of behavior and social relationships. The Church attacked the lodges also. However, owing to the selective tendency shown in the recruitment of their members and the clerical reaction toward the end of the century (cf. Rivera y Garrido 1897, 303), membership was limited to the dominant groups and the influence of the lodges was considerably weakened. They persisted throughout the nineteenth century with purposes that were primarily honorific.

In fact, the economic situation and the conditions of public order in the postwar period did not allow greater experimentation or risks. This prudent attitude is summarized in the annual report to Congress by the Secretary of the Treasury of President Santander, Don Francisco Soto, in 1833: "It is not as important to be creative as it is to preserve that which exists." This dictum gave support to the protectionist policy of the state and helped to preserve the status quo. But it was not an obstacle to the imposition of individualistic counter-norms and the weakening of the norms of communal stability whose principal expression was to be found in the Indian reservations and their towns (*reducciones*). Those who had by tradition sown the soil under the protection of collective concessions from the Crown were turned into fee-simple, individual proprietors by law. It is possible that on these reservations the situation had already degenerated, with there being instances of individual exploitation of the land; but this did not threaten the existence of communal lands as such, like the *ejidos* and pasture areas from which all the *comuneros* benefited (Fals Borda 1957). Moreover, the basic goodness of the philosophy of common usage had not been doubted until independence opened the gates to liberalism and the myth of individual private property. The economic effects of the measures that undermined such norms of communal stability have already been mentioned. These norms had to take the alternative patterns of the present *vereda* (rural neighborhood) in which minifundists or small farmers prevail.

The fact that the anti-Spanish reaction of the postwar period did not go beyond the normative framework, as we have seen, leaving the more vital area of values untouched, was a development that could easily have been foreseen. Nevertheless, it prepared the way for and reinforced the transformations that occurred a little later when not only were the seigniorial norms attacked, but also the values, thus engendering the rebel organisms necessary to carry out the subversion. This stage, which will be studied next, was more exogenetic because it was concerned with the new economic and cultural exchanges with Europe and the impact of the democratic revolutions of 1848 in France, Austria, and Germany.

Economy and Ideology

The arrival of the liberal subversion was announced by a change in the national economic policy and the social reaction it produced: the adoption of free trade and manufacture about 1847 by the first government of General Tomás Cipriano de Mosquera, while Florentino González was Secretary of the Treasury.

González, an economist who had recently arrived from Europe (where he had become enthusiastic about the innovations of English free trade), insisted on maintaining the *latifundista* agrarian structure of the country in order to intensify the export of its products (Galindo 1880). Adopting a neo-mercantilist and *laissez faire* position, he withdrew support from local industries that had been developing since the later days of the colony (in Socorro, for example) and thus alienated the artisans and manufacturers. This decision, naturally, opened the door for subversion and prepared the scene for significant events.

The most important economic measures were related to stimulating international trade and internal transportation. Macadam roads were built, certain canals began to be improved (those of Dique and Puebloviejo on the Atlantic coast, for example), navigation by steamboat was expanded on the Magdalena River, and the first railroads were designed and planned. Furthermore, certain state monopolies inherited from the colony, such as that of tobacco, were eliminated in order to open the way to private initiative and to encourage the development of the first great agricultural enterprises.

Three years later, President José Hilario López ordered a national inventory of natural resources to be conducted by a Chorographic Commission headed by Colonel Agustín Codazzi. This group performed an extraordinary feat comparable only to that of the Botanical Expedition of the late eighteenth century. The Chorographic Commission fostered localism and an incipient nationalism (now regarded as a new value), imparted greater confidence in the worth of native things, and encouraged the dominant groups to go ahead with their efforts toward economic transformation (Morales Benítez 1957, 210–12).

These initiatives were further stimulated by the tumultuous events of the French revolution of 1848, that which toppled Louis Philippe. The local groups chose not the concrete form of this revolution, which was to a certain point anti-machine because it stemmed from artisans and students who looked more toward the past than toward the future, but rather its content, expressed in ideologies such as socialism (of the "utopian" kind), anarchism, and positivism.

Alphons de Lamartine and his *Histoire des Girondins* became the prophet and Bible of the new utopias. The educated elites also adopted, in passing, the nationalistic conscience that was bursting forth in Europe, especially in the Italian and German states, for the ostensible purpose of integrating the country. Through this effort at self-examination and ideological comparison the incongruities and tensions of the seigniorial order became apparent in a significant way—that is, the country entered into a period of subversion (cf. Nieto Arteta 1962, 115–19, 229–38). Specifically, the seigniorial values of nature, otherworldliness, and neo-Manicheism were attacked.

By virtue of the advances of industrial mechanistic attitudes, the first counter-values of the old idea of nature began to be vaguely discernible. These new counter-values would lead to the articulation in Colombia of technological behavior elements in the twentieth century. The knowledge that there existed the possibility of controlling natural processes even partially did not fail to occasion expressions of incredulity on the part of the humble people. But it had immediate effects on the society and culture. The proof of this was the defiant attitude of a large part of the artisans of Bogotá who confronted the traditional institutions during the critical years of the subversion. The elementary manufacturing installations of Socorro and Boyacá began to be displaced by small industries such as those established on the savannah of Bogotá (Ospina Vásquez 1955, 138–39 *et passim*). Nevertheless, this technological development was limited and the discouragement to industry caused by González's free trade policy did not permit its complete fruition. As we shall see, these mechanistic counter-values were later absorbed by the bourgeois order.

Otherworldliness was attacked by way of the patterns of submission that prevailed in colonial days. With the formal structure of the Hispanic society in doubt the appearance of *caudillos* and other new leaders led to a re-evaluation of the relations between superior and subordinate. In the rural area these relations remained almost unchanged, but this was not true in larger towns such as Bogotá, Buga, Cali, and Medellín where a strong movement was organized. At times rebels made incursions into the countryside where they created an atmosphere of terror. The general result was a challenge to otherworldliness stemming from the counter-values of the liberal utopia.

Similar was the relation to the seigniorial values of neo-Manicheism. While the latter led to scorn for man as a source of sin and evil and to seeking passive refuge in God, the counter-values of the liberal utopia presented a contrasting goal of improving the human condition in the here and now. Man could achieve progress and happiness in this life through cultivating his intelligence and reason and could achieve perfection through new patterns of social interaction. Therefore, the idea of equality according to its new advocates should no longer be myth and the local society should begin to think more about enriching life than about the tortures of hell.

The exposition of these heretical ideas led as well to the weakening of the old norms of prescriptive rigidity and acritical morality, inasmuch as they implied the opening of channels of social mobility that were formerly closed, the acquisition of a class consciousness, and a challenge to the customs emanating from traditional institutions. For example, one counter-norm that was beginning to become common already had the Church worried: it was the theological mania of laymen who "believed they had the right to decide on matters of the Church, [qualifying] its teachings or repudiating with scorn those they wished to" (Mosquera 1858, II, 700 ff.). A state minister, Don José María Plata, could laugh with impunity at the canons of the Church in the House of Representatives in 1852; at about the same time the radicals used the epithet "purple puppet" to describe the Primate Archbishop of Bogotá, Monsignor Mosquera (Cuervo and Cuervo 1954, II, 1356, 1377); and in Mariquita and other towns the suppression of the ancient catechism by Father Astete was decreed (Mosquera 1858, II, 339ff.). Thus the position of the Church was becoming ever weaker as representative and defender of the seigniorial norms because other dominant groups wanted to clear the channels for the liberal counter-norms to move in.

Political parties underwent a series of ideological confusions that eroded their organizational structures. At first, the conservative party could call itself liberal and vice versa. There were also "Golgothians" (utopians) and "Draconians" (old liberals). The lack of cohesion in the parties led them to a chaotic situation in which some of their notable leaders and representatives lost authority.

The Liberal Subverters

The liberal ideology made its main impact on the social organization through two associations: the Democratic Society and the Republican School, which became active subverters. The Democratic Societies, in particular, were the most important innovational mechanism of this period of acute transition.

Thorough and impartial studies of these Societies have not been made. However, through isolated clues it is known that they were not new to the country, for an ex-minister of General Santander, Don Lorenzo María Lleras, had already founded a Democratic-Republican Society of Progressive Artisans and Farmers in Bogotá in 1838, with affiliates in Tunja and Villa de Leiva, that limited its activity to the dissemination of cultural information (Arboleda 1933, I, 300–02). These groups combated President José Ignacio de Márquez, whose government was pro-clergy in the civil war that originated in the convents of Pasto (1839–1841). Nonetheless, their function was essentially an informational one, by which they were distinguished from the strategic cells organized about 1848, which were perhaps their successsors. In this new period, even though they were still under the direction of Don Lorenzo María, the Democratic Societies consisted of artisans who were unhappy about the free-trade measures of the government and of students of the new National College (university). By uniting in the new historical context, as their French counterparts had done a short time before in the Champ de Mars, these groups made a subversive impact of considerable import. They had a national organization with about two hundred local societies established between 1847 and 1852 throughout the country in places such as Cali, Buenaventura, Cartago, Popayán, Pasto, Tunja, Sogamoso, Zipaquirá, Chocontá, and Cartagena (Restrepo 1963, II, 169–72; Galindo 1900, 43; Gilmore 1956, 200–03).

In these societies, progress and the democratic ideals of the last French revolutions were discussed and, in passing, support was given to the interests of the artisans who wished to protect their small industries. Thus, they were not communalists but rather respected (along with Bentham and Locke) the principle of individual private property. The noted politician and economist of the period, Don Aníbal Galindo, declares that "the most exaggerated theories of liberty and equality" were preached therein, "in contempt for the domination of the upper classes of society," which led to "innumerable assaults and violence against persons and property" (Galindo 1900, 50–54; cf. Camacho Roldán 1892, 82–84, 87; Cuervo and Cuervo 1943, II, 134 ff.).

The critical fact that the Democratic Societies achieved a certain local diffusion and their members reached the level of the local community (and therein lies their significance) was shown by the organization of gangs, bands, and guerrillas in the capital and in some other regions such as the savannah of Bogotá, the greater Cauca, and the Valley of the Cauca, where there were violent confrontations and acts of war. Prominent were the bands organized by Dr. José Raimundo Russi, an "unusual character" according to Henao and Arrubla (1952, 668), who was a teacher, parish judge, and secretary of the Democratic Society (Cuervo and Cuervo 1954, II, 1365). Russi fought in the savannah of Bogotá and did certainly initiate ferment among the poor people of the capital with whom he personally identified himself. In the Valley of the Cauca appeared bands that were quite fearsome and well organized, some of which were founded by freedmen as described by the local historian, Don Luciano Rivera y Garrido (1897, 206–11). These bands spread terror among hacienda owners and peasants from Cali to Cartago (cf. Cuervo and Cuervo 1954, II, 1366–70). There were also popular movements directed against certain province *gamonales,* such as that which developed in Chocontá in 1853 against the dominant family, the Maldonado Neiras (Fals Borda 1961a, 24), and collective displacements caused by local acts of violence, such as occurred in Cartago (Cuervo and Cuervo 1954, II, 1372–73).

The intervention of the Democratic Societies was also important in national politics. In first place, their tumultuous participation in the halls of Congress was a factor that led to the election of General José Hilario López as President of the Republic on March 7, 1849. Furthermore, without the support of the Societies, General José María Obando would not have ascended to the Presidency of the Republic in 1853. Undoubtedly, the liberal subversion had an element of fundamental importance in these active popular associations.

Yet the Democratic Societies did not move alone, at least not at the beginning. They had a subversive reference group in another association called the Republican School, founded on September 25, 1850. This group was made up of the elites but it was attempting to dissociate from them because in the light of the liberal utopia it had perceived the incongruities and inconsistencies of the seigniorial order. Thus it confronted the elite with the support of the new ideologies then in vogue in the prestigious circles of Paris. It was a counter-elite group with revolutionary airs and apparently committed to sponsor the transformation of the established order (see Appendix B for theoretical discussion on counter-elite).

The members of the counter-elite of the Republican School were then between twenty and thirty years of age. They were: Salvador Camacho Roldán, Santiago and Felipe Pérez, Aníbal Galindo, Manuel Murillo Toro, José María Samper, José María Rojas Garrido, and Foción Soto, among others. They sought rapid social change by looking to anti-colonial, anti-Hispanic, and anti-clerical formulas, as one of them confessed toward the end of the century. In this way they challenged the opinion of the mature members of the elite that judged the rapidity and accumulation of the reforms to be imprudent. They did not respect traditional institutions such as the Church. In fact, some members like José María Samper maintained that "Catholicism contradicts the republic" and called the clergy "clerigalla" (in contempt) (Ortíz 1907, 239; cf. Samper 1946–1948, I, 237–39). These young men of good breeding believed that "in all things appeal could and should be made to human reason through free discussion" and that the most important thing was to seek the power of public opinion "as the firmest support for republican institutions," ideas with which they promoted and secured freedom of the press (Camacho Roldán 1889, xii–xiii; 1923, 75–76, 195–96). According to Don Aquileo Parra, these rebellious boys lacked "political experience," implying that they would learn their lesson in time and that following their misguided efforts they would return to the mother group (Parra 1912, 146–47). This in fact was to occur.

On the rebound, the Jesuits, who had returned to the country in 1844, also organized groups for the opposite side, the Conservative one, to counteract the action of the Democratic Societies. They called them Popular Societies and their elite reference group was identified as the *Filotémica*, while their president was the expert politician, Don Mariano Ospina Rodríguez (Ortiz 1907, 203). But these groups as such were not as effective as their opposites (Cuervo and Cuervo 1954, II, 1353–54; Henao and Arrubla 1952, 667, 668; Morales Benítez 1957, 213).

The impetus of the subverters was so great in the beginning that the Congresses of 1850 and 1851 found themselves forced to dictate measures, one after the other, that affected the values as well as the normative framework and the organization of the seigniorial order. This becomes obvious through listing these measures: the law decentralizing state revenue (April 20, 1850); the law abolishing the necessity of a science degree to have a profession and establishing schools supported by the state (May 15, 1850); the law that expelled the Jesuits (May 24, 1850); the law establishing free institutes of arts and trades in the national secondary school system (June 8, 1850); the law providing for free alienation rights of reservation lands, and the definitive end of the Indian tribute (June 22, 1850);

the law concerning the abolition of ecclesiastical privileges (May 14, 1851); the law giving definitive freedom to slaves, that which according to Joaquín Mosquera (Cuervo and Cuervo 1954, III, 1373) had the effect of "an earthquake" at the level of rural communities (May 21, 1851); the law which gave town councils and parish residents the power to elect their priests (May 27, 1851). In this manner some of the compelling ideas of the liberal utopia were translated into norms.

The last law mentioned should be emphasized, not only because it attacked the traditional bases of ecclesiastical control—affecting even the basic ecological groups and fostering active participation of the parish in its administration—but also because it was the cause of a schism in Antioquia the following year and the exile of Archbishop Mosquera of Bogotá, and the bishops of Cartagena and Pamplona, for disobedience (Mosquera 1858, II, 497 ff.). There was shortly a discussion in the House of Representatives of total schism of the national Church to separate it from Rome, in an unusual movement headed by a priest and deputy, Don Juan Nepomuceno Azuero (Cuervo and Cuervo 1954, II, 1409).

Furthermore, the subversive impulse was starting to challenge the agrarian property structure and to question the seigniorial ethos in the countryside. The novelist Eugenio Díaz testified that this was beginning to happen: friends of the new local *gamonal*, Don Tadeo, as described in the novel *Manuela*, were already pressing for land, protesting the conditions of the leases and denouncing the hacienda owners and priests united against them (Díaz 1889, II, 181–82 *et passim*). The violent events in the greater Cauca region and the Valley of the Cauca referred to as "democratic frolics" clearly indicated the same situation (Ortíz 1907).

The subversion could not have been more decisive and dangerous than it was at this time, so naturally it gave rise to immediate efforts to contain it. Nevertheless, its force had become so great that it led to the election of a popular rebel, General Obando, as president in March 1853, and to the extraordinary phenomenon of achieving a successful revolution by which the subverters wrested total political power from the traditional oligarchy. Even though it lasted only a few months, until December 4, 1854, it is the only successfully completed revolution in the history of Colombia. The date marks the end of the acute phase, or climax, of the liberal subversion.

The Cooptation of the Counter-elite

The historical events that occurred during this period illustrate a social process of wide importance that is seldom studied: that of the cooptation of the will of the counter-elite by dominant groups for the purpose of holding back the subversive movement or changing the course of its direction to head it toward adjusted goals. In the present case, a cooptation of reactionary type occurred since the rebels ceded under pressures from their elders, peers and agents of the dominant groups, through fear of the loss of position, prestige, or resources, through attraction by offers of sinecures and privileges, or through physical violence. This led the erstwhile rebels to ideological compromise and prostitution of the principal ideals of the subversion. As a consequence of this process they returned penitently to their families and the original primary groups, as prodigal sons who had become temporarily bewitched by the zeal of protest (see Appendix B).

During the climax of the subversion, between 1849 and 1854, as could be expected, there was a reaction. As a result of such "extraordinary and scandalous" events engendered by the liberal subversion, the traditionalist groups awakened, becoming articulated ideologically and aware of their own tradition, perhaps for the first time. They took authority, order, and religion as key ideas to lend support to seigniorial values and norms, acting just in time to avoid assimilation of the subversive precepts. Their task of arresting the revolution was completed in the short period of fifteen years.

Braking of the process began with an armed uprising in Pasto (the most conservative and Catholic province of the country), in May 1851, which was promptly put down. Immediately afterwards, the conflict became more acute in the capital itself where it took on the characteristics of a class struggle in which the groups were identified by their dress: *los de ruana* (those in ponchos) on one side, consisting of members of the Democratic Societies, their friends, and relatives, and *los de casaca* (those in frock coats) or "dandies" on the other, consisting of members of the upper, wealthy, and educated classes. These groups came into conflict several times in the streets and plazas of Bogotá, in the galleries of Congress, and at bullfights (Ortíz 1855, 22–25). The same tensions, with similar symbols, spread to the peasants. Among them it was the possession or lack of boots that mattered; that is, there were "the barefoot," consisting of tenant farmers and the masses in general, and "the shod," who were mainly hacienda owners, the clergy, and their respective families (Henao and Arrubla 1952, 683–84; Díaz 1889, I, 111 *et passim*).

It is obvious that the revolutionary, class-oriented movement fostered by these subverters could not have been looked upon with approval by the colleagues, wives, and relatives of the dominant class, much less had it reached its ultimate consequences, changing the agrarian structure and upsetting the values of the seigniorial order. Therefore many fathers ordered their sons to withdraw from the Societies, and in the National College the course of superior studies was eliminated. This reduced the size of the Societies (Cuervo and Cuervo 1954, II, 1367–70, 1420; Ortíz 1907, 204–14).

The exact moment at which the attitude of the young counter-elite began to change is not known. The phenomenon became manifest in 1853 when symptoms of withdrawal in the Democratic Societies could be observed—as if the "mature men" of liberal families had successfully exercised pressure to halt the revolutionary march and coopt the members of the counter-elite. In the class conflicts of that year, those of the Republican School took the side of the "dandies" and became embroiled in a hand to hand fight with "those in ponchos." That is the way Rufino Cuervo tells it in a letter of August 3, 1853 to Joaquín Mosquera (Cuervo and Cuervo 1954, II, 1421). The withdrawal of the upper reference group was especially observable when *gamonales* of a new type began to appear in the countryside. They were opposed to the traditional ones who were generally hacienda owners with a large number of tenant farmers or sharecroppers under their orders. Apparently, control over people in the countryside was falling into the hands of persons who often did not inspire trust: regional government functionaries who lacked connections with the traditional oligarchical group. Such was the case of Russi, Tadeo, and the governor of the province of Cartago, Don Carlos Gómez, which soon became the scene of bloody local repressions (Cuervo and Cuervo 1954, II, 1371–72).

On April 17, 1854, a lower class military officer, who had earlier been a businessman in the provincial city of Ibagué, General José María Melo, usurped power with the support of the Draconians and artisans. With this act the liberal subversion reached its revolutionary culmination. The move may have been a tactical error, since President Obando sympathized with the subversives, but it was perhaps inevitable in view of the threat of an attack on General Melo (after an incident with a subordinate in the military quarters of Bogotá) which functioned as a precipitant for the revolution. The rebels surely thought that taking power was the only way to defend the liberal subversion and the victories won, already threatened by the strong traditionalist reaction.

Evidently the imminence of a revolutionary change in the class system and the power base had to arouse the counteraction of the whole dominant group, united as it was against the new "tyrant" and "the dregs of society." With the excuse of restoring the myths of "democracy and legality" the traditional elite promoted a military campaign commanded by the same men who had initiated the reforms, who now repented of their deeds: Generals Mosquera and José Hilario López, Manuel Murillo Toro, Tomás Herrera, and others. Former members of the Republican School such as Camacho Roldán, Galindo, and the Sampers once again identified with the elite and became more orthodox writers and orators (Galindo 1880, 295–307; Samper 1898, II, 762–64; Lozano and Vega 1939, 227; Ortíz 1907, 202, 240).

The weakness of General Melo as a revolutionary leader was added to the force of the repression to dull the impact of the liberal subversion. According to his own friend and collaborator, the former rector of the National College, Don Juan Francisco Ortíz, Melo turned out to be a weak and indecisive leader. He surrounded himself with ineffective and immoral persons who did not command respect, and he became immobilized in the minor town of Facatativá while his enemies took the more important Honda and met in a Congress in the city of Ibagué. This was a grave error of political strategy and military tactics. Cornered more and more in indefensible positions, Melo finally had to capitulate in his own cavalry quarters in the heart of the capital on December 4, 1854 (Ortíz 1907, 219–21).

At the fall of Melo's dictatorship, young Camacho Roldán was assigned, as President Obando's prosecuting attorney, to investigate events of the preceding years. Vice President José de Obaldía, also formerly a most enthusiastic supporter of the Democratic Societies, was given the task of eliminating their leaders, which he did without qualms; more than one hundred fifty artisans, arrested earlier with arms in hand, were sent to Panama as prisoners (Cuervo and Cuervo 1954, II, 1401). These political acts of Camacho Roldán and Obaldía, who were already coopted by the elite, mark the end of the Democratic Societies in that intense period (although they continued to function intermittently until perhaps 1880). The surrender of the counter-elite is also a symptom of the firm beginning of the arrest of the subversion and the quite appropriate advent of the conservative governments of Presidents Manuel María Mallarino and Mariano Ospina Rodríguez. With these presidents began the adjustment process which was to end in the new bourgeois order. This trend, interrupted only during the interregnum of the presidencies of Mosquera (1860–1867) will be studied in the next chapter. Meanwhile, the disillusionment at the popular level was well expressed by the words of Francisco Novoa, the "Melist" blacksmith of *Manuela,* when he exclaimed: "The same ones who taught us in the Democratic Society that neither property nor authority should be respected were the first to arm themselves to question us abusively for the uprising against the government and for the expropriation."

And the return to the ethos of passivity was underscored by Francisco when he accepted that "I can be a liberal without being a village revolutionary" (Díaz 1889, II, 240–41).

The Meaning of the Frustration

From the study of the acute stage or climax of the liberal subversion certain conclusions are derived that may help not only in understanding the phenomenon from the projective point of view but also the implications it has for other social movements of similar scope.

Obviously, a subversion is not necessarily irreversible even though the incongruities it fosters among the components of the social order be radical and the conflicts intense, to the point of revolution. Much more than the will to initiate the changes is needed. The subversive elements—counter-values, counter-norms, and disorgans—may disappear, not only through assimilative absorption as was the case of the colonial transition, but also through effective repression, dispersion, and reactionary cooptation exercised during the acute period of the transition.

The period under study also shows that owing to the mere fact of subversion, the intensity of the conflicts it unleashes, the discovery of the incongruities, injustices, and aberrations of the established order, there is never an absolute return to the *status quo ante*. A social order that is similar to the prior one may emerge, but distinct from it in significant qualitative, material, and technological aspects. Thus, in the present case, the traditionalist Colombian groups were not able to recapture the essence of the seigniorial order that had reigned up until 1848, even though they triumphed over the revolution of 1854. On the other hand, after the initial violent repression, the vested interest groups promoted an adjustment between subversive and traditional elements which led society to the bourgeois order.

Headway was made by certain values and norms that distinguish this period from the prior social order and that were at the root of later adjustments. Outstanding were some mechanistic values that made possible the introduction of various technological innovations; those nationalist attitudes that had greater implication for the elite in view of their importance in relations with other states; and the values of entrepreneurial individualism. As will be shortly discussed, these values found adepts among the *nouveaux riches* of the capitals and the Antioquian group, with secondary and sometimes self-defeating repercussions among the peasants of the former Indian areas. These values were manifested as norms of *laissez faire* and formal democracy, with the ubiquitous *caudillista* deformation which was an impediment for the integration of the country. The adjustments in the norms of prescriptive rigidity imposed by the formal advent of the Republic also persisted.

It is important to stress the innovational and at the same time repressive role played in this case by the counter-elite, even though it allowed itself to be coopted in a reactionary manner. For a moment, a glimpse was caught of the tremendous consequences that a schism of this type in the dominant groups could occasion for the rest of the society. This phenomenon of internal rebellion (which may take positive forms, as studied later) has occurred several times in history, especially when the counter-elites are composed of nonconformist intellectuals and ideologues who protest the normative inconsistencies and moral contradictions of the social order in which they live.

The revolutionary outset and the later dispersion of the liberal subversion underscore once again (as in the case of the Christian subversion and the seigniorial order) the crucial role played by mechanisms of compulsion and by stabilizing factors to secure enduring transformations in society. Of the three mechanisms of compulsion necessary to bring about the adjustments of the subversion (Chapter Four), only two were present in this case, with a serious failure of the third. Actually, during the period of the liberal-democratic transition a satisfactory revolutionary level of hegemonic domination of the political machinery was achieved. A new ideology was disseminated and adopted, even though only halfway, and the rebel groups and organs were established in order to saturate with subversion all levels of society including the communal. This task of revolutionary development began to be carried out in satisfactory manner.

Unfortunately—and this was crucial—the movement's leadership made serious mistakes which weakened it, left its flanks unprotected, and prevented it from maintaining the initiative.

Worse yet, in addition to suffering the effects of the demoralizing flaw in leadership, the liberal revolution was unable to call to its aid the stabilizing factors that would guarantee the advancement of change in the desired direction. Thus the subversion was cut off before it even completed the first cycle of socialization, having had no time for the essential transmission of the new norms and attitudes from fathers to sons. There was failure in the control of power, and the legitimation of coercion was not achieved. Thus unnecessary chaos and much disorder were produced instead. This necessarily weakened coherent action and the effectiveness of the subversion. And there did not exist total constancy or persistence in action, or loyalty to the ideology in the subversive groups, so that compromises were made between the rebels and the traditional groups.

Furthermore, the absence of a new technology capable of breaking down tradition and encouraging popular participation in the technological innovations of the period precluded these factors' playing a positive supportive role during the period of the subversion to consolidate the power of the rebels. The technological innovations introduced were not under the control of the rebels, but rather fell into the hands of the groups that were committed to maintaining the seigniorial order. The *señores* used them not only to defend the condition of tradition but also to promote the already inevitable adjustment from which there emerged a society more suitable to necessities in the new circumstances: the bourgeois order.

CHAPTER SIX

Adjustment and Compulsion
in the Bourgeois Order

THE mechanisms applied to arrest the liberal revolution and prevent the disintegration of the seigniorial order—the reactionary cooptation of the counter-elite and repressive violence—were insufficient to turn back the clock of history and secure the *status quo ante.* The very force of the new ideologies as a reaction against the colonial heritage prevented this A compromise was reached between the vestigial elements of the subversion and those of tradition: they moved forward together toward a "modern" state with democracy, liberty, and *laissez faire* as the new valued goals for economic and social development (cf. Mannheim 1941, 179). This compromise established the basis of the necessary adjustment for reconstructing the society and reaching a topia, in view of the impossibility of achieving the absolute liberal utopia. The compromise was strengthened by the appearance of a new technology (steam), the elements of which contributed to consolidating the emerging social order.

The revolutionary accents of the liberal subversion would lead one to expect that its agents would become key groups to impose their will on the compromise solution for the nascent social order, and that the main adjustments would have to be conceded by tradition. This, at least, is what occurred in the case of the sixteenth-century conquest. However, in the period which we are now studying, there occurred an extraordinary switch in the historical roles. The liberals, to whose influence and initiative the subversion was owed, in the long run experienced the most significant reversals; they allowed reactionary cooptation among their followers. The traditionalists, who were at first trapped by change, turned their panic into victory by assimilating into their own ranks those key groups that imposed their innovating ideology. The traditionalists responded to the liberal challenge with bourgeois compulsion.

The new strategic groups were those who benefited economically from the post-colonial reaction and who incidentally supported the return to clericalism as the defense of law and order. They were trading and commercial groups that appeared in certain cities (Bogotá, Medellín) as a result of the abolition of the state tobacco monopoly and the production and export of new products such as cinchona and coffee. The Antioquian rural migrant families accompanied them. These groups became fundamental to the development of the new social order. They began to fall into the ranks of the conservative party, which thus took on the role of a motor for change and architect of the new society.

After the anticlimax of the subversion in 1867, the adjustments in the liberal camp were the political business of men like Rafael Núñez, General Julián Trujillo, and José María Samper, giants of strategy and architects of compromise. Inevitably they became victims of the risks they took with their more experienced and persistent opponents. Meanwhile, the important tasks of determining the direction of social change and applying conservative compulsion were the responsibility of Miguel Antonio Caro and Carlos Holguín. The work of these leaders completed the metamorphosis of the colonial society in order to make way for the bourgeois order in Colombia.

The present realities of Colombia have their foundation in this nineteenth century synthesis, when a significant socioeconomic advancement was gained. This advancement was brought about on the basis of the partial disintegration of the seigniorial order from which there remained only those values and norms required by innovations in the political (representative democracy, nationalism), commercial (*laissez faire*), and technological (mechanistic counter-values) realms. In this way the caste system was weakened to allow the emergence of a new type of peasantry and a new money-trade aristocracy. The two-party, open class political system of today was also created during this period as a result of acute local conflicts.

It is on these crucial elements of the social organization of the bourgeois order as products of an intense process of economic adjustment and political compulsion that our attention is concentrated in the present chapter.

The Creation of a Rural Middle Class

It was said earlier that the seigniorial order had its representatives in certain places, such as the capitals of the viceroyalties, where high-ranking persons most closely connected with the dominant institutions of Spain gathered. In those places they were able to easily impose their aristocratic, caste-like patterns of living. But in the marginal provinces it was not possible to fully establish the seigniorial order, at least not with the intensity with which it was done in important cities like Santa Fé de Bogotá, Cartagena, and Popayán. Such seems to have been the case, for example, in the province of Antioquia.

The origins of the Antioquian society are still shrouded in mystery. From the available descriptions (such as the reports of authorities and the writings of local scientists and historians) it appears that from the beginning a society was formed there of crude landowners, miners, and traders centered around cities like Santa Fé de Antioquia, Rionegro, Marinilla, and Medellín. For them, agriculture was not a sacred way of life with Indian laborers and tributes, as it was elsewhere, but a profitable business with a guaranteed internal market in mining communities (Santa Rosa, Yolombó, Cancan). Antioquians did not mind working with their hands. They were capable of heterodox behavior, as shown by such deeds as the very early (1781) liberation of slaves (Restrepo 1849, 210–15; Posada 1933, 26) and clearing the forest in order to settle the land, as occurred in Don Matías and Yarumal in about the same period. Evidently, freeing the slaves was not a general practice, and pioneer jungle settlements were a contradiction of the classical form of Spanish colonization, for the conquistadors preferred the open country and esplanades that had already been tamed by the Indians. For this reason there is a feeling that the civilization of Antioquia was somewhat different. It seemed to be somewhat autonomous, marginal, and semi-isolated in the vice royalty, except with regard to the production and exportation of precious minerals (Hagen 1962, 364–78).

Several factors seem to have impeded the flourishing of the seigniorial order in Antioquia: (*a*) the rapid disappearance of the Indians owing to epidemics and toil in the mines which also prematurely voided local *encomiendas* (Zavala 1935, 329); (*b*) the predominance of mining over agriculture as an economic activity (so that many food products had to be imported), which frustrated both the development of the hacienda and the adoption of plow technology (Restrepo 1849, 216; Parsons 1949, 62); (*c*) the humble origin or former commoner status of many of the families that arrived in the region between the sixteenth and eighteenth centuries —Basques, Asturians, Andalusians, Sephardic Jews, gypsies, soldiers, and new Christians (Simón 1882–1892, V, 322)—who had different attitudes toward manual labor and land exploitation.

These facts are basic to understanding the subsequent and autonomous move of the Antioquians to the forested fringe in the south. They help to explain why it was from this area that there emerged a rural middle class, the first in the country, and perhaps in all of Latin America as well. The movement of settlers began to take full shape soon after the Great Colombia was founded and the new anti-colonial institutions had been established. The Antioquians migrated because of the decline of agriculture and mining in their original communities, population growth, famines, the illusion of hidden treasures of Indian gold, and the legend of the Pipintá deity. Especially important was the reformist pressure of a group of Medellín businessmen established in colonization and road construction companies such as the Caramanta venture of 1835 (Parsons 1949, 85–95). These tradesmen, entrepreneurs, and contractors were interested in the promotion of commercial products such as coffee, neither bound to nor stigmatized by the seigniorial order, for export to Europe and the United States; they had discovered already that it was a good business in Central America (Ospina Vásquez 1955, 244–46; Parsons 1949, 137).

This new bourgeois mentality appears to have developed here endogenously and in political and economic isolation (Hagen

1962, 370; cf. Weber 1858). It spread rapidly although it did not attack the system of land tenure. In Antioquia, the traditional agrarian structure remained intact: the pioneers, in fact, wanted lands in the public domain or abandoned latifundia that were overgrown with forests. In reality this epic was an expansion of the Antioquian civilization and, as such, reproduced the value systems as well as the normative, organizational, and technological characteristics of this particular society. However, the different attitudes held by these peasants with regard to land allowed them to exploit their new possessions by means of experiments like the family corporation. This opened autonomous possibilities of economic independence to them, with an aura of dignity attached to work such as did not exist in other parts of the country. In this way, the old norms of prescriptive rigidity were largely broken. The rest of the Colombian society had to compromise with them, although the subsequent adjustments were to foster acts of violence in the newly colonized areas.

The occupation of the forests of the Quindío region and adjacent areas, that later came to constitute the department of Caldas, was classic. This stream of colonization moved southward to culminate between 1880 and 1890 in distant parts of the Valley of the Cauca and Tolima. The twenty heads of families who founded Manizales in 1848—all of humble origin, some being muleteers—organized themselves into a community based on the institutions of mutual aid and exchange of labor. The powerful interests of the latifundists who possessed the deeds of royal grants, dating as far back as 1801 (to José María Aranzazu), were challenged by peasants armed with their axes and able to prove the reality of their occupation of the lands. The descendants of Aranzazu, among them the president of the state of Antioquia itself, opposed this *de facto* occupation, which led to bloody encounters. In 1851 a settlement was made over the land and the litigation ended with a Congressional decree two years later by which the interests of the settlers were supported and certain rights of the legal owners of the land were recognized (Morales Benítez 1951, 24–27, 70–80). Thus the subverters, then in power, came to support the groups of Antioquia in their struggle against the colonial latifundium system. This was in order to create

small-property owners, a goal consistent with the ideology of liberal
subversion. Similar processes were observed in El Líbano, north of
Tolima (Santa 1961), and in Támesis, south of Antioquia (Havens
1966). The official tendency to support the rural *petit bourgeoisie*
continued until the passage of Law 61 in 1874, by which the settlers
gained juridical recognition, and of the decrees of 1882 by which
colonization was officially encouraged. By the end of the century
the government had granted all the lands in the public domain that
the new Antioquian communities had requested, totaling more than
200,000 hectares (Parsons 1949, 98).

One result of this struggle was the creation of a new type of
middle-class man whose mission was the production of wealth. He
was not ashamed of working, and he educated himself. He could
prove that "one can live as a poor man and die rich." Persons with
this attitude could not help developing a special civilization, the
bases of which would be anti-colonial, anti-clerical, and mechanistic.
But owing to the defeat of the liberal revolution and the defensive
attitude adopted by the elements of the liberal party, the majority
of Antioquians followed the current that combined socio-political
compulsion with the survival of the principal aspects of tradition.
The authoritarian government of General Pedro Justo Berrío as
governor of the province and that of his successor, Don Recaredo
Villa, a noted banker, played important roles in this. They turned
Antioquia into a conservative, bourgeois bastion and a pillar for the
Catholic Church (a development which on the other hand led the
liberals to seek geo-political balance through developing the state of
Santander across the Magdalena River as a liberal bulwark; Samper
1898, I, 259, 298).

With the backing of the bourgeoisie of the Antioquian and
Quindian cities—first through their export traders, businessmen, and
road construction companies and later through their small industrialists—the minifundia system based on coffee and planted pastures
flourished in the countryside. Small farmers achieved an acceptable
level of prosperity. Without the stigma of the row crops planted in
the regions with a seigniorial tradition, the Quindian peasants were
able to create a rural middle class whose influence is still felt today,
in spite of the social erosion motivated by the successive partition-

ing of their lands through inheritance. These small coffee growers were progressive with regard to the economy and commercial ventures, but they were traditionalists concerning religion and other norms of behavior. In this way they played a fundamental role not only in the development of the national economy with their own Calvinistic ethic, but also in the political game. They formed a self-generating reservoir for the deep conservatism of the Colombian people. A large part of the initial battle for the bourgeois compulsion in Colombia was won with their help.

The Formation of the Upper Bourgeoisie

Just as the common people of Antioquia awakened and took advantage of the post-colonial situation to partially destroy the caste structure, about this time there also emerged a new class of entrepreneurs. This effort produced an autonomous economic advance without the need to import capital or to stimulate large-scale foreign immigration.

Two activities were particularly attractive to the entrepreneurial groups in this context: (*a*) plantation agriculture and forest concessions with a view to exploiting and exporting primary products; and (*b*) trade, represented by the import of foreign manufactures and the export of national products, especially tobacco, indigo, cinchona, and coffee. Later they also embarked on manufacturing industries.

These economic activities imply at least the following elements: (*a*) the acceptance of the new mechanistic counter-values; (*b*) a nationalistic orientation, with greater identification with the native soil; (*c*) a greater awareness of the machinery of the state and its bureaucracy for the purposes of social manipulation and economic control; (*d*) a centrifugal orientation with regard to economic ventures, with increasing connections with foreign markets and economic groups; and (*e*) the displacement of the colonial aristocracy by the bourgeois groups which belonged indiscriminately to the main political parties, the liberal and the conservative.

Plantation agriculture became possible once the custom houses were opened and the free trade policies of Florentino González prevailed. The product that most lent itself to this type of exploitation at that time, with a guaranteed market in Europe (especially Germany), was tobacco. Thus the state tobacco monopoly was ended and the young sons of the *nouveaux riches*, especially, were charged with its exploitation and export: the sons of the Samper, Camacho, Montoya, Sáenz, Nieto, Latorre, Umaña, Brigard, Argáez, Pizano, and Tanco families and others, as the writer of the period, Don Medardo Rivas, describes in detail (1946, 117, 119, 130–36, 144, 205, 262–63, 277, 282).

About 1850, these young people began to descend the mountainous area within the watershed of the mid-Magdalena River, felling the forests of the region and preparing the land for tobacco planting. They also established a large factory in which the product was prepared for export from the nearby port of Ambalema (Diaz 1889, II, Chap. XX). Some paddle wheelers brought from the United States were already plying the river and serving the new trade. All of this was but a capitalist expansion of the hacienda system, since basic elements of the old seigniorial order had been transferred to the tobacco sector (Ospiná Vásquez 1955, 196, 198). This economic development was to last until 1870 when the purchase of Colombian tobacco in Bremen was ended.

However, the active group of agrarian entrepreneurs was not discouraged by this crash. Their plantations were converted into pasture lands for cattle, into sugar cane, or coffee-growing lands, or were kept as farms for recreation purposes. Land was already seen as an asylum for capital and as security in times of civil war. The new hacienda-owning aristocracy then took over uncultivated lands, exploiting the new export products of their forests such as cinchona, indigo, and rubber. They began to buy at low prices and consolidate the lots received by the "Indians" when reservations were partitioned, and they acquired the lands that the state had taken from the Church by means of disamortization decrees. New *latifundia* were formed in this manner.

There was an element that prevented the complete return to the seigniorial order, once the liberal revolution was put down; it actually facilitated the advent of the bourgeois order. This element was technological in nature. Beginning with improvement of navigation on the Magdalena River, the mechanistic impulses expressed themselves in the urgency to construct modern means of transportation for export products, as this type of trading constituted the basis of the national economy and the source of prosperity for the dominant groups. Thus large sums were dedicated to the technical improvement of the existing river channels and to the construction of railways connected with the "spinal column" of the Magdalena River. So important was the technological movement that it led to the presidency of the republic those whom historian Manuel Briceño called "the railroader presidents" (1878, 9): Manuel Murillo Toro, Santiago Pérez, and Aquileo Parra. These liberal leaders of not very wealthy but distinguished families became important businessmen, stockholders, and entrepreneurs of consequence in conjunction with other members of their party.

With the exception of the special early case of Panama, construction fever began with the railroad between the new and flourishing river port of Barranquilla and the nearby beach of Sabanilla (1869–1871) which was later extended to Puerto Colombia between 1888 and 1893 (Ortega 1932, Rippy 1943, 650–63). In 1874 the railroad between Medellín and Puerto Berrío was begun; in 1878 the port lines of Cali and Cúcuta were begun; and between 1881 and 1891 the railroads from Bogotá to the Magdalena and from Bogotá to Nemocón in the north began to be built. About the same time other unconnected lines were constructed that by 1915 totaled 1,082 kilometers.

Almost simultaneously, the first telegraph line was installed between Bogotá and Conejo on the Magdalena River (1865); the cable connection with the exterior was completed in 1882. The first telephones and trolleys appeared in Bogotá in 1884. A few mechanical mowers and threshers were imported to haciendas and the purchase of land vehicles and other steam-driven apparatuses was urged (Camacho Roldán 1893, 442–48; Samper 1898, I, 136).

The accumulation of savings permitted the key bourgeois groups to take one more step in the direction of social differentiation: the development, at last, of national industry. At that time it was thought that a modern nation could not exist without factories. The few minor industries of mid-century (iron, earthenware, paper) had been very rudimentary and short-lived. Thus, the first serious attempts to industrialize came in the textile field in Samacá (state of Boyacá) and in the city of Medellín about 1886. But in Antioquia a factory making coffee-processing machines of native invention also appeared. These innovations emphasized the impetus given industrial development by the peasant middle class that had settled the Quindío and neighboring regions. Facilities for processing chocolate and agave fiber and for making both glass and beer (a brewery called "Bavaria" was founded in 1891) began production. A factory producing chemical fertilizers appeared in Bogotá in 1894 but it was closed soon afterwards for lack of a market among the farmers; the peasants had not yet developed much interest in technological counter-values, and innovations in this field were the privilege of the elite (Ospina Vásquez 1955, 307–13).

Almost simultaneously, the banking institutions appeared: in 1864 the Bank of London, Mexico, and South America arrived; the first Colombian-owned bank, the Bank of Bogotá, was officially established in 1871 and the National Bank in 1881. The Colombian Insurance Company began operations in 1874. The *nouveaux riches* of both parties, especially those of the liberal group that had been coopted, became stockholders in all of these institutions.

This extraordinary socio-economic advance occurred in spite of the civil wars that plagued Colombian society during this period. The developments made the dominant group wealthier and benefited the lower classes only marginally for they did not open new effective channels to upward social and economic mobility. In fact, the socio-economic advance of those decades did not have multiplying effects among the basic ecological groups. The history of the technological invasion of the sixteenth century was partially repeated as the most advanced and efficient elements (such as iron tools, horses, and arms during the conquest) became again the exclusive property of the elite. This time the dominant group became the direct or indirect owners of the means of transportation and communication and of steam-powered machines that were as strategic in the new economic structure as the horse and cart had been in the seigniorial order.

The technological advantage made the upper bourgeoisie ever

more prosperous through their export and import business, connections abroad, and control of the political machinery. The economic advancement fostered compromise and accomodation among the ruling classes of both parties, the liberal subverters and the conservative traditionalists. For this reason liberal as well as conservative persons were found among the *nouveaux riches*. And since peace was a necessity for the full exploitation of the new opportunities, those involved in business began to put aside their warring impulses, shedding their epaulets of rebellious generals in order to become promoters of order, or to become entrepreneurs. Perhaps this bourgeois accomodation was one of the factors that made Aquileo Parra, already a prosperous businessman, indecisive and weak as the director of the liberal party during the difficult days between 1890 and 1900 when the party had been intimidated and young liberals pressed for civil war.

The process of circulation, displacement, and assimilation that the entrepreneurial group carried out with the old aristocracy was of the greatest importance. When the local nobility was ruined because it clung to the colonial imperial structure, then incongruent owing to its incapacity at direct business administration, it sought to mix with the *nouveaux riches*. One way was through matrimony. The Quijanos became related to the Nietos; the Valenzuelas to the Sampers; the Torres family to the Sáenz; the Rivas to the Montoyas. All—the new rich and the aristocrats—kept their basic attitudes of the seigniorial order; but the parvenus rose above the crowd with their commercial ventures, their new world outlook, and also their hunger for profit which was quite impressive, according to the visiting French botanist Edouard André (André 1884, 531; cf. Von Schenk 1953, 25).

Inevitably, the fulcrum of power moved toward the upper bourgeoisie. They formed the key groups in the new order. Furthermore, the liberals discovered a spiritual and literary affinity that made it possible for them to organize the local society identified as "Radical Olympus" between 1865 and 1875 (Rodríguez Piñeres 1950), which in turn allowed them to exercise some political influence. The conservatives had their societies also. Through personages in these societies, through relatives in the army, or through those who belonged to both parties the wealthy aristocrats, regardless of party affiliation, managed to manipulate the state machinery at will. The ruling positions of society came to be transmitted as if they were matters of family inheritance: from Pedro Alcántara Herrán to his cousin Francisco Javier Zaldúa; from Santiago Pérez to his brother Felipe; from Felipe Zapata to his brother Dámaso; from Manuel Murillo Toro to his stepson Nicolás Esguerra; from Francisco Soto to his son Foción; from Salvador Camacho Roldán to his brother-in-law Nicolás Pereira Gamba; from Miguel Samper to his brother-in-law Manuel Arcízar or to his influential brother José María; from Mariano Ospina Rodríguez to his grandson Pedro Nel (and from Pedro Nel to his nephew Mariano Ospina Pérez); from Carlos Holguín to his son Jorge; from Miguel Antonio Caro to his cousin through marriage, Marco Fidel Suárez. (This is an antecedent of the same tendency to legate political positions in more recent years: that of Alfonso López to his son Alfonso López Michelsen; that of Laureano Gómez to his son Alvaro; that of Gustavo Rojas Pinilla to his daughter María Eugenia de Moreno Díaz; that of Jorge Eliécer Gaitán to his daughter Gloria de Valencia.)

In turn, this transition in political and economic power was the prelude to the decline of noble cities: Santa Fe de Antioquia, Pamplona, Buga, Popayán, Cartagena, Mompós; and the rise of the commercial centers of Medellín and Cali and, toward the end of the century, of Barranquilla and Bucaramanga.

Nothing could better demonstrate that there was a new social order in Colombia, one in which action was based on new values oriented toward the machine, the world, the nation, and the bank account.

Religious Compulsion and the Bipartisan System

While the coups of the reactionary groups led the liberal party to make successive adjustments in its politics and doctrinaire positions, the conservatives successfully fulfilled their function of compulsion so that development followed the direction that suited them, in support of the bourgeois élan. For this purpose the conservatives had not only the lever of tradition, an advantage in itself, but also an extraordinary mystique that permitted them to persist without wavering. This mystique did not derive from the political platform adopted by the former supporters of Bolívar. It derived principally from personal convictions, from confidence in the morality of their ideas, from a certain chiliastic tendency that sharpened confrontations with other groups; in short, it derived from religious fanaticism.

The way in which conflicts become more intense when religious convictions are involved is well known. It was the experience of Europe during the Middle Ages (the conflicts among Christians and between Christians and Moslems), and in a singular way during the wars between churches in the sixteenth century. The two sides were completely defined in Manichean terms: one was either for or against the Church, on the side of God or the devil. Intermediate positions were not permitted. This became a tremendous conflict in which personal animosities, family feuds, and intolerance played their part and in which hatred acquired its own dynamic to polarize individual and family positions.

This emotional religious battle, which was at the same time rancorous and personal, relegated class consciousness to a secondary level and inhibited conflicts based on self-awareness of the people. Thus Colombian political parties became agglomerations where not only members of the elite but also persons of the lower classes who shared their orientation were sheltered (giving the latter a certain sense of satisfaction and the security of accommodation). The party became a multi-class system, dividing Colombian society vertically and grouping persons in opposite camps according to formal clerical or anticlerical, traditionalist or progressive, conservative or liberal conviction. Moreover, a regional differentiation by parties was also produced, creating homogeneous enclaves of liberals or conservatives in towns and villages, which fostered the same feeling of belonging and security within the party that was derived from the identification with the upper classes. This led to a resurgence of neo-Manichean passivity in order that rules of political and social behavior based on conformity might be adopted. Such conformity soon saturated other spheres of social life (Torres 1963).

This multi-class, conformist bipartisan system of community identification and defense had its origin in the religious confrontations of the liberal subversion from 1848 to 1867. Until then political parties had been personalistic groups that followed *caudillos* or *gamonales*, but without much sense of urgency concerning ideological identification and differing very little as far as principles were concerned (Samper 1886, I, 206). This can be seen through reading the first manifestos subscribed to by the ideologues of the parties in 1849, José Eusebio Caro and Mariano Ospina for the conservatives and Ezequiel Rojas for the liberals (Santa 1964, 44–52). However, the intensity of the conflicts fostered by the subversion was of such magnitude that the people had to clearly align themselves with one side or the other, and decisions were made on the basis of excited emotions or offended religious belief. The wounds inflicted on each other by subversive groups and traditionalists were so deep that they could do no less than cause a serious schism in the social body. The liberals in power declared their anti-colonial and anti-clerical revolutionary position that was a challenge to the norms and values of the seigniorial order, especially those of otherworldliness, naturalism, prescriptive rigidity, and acritical morality. Their opponents could not do otherwise than articulate their own ideological position and for this purpose they turned to the sources of tradition in which the religious factor stood out prominently. Thus, far from this being an "element of national unity" and "social order" as the Colombian Constitution states, the Catholic religion has been rather a source of conflict and bloody disunity among Colombians.

The crucial moment of this ideological articulation of conservatism occurred on May 5, 1853, when Don Rufino Cuervo, a well-known conservative official, circulated the "Catholic Manifesto" which he had edited after consulting with the hierarchy of the Church. In the Manifesto reference is made to the "series of acts against the Church of Jesus Christ in New Granada since 1850" and enumerated are certain "foul deeds," such as the expulsion of the archbishop and bishops, the delegation of the appointment of parish priests to communal associations, the suppression of ecclesiastical privileges, the cancelation of titles, and the expropriation of the archbishopric's seminary. It declares that these deeds were "serious offenses and excesses against the most sacred of our convictions and the dearest of our affections." This led to the defense of the Roman Catholic Apostolic religion:

. . . because it is the religion of our conscience, the religion of our heart, the religion of our minds, the religion of our hopes: we support it because we consider it as if it were family property . . . because it is the only powerful element of morality and civilization for our ignorant and heterogeneous popular masses . . . because it is the true, conservative principle of the social order that is so seriously threatened by the groups and factions that contest for power in our beloved country. Professing, preserving and defending our august religion is something more . . . than an option; it is a duty—a sacred duty, a duty of honor and of conscience, a duty for whose fulfillment we shall have to respond before the Eternal Judge.

It then suggests different forms of action for maintaining unity among Catholics in the face of their enemies, ending by committing Catholics principally to the following:

To believe in, confess, and defend until death the dogmas, mysteries, and doctrines of the Catholic religion. . . ; to recognize, accept, and obey the authority of the Roman Pontiff, Vicar of Jesus Christ on earth . . . without submitting to fear, flattery, or to the threat of damage to one's interests, loss of position, poverty, persecution, or any class of suffering. . . ; to employ our efforts, resources, and relationships with others so that with the revocation of the anti-clerical laws the Church might be reintegrated in full enjoyment of its freedom, authority and rights. . . ; to commit ourselves in the most solemn way to support Catholic worship with our own fortunes whenever the nation does not completely contribute to these ends; never to agree that the interests of religion be submitted to those of politics; and accordingly, not to support any of the political parties that today or later may appear in New Granada that are antagonistic to the religious principles and interests stated in this manifesto (Cuervo and Cuervo, 1954, II, 1411–16).

The declaration of holy war could not have been clearer. The Catholic Manifesto of Rufino Cuervo, read in the churches of the capital, was distributed all over the country and subscribed to by hundreds of persons. Note that it was communicated to the basic units of society, to the rural community and country neighborhoods by parish priests.

The struggle also spread to these basic levels, manifesting itself in personal and community life. Peasantry and city folk were both compelled to identify with the religion of their ancestors as a means of achieving a minimum sense of security; and when this attitude was sufficiently socialized it was transmitted to the subsequent generations. For this reason the political affiliation of the Colombian, for the first time, became a matter of family inheritance. From this moment on it became a horrendous crime, an immoral act, to adopt the ideas of the opposite group. For this reason villages and communities began to be homogeneously conservative or liberal, organized for self-defense as a result of this politico-religious conflict, a social characteristic of disunity and tension that persists until today. Such was the case of the liberal community of El Cocuy, pitted against the conservative Guicán, a conflict that played such an important role in the civil war of 1885. It is true also of almost all the Andean regions (Martin 1887, 84–86; cf. Fals Borda 1961a, 297–302).

In general, the internal conflicts after 1853 that were fought ostensibly for the control of the state and disposition of the budget, or for changing the Consitution, were really fought on religious grounds. It could not be otherwise if the watchwords of Rufino Cuervo, that became the cornerstone of the movement for revitalization of conservatism, were to be followed. The observations of contemporary actors in this respect are valuable. They do not hesitate to affirm that the element of holy war was present in the frays between liberals and conservatives, making of them bloody and ruthless conflicts. Let us look at random at the descriptions of Juan Francisco Ortíz. He says that about 1857 the two parties went to war with one side shouting "Long live Liberty!" and the other "Long live Religion." The former were called "reds, heretics," and the latter, "*godos,* fanatics" (Ortíz 1907, 301). Luciano Rivera y Garrido, who observed the intensity of the conflict at the family level, made similar statements, pointing out how former friends did not even greet each other and how antipathies and hatreds were transmitted among families to the next generations. The principles invoked on one side were those of religion, morality, property, and family; and on the other, the counter-values and counter-norms of "liberty," "progress," popular sovereignty, and the right of suffrage (Rivera y Garrido 1897, 307–08). The same characteristics of holy war were observed by foreign diplomats, concerning the war that ended in 1861 (Shaw 1941, 581).

Religious tensions increased when Mosquera freed Church properties from mortmain in 1861. Tensions reached a climax when an "atheist" Constitution, with restrictions on clergy and a challenge to acritical morality, was promulgated in the city of Rionegro in 1863. Furthermore, Archbishop Antonio Herrán of Bogotá was expelled. The conservative forces quickly coalesced, encouraged by the condemnation of liberalism by Pope Pius IX in 1864. They took advantage of an internal split in the governing party and various incidents involving the president, and a coup d'état to overthrow General Mosquera was plotted. He was taken captive on May 23, 1867, before he was able to take additional measures that would have worsened relations between the two parties and would have hindered the necessary political adjustments. This marks the definitive end of the liberal subversion (Liévano 1966, 49–84). With regard to the adjustments, the agreements at which the leaders of the "radical" faction of liberalism arrived with the leader of conservatism, Don Carlos Holguín, to rectify Mosquera's policy concerning ecclesiastical communities were important (Liévano 1966, 62).

The religious conflict flourished anew and with complete openness during the civil struggle that originated in Cauca in 1876. This was considered by many to be a veritable "clerical revolution." In fact, its motto was "God, Country, and Liberty," and it seems to have taken inspiration from the second Carlist war in Spain and the restoration of the Catholic monarchy with Alphonse XII, when the Spanish Republic collapsed in 1875 (Lema 1927, Strobel 1898).

The pro-clerical conservatives accused liberalism of winning the 1876 elections by fraud, invoking the aphorism, "he who counts, elects." This was answered with "the sacred right of insurrection" (Briceño 1878, 3, 59). But above all, the pro-clerical group protested the imposition of the new educational policies of President Eustorgio Salgar and his Director of Education, Don Dámaso Zapata, whose initiatives in establishing normal schools (under the direction of German Protestant teachers) and freedom of teaching smacked of Freemasonry and of a "takeover by the Prussian monarchy" (Zapata 1960). In the state of Cauca, the bishops organized their own schools and societies, disobeying the dictates of the president of the state, Don César Conto, who therefore closed the Catholic Society of Popayán (that had been established to counteract the local Democratic Society) by armed force and war was thus sparked in the southern part of the country. By this time, Don Aquileo Parra was president of Colombia.

The Cauca Catholics immediately sought the support of those of Antioquia, claiming that the promulgation of laws or decrees affecting the autonomy of the Church or insisting on free education be considered *casus belli*. A guerrilla group began to function almost simultaneously in the town of Guasca (Cundinamarca) and their formal "Declaration of Insurgence, in the name of God" dated August 22, 1876, synthesized Cuervo's Manifesto (Briceño 1878, 212). This aspect of holy war is also encountered in the diverse proclamations that alleged action to be "in defense of our religious beliefs" (Briceño 1878, 289). It was dramatized even more by the appearance of soldiers who went to battle at Los Chancos with banner pictures of Pope Pius IX and of Christ wearing epaulets. Some even bore crosses and wore their hair long, in imitation of the Nazarene; and others insisted on wearing a scapular over their uniforms, which irritated the liberals even more (Briceño 1878, 228, 281).

The threat of a conservative "theocratic government" at that time served to unite the liberals around the government of President Parra. This had not been anticipated by the rebels; they also had against them the bourgeoisie that was beginning to become wealthy and whose prosperity was seriously threatened by the war. Thus, at the first sign of setbacks, the small Antioquian fort surrendered and President-banker Recaredo Villa, leader of the state's bourgeoisie, urged his generals to make peace and keep the war from entering Antioquia (Briceño 1878, 244–48). The war was soon ended, but it managed to confirm the deep partisan divisions that the religious element had produced among the Colombian people. Religion became a mechanism of compulsion that in the long run guaranteed the conservative victory in the new bourgeois order.

Liberal Adjustment and Reactionary Cooptation

The fact that the conservative forces were defeated in 1877 did not mean that the subverters triumphed. On the contrary, there was already at that time a strong tendency within liberalism—especially among the liberal bourgeoisie—to make compromises with their ideological opponents, with José María Samper, the former enraged anti-clericalist, one of the most obvious heads of this movement. Samper stated that the liberal party had gone astray "through excessive use of force and lack of responsibility," thereby producing a "frogish oligarchy" (from the nickname "The Frog," given to Ramón Gómez, who organized a corrupt political machine in Cundinamarca around 1862) that did not deserve to be perpetuated in power (Briceño 1878, 115–22). A little later, politicians like Camacho Roldán, Camilo Echeverri, Ramón Santodomingo Vila, and Nicolás Pereira Gamba were incorporated into the conservative group (Briceño 1878, 44). Reading the future correctly, the same man who was the victor at Los Chancos, General Julián Trujillo, agreed to carry out as president of the Republic the following adjustments: (1) freedom of suffrage; (2) respect for the sovereignty of the states (which one by one were becoming conservative); (3) religious freedom for the Catholic majority; and (4) teaching of the Catholic religion in the schools (Briceño 1878, 69).

In 1878 it fell to Dr. Rafael Núñez, then President of the Senate, to swear General Trujillo into the Presidency. At this moment Núñez articulated the watchword of the political adjustment: "Fundamental regeneration or catastrophe." Núñez, in fact, represented the prototype of reactionary cooptation realized during the postsubversive period (Soto 1913, I, 27). He encouraged the definitive triumph of the adjustment that modified the liberal party of the end of the century by bringing it closer to the conservative pattern of power manipulation.

Núñez had begun as a rebellious liberal in his native Cartagena, where he was president (1849) of the Democratic Society, editor of *La Democracia* (a passionate tribune for the freedoms proclaimed in the last French revolution), a supporter of rebel General José María Obando, and a rabid anti-clerical (Lozanoy Lozano and Vega 1939, 124–25). He sanctioned the Constitution of 1853 and implemented with his own signature the decrees that freed Church properties from mortmain.

A trip to Europe opened his horizons and led him to read the works of sociologists then in vogue such as Herbert Spencer whom he came to consider the "true founder," rather than Comte, of sociology (Núñez 1885, 393–416). This discovery of the social sciences brought with it an ideological ingredient that permitted him to better project himself politically upon returning from Europe. Not only Núñez but also others of his orientation, such as Camacho Roldán, discovered in Spencer a bridge for uniting conservative traditionalism with the renewing, technological, and scientific impulse of liberalism (Torres 1935, 155–57). Eager for a partial compromise with conservatism, Camacho Roldán rejected the irreligious (and anti-clerical) positivism of Comte (Jaramillo Uribe 1964, 440–44), and popularized instead the English sociologist, who became a cultural hero to the bourgeois generations of the end of the century. In 1882 Spencer's books replaced those of Bentham and Destutt de Tracy in Camacho's university course. It was a symbolic decision that had the blessing of Núñez (Camacho Roldán 1892, 204–44).

Little by little, Núñez derived "a more serene ideology" to succeed "the pernicious prevalence of strange theories, the undigested assimilation of utopian principles" (Lozano and Vega 1939, 177). Núñez had already begun to concede in 1874 that "the Jacobin entreaty against Catholicism in a Catholic nation does not sound good," and a little later he admitted in a letter to Carlos Martínez Silva: "I am not decidedly anti-Catholic" (Lozano y Lozano and Vega 1939, 185). In this way, subtle politician that he was, and with the *libido imperandi* noted in him by Professor López de Mesa, he prepared his ascent to power, courting the liberal and conservative bourgeois leaders.

Ideologically, Núñez rationalized his own cooptation in accord with the tendency of the times. He already thought that "the conservatives have become more liberal and the liberals have come to understand that no seed turns into a productive tree overnight" (quoted by Lozano y Lozano and Vega, 1939, 206). In his commentary on the French Republic he notes that:

Republics have frequently aborted because their founders and administrators have thought that they marched further by merely hastening their step, while everything in nature indicates that progress in reality implies gradualism; that is, slow, ordered movement [toward a goal]. Every dynamic mechanism should have a controlling regulator; that is, a counterweight, something to counterbalance the main impulse. Monarchies required accessory liberal institutions and republics [need] restraining or conservative institutions (Núñez 1885, 456).

Núñez married a conservative matron in 1877, a fact which was not without influence on his later cooptable behavior (Liévano 1946, 125–31). He thus began to discard his former radical trappings, creating confusion in the minds of the people. With just cause, there was controversy at the community level as to whether Núñez (now President) was in reality a liberal or a *godo* (a contemptuous term for a conservative) as General Foción Soto said in Zipaquirá in 1884 (Soto 1913, I, 201).

Núñez and his coopted followers definitely joined the rightists when the civil war of 1884–1885 was lost by the radical liberals who provoked it hoping to overthrow the man they considered a traitor. It was a war in which the religious element also played a role, as noted by the general and physician, Julio Corredor (Martín 1887, 325) and the Argentine ambassador to Bogotá, Miguel Cané (1907, 138).

The conflict of 1884–1885 is a case study on how not to carry out a revolution. There were errors of strategy, mistakes in organization, a scorn for technology, lack of resources, wavering leadership, and a lack of consistency. Moreover, it revealed the futility of using violence when people do not respond positively to it. The descriptions of General Foción Soto concerning the lack of enthusiasm among his fellow party-members for the war against Núñez are incredible and disheartening. This lack of enthusiasm hindered his attempts to raise the army's morale, to obtain money for food and pay, and to sustain the momentum of the conflict. It is difficult to understand how a party could throw itself into a war with only one small-town mechanic to make weapons and with carpenters who were incapable of making ladders adequate for scaling the walls in the seige of Cartagena (Soto 1913, I, 148; II, 64–65). The inconsistencies and desertions of the liberal director of the war, General Sergio Camargo, were comparable only to the ineptitude of his subordinates. With tragic errors behind them, they arrived at the holocaust that was the battle of La Humareda where the liberal rebel forces were decimated.

The defeat of the liberal party while Núñez was in power compelled him to move toward the conservative party, with whose weapons he had defended himself. Don Carlos Holguín, an able conservative leader who propitiated the cooptation of Núñez and his group (and who had taken state after state through local elections), ceded his leadership to his brother-in-law, Don Miguel Antonio Caro. Caro was the architect of final compulsion, whose historical mark was made indelible in the Constitution of 1886 and in the adoption of the civil code. Of course, Núñez communicated his instructions as president to the Council of Delegates in 1885 on writing the new Constitution that was to supplant that of 1863. But it was Caro whose ideological viewpoints prevailed there to secure the triumph of the bourgeoisie and the clerical party (Torres García 1956; Lozano y Lozano and Vega 1939, 33–34).

While Núñez—in the end left at the political sidelines at home in Cartagena—was deciding whether or not he would return to power (and if so, with which group he would govern), the conservatives took over the reins of the state. They imposed political centralization, the presidential regime, and, above all, they legalized the alliance between Church and state. A Concordat with the Holy See was approved in 1888 which granted the Church full control over national education, total autonomy for self-government, ecclesiastical privileges that had been disputed, and fiscal advantages. It also provided for recompense to the Church for damages suffered when its property was disamortized, through annual payments *ab aeternitatem*, and that the Catholic Church be protected from competition from other churches.

Consequences of Cooptation

Inevitably, the result was an attempt to return to the old patterns of the seigniorial order, without going as far as a return to the precolonial stage, in which the first synthesis between subversion and tradition had been achieved. The old seigniorial patterns began to be felt on all sides: the Jesuits returned for the third time and reconstructed their institutions within the framework of the bourgeois order; the colonial resident-serf system of the *concertaje* reappeared in areas formerly comprising reservations where owners had built latifundia (Fals Borda 1961a, 137–38; Triana 1951, xii). The rebirth of the clerically dominated Hispanic society was also felt in the intellectual sphere owing to the influence of Balmes and the Greco-Roman movement led by Caro and Rufino José Cuervo, Rufino's latinist son. This reactionary movement occasioned the complaint about "the return to . . . Spanish [patterns]" by a liberal scholar, Ezequiel Uricoechea (1871, xlvii–xlviii). The reactionary tendency was further manifested in the abrogations of liberal policies by the conservative presidents that succeeded Núñez. It was revealed in the abuses and persecutions repeatedly discussed by writers such as Fidel Cano, Nicolás Esguerra, and Miguel Samper. They were actions such as the decree regarding subversive acts of February 17, 1888 (concerning publications against the Church, the government, and the monetary system, and incitement of class strife) and the so-called Horse Law of May 25, 1888. The reaction was also shown in the attitudes of scorn for the common people—"the Indians" described in literature of the period—that signaled the rebirth of the caste spirit.

The reactionary cooptation of Núñez and his group reveals to what extent ideological surrender may lead when power is lustily sought as an end in itself. One may rationalize the situation and consider it to represent an "evolution" of Núñez' thought, as many of his friends have done. The dominant tendencies of the bourgeois society in the direction of a "Catholic democracy" (supported by the triumph of Carlist-Alphonsist forces in Spain) may of course be pointed out; they may have led Núñez to ideological surrender in order to "avoid greater harm to the country" and maintain its threatened political unity (Liévano 1946, 430). It may have been "realistic politics" that purged liberalism of its utopian elements (Jaramillo Uribe 1964, 289). However—and this is fundamental—the reactionary nature of cooptation may also be judged by its results in the governments that followed that of Núñez. These regimes were intolerant and ruthless. They were the reactionary affirmation of many theses to which the liberals were opposed, even during the calmer period of the adjustment.

The conservatives and the bourgeoisie, with Caro and Holguín as their champions, employed all the elements at their disposal to achieve such results: offers of positions, prestige, and economic advantage or threats of social sanction based on fear and violence. They knew how to achieve cooptation with both ideas and weapons. But they did so without realizing that in seeking the annihilation of their ideological opponent, they closed the channels and destroyed some of the mechanisms which would have made Colombia a much more advanced modern, and prosperous country. The bourgeois order was not entirely successful, for it retained unacceptable incongruities that later broke forth.

Thus this process shows also how easy it is to move from adjustment to surrender and from surrender to reaction retarding progress.

Obviously, this process of adjustment and compulsion was not a children's game. It was a test of persistence, pressure, and force calculated to lead the opponent into indefensible positions. As was explained before, through adjustment, advantage was taken of the opportunities to stress certain points of view, either those of the elements fighting for transformation or those favoring tradition. Through compulsion, an attempt was made to impose a direction and a dynamism on change. Both processes implied a flexible strategy that combined the application of persuasion, coercion, and violence, the formation of leadership cadres (both technological and ideological), and the dissemination of ideas at the precise moments demanded by the social circumstances and the state of the conflict itself. These processes demanded a leadership of multiple resources, with constancy, tenacity, and the capacity to attack and to retreat, to feint and to counter-attack, in order to demonstrate the use of mechanisms and factors of social change analyzed herein.

Judging by the case of Núñez and his group, there is a danger in this vital play of power that adjustment become a compromise or retreat from a position; and that compulsion become imposition. This possibility depends in great part on the factors of power and strategy that lead the opposing groups to the arena of confrontations. It depends on the response of the people themselves to subversive attempts and also on the personalities of the leaders. Adjustment is a long-range effort, with adaptations to the historical tendencies of a people made in harmony with the visions of statesmen. On the other hand, compromise is a maneuver that tends to obscure the vision of the whole and to confuse the general strategy of the movement; this as much as the imprudent use of violence at times and places in which it is self-defeating also obscures the central issues of subversion.

The bourgeois order was finally established. The triumph of the rightist groups and the clerical party could not be taken away from them in spite of the bloody and destructive civil wars that occurred in 1895 and from 1899 to 1902, almost annihilating the liberal party and ruining the country. In this new historical period, even though such wars were imprudent and self-defeating, for the liberal party there was no other possibility except violence, since all other means of legitimate political action had been closed to them by intolerant governments. The apocalyptic "war of a thousand days" (1899–1902), followed by the North American intervention of 1903 that culminated in the secession of Panama, told the country that it was in fact living in a new social order. To guarantee the transformation, it was necessary to achieve peace and to initiate a new cycle of development beginning with the search for a new utopia to lift the spirits of the people and justify the eventual rebellion. It was also necessary to take a nationalistic stance in the face of the "Colossus of the North." This was achieved later.

In any case, the political and economic predominance of conservatism that developed in this period helps to explain the basic intolerance, the profound resistance to change, and the tendency to maintain obsolete patterns of political and social behavior that are observed in many parts of the country today. It also permitted the bourgeois order to survive until the decade of 1920 to 1930 when new social and economic forces made a more radical challenge to the established social order, thus beginning the cycle of subversion all over again.

CHAPTER SEVEN

Subversion and Frustration in
the Twentieth Century: The Socialists

SINCE the end of the last century there has been almost imperceptibly, an accumulation of marginal changes within the leeway of tolerance of the bourgeois order, which presaged profound transformations in society (cf. Moore 1963, 50, 71; Cooley 1909, 328). Some politicians, including Núñez and Caro, inclined toward different conceptions of the state, preferring, in theory, interventionism and certain forms of "Christian socialism" (Torres García 1956, 226–28). These goals were partially adopted by the conservative party. However, the accumulation of marginal adjustments can be more clearly seen in the technological component. Owing to the very nature of technological innovations, "instruments" for producing certain social and economic changes were discovered. They were conceived within a new rationale: that of the modern ends (such as the goal of a "civilized nation") related to certain means.

This instrumental tendency was reinforced by the adoption of the entrepreneurial ethic. However, new attitudes did not saturate the whole society. Only certain segments of the society, such as the upper bourgeoisie and the middle class Antioquian settlers (the majority of whom were conservative), followed the instrumental tendency of the era. Others, particularly seigniorial-type rural communities, continued to be guided by the ethos of caste urbanism.

The social processes that have made their appearance in this century have a dynamic that is similar to that of the social processes of the middle of the last century. But there exists a basic difference between them: the introduction of the liberal utopia in 1848 failed to assure the support of technology for the subversive groups of the time and rather gave control to the bourgeoisie, while in the early twentieth century there was an autonomous accumulation of elements in the technological component that multiplied the disintegrating potential of another utopia. This one appeared about 1904 enshrouded in socialist thought, but it did not have concrete effects until after 1919. To a certain point, the total effect of the socialist utopia was conditioned by prior economic and social advance. Its potential for change, based on the tensions and incongruities inherent in the existing social order, eventually led to a subversion.

This disruptive impulse of change made cleavages that permitted the adoption of new attitudes incompatible with the traditional ones. A new ethos began to emerge, that of instrumental secularism, which incorporated the new counter-values and counter-norms. This ethos emerged at the same time that the first utopian inroads by socialism appeared, and so secularism came wrapped in the ideological cloak of socialism. But the two complexes should not be confused. Secularism is a way of life and an analytical category of sociology; socialism is a political ideology with concrete expressions in social organization. The analysis which follows attempts to recognize the importance of secularism and the consequences of instrumentalism that had been incubating, causing the bourgeois Colombian society to arrive at a critical point. This point required significant changes in values, norms, and social organization and therefore another subversion appeared.

The seigniorial-bourgeois order, which established itself in two generations, was unable to resist the combined impact of the socialist utopia, secularism, and technological accumulation, and it began to disintegrate. Traditional elements were again confronted by those of the new situation of subversion, leading to one of the most tragic and confused periods of Colombian history that included the short revolution of 1948 and the subsequent frustration implied in *la Violencia*. A tactical synthesis was achieved in 1957 with great difficulty: the liberal-bourgeois order of the National Front. In order to achieve the new topia, the basic processes of adjustment and compulsion, cooptation and arrest were employed to gain control of the compulsive and stabilizing mechanisms.

Technical Accumulation and the Critical Point

Technical innovations in agriculture, in the use of energy and in the cultural complexes related to industry, transportation, defense, communication, medicine, and similar activities led imperceptibly to a critical point that brought about and made mandatory important transformations in the values, norms, and social organization of the bourgeois order.

In the last chapter some of the principal innovations that were basic to mid-century development and concomitant economic growth were described. Accumulation of technological elements in the new social order and of the wealth of the country (which was not well distributed among groups that made its accumulation possible) accelerated when the government of General Rafael Reyes (1904–1909) revoked earlier laws and implanted a protectionist system. With the aid of Reyes, whose ideal means of progress was the machine and whose paradigm was Mexico's dictator, Porfirio Díaz, the great companies that now exist in Colombia began to flourish: Telares Medellín (1906), Coltejer (1908), Obregón and Cervecería Bolívar (1908), Cemento Samper (1909), and many others founded later. Meanwhile in the countryside, the great banana and sugar plantations and sugar cane refineries were firmly established (Ospina Vásquez 1955, 326–44; Eder 1959). The tendencies toward industrialization were sustained during the First World War.

There was also an acceleration in the rate of population increase after the last civil war. Population rose to nearly six million people in 1918, a remarkable rise if it is compared with the very modest increases during the nineteenth century. This rapid demographic growth also led to modifications in the social order because the conditions of the social scale varied (Wilson and Wilson 1945, 24–26).

With the change in the relations of production and the promotion of "instrumentalism," in addition to the population increase, technological innovations began to demand a natural process of social differentiation. They gave rise to new groups and institutions that functioned as mechanisms for maintaining the innovations themselves: banks, insurance companies, business firms, factories, and transportation companies. With social differentiation, certain new channels of social mobility were created; the urban *petit bourgeosie* and a proletariat began to be discernible. This whole process of differentiation and disruption, of course, occurred within the margins allowed by the survival of caste urbanism. Nonetheless, the fact of forming a more complex structure in society, breaking certain traditions, fostering new attitudes that were adaptable to the bourgeois order, and above all, being nourished by the "demonstration effect" of the salaried groups could not help but have consequences for the relations between castes. Differentiation led them to a greater self-awareness and turned them into more open and flexible classes. The discovery of class consciousness was in these circumstances a critical point that determined the course of later events (for which the affected groups sought pertinent ideological support).

Always alert to their own interests, the intellectuals of the upper bourgeoisie had already observed the socio-political movements that had shaken Europe toward the end of the nineteenth century, especially the creation of the first Spanish Republic, with its leanings toward anarchic syndicalism and socialism. The tendencies toward parliamentary government in other European countries were symptoms of great changes. The writing on the wall was ever clearer: a great revolution was coming, one that would challenge the caste structure of the bourgeois order through simultaneous action affecting two of its components: the technological and the valuative. The economist-politician Aníbal Galindo expressed it this way in 1880:

The characteristic phases of this economic revolution are three in number: (1) the access of all classes—down to the very lowest—to the goods and comforts of wealth through the extraordinary growth of production and through the extreme inexpensiveness of products made with the assistance of these automatons who work for infinitely small salaries. Photography, oleography, telegraphy, lithography, printing; the sewing machine and machines for spinning and weaving cotton have made comfort, pleasures, and benefits available to the lowest social classes that were previously the privileges of the land's potentates; (2) the decreasing use of manual labor, and replacement of the beast-of-burden role imposed on the worker by the intellectual and moral work of supervision and vigilance to which the functions of the worker in the modern workshop are being reduced. On all sides, *mutatis mutandi,* the porter moves into the category of the railroad guard or watchman. . . ; and (3) the migration to great population centers in the search for work and salary levels available in the world market owing to the rapidity, the facility, and the economy with which trips may be made by modern means of transportation (Galindo 1880, 308).

The *petite bourgeoisie* that was the product of this initial process of economic transformation tended to identify with the upper classes on which they depended for subsistence. But it did not yet dissociate itself from its humble origins and during the first moments of crisis took the side of workers and craftsmen. Only later, when their ranks were filled out and they were more thoroughly assimilated, did the new middle class become conservative and a decided partisan of social accommodation. Its emergence had indirect but profound consequences in the class consciousness of proletarian and peasant elements. These were groups beginning to understand the difference between their own social position and that of other groups. The discovery that it was possible to achieve a way of life that differed from the routine through effort, education, business, or industry aroused the latent energy of the people and made them alert to the opportunities for betterment. This new consciousness has been identified by elderly members of the proletariat and peasants today when they recall past events and exclaim: "When progress came. . . ." "Progress" resulted from the "demonstration effect," instrumental opportunities for advancement, the new mechanisms of employment, and the possibilities for leaving the provinces and the communal niche.

Not all of this could be intentional. The dominant groups were unable to anticipate the consequences inherent in the technological and economic process they fostered except in the remote and theoretical way in which Galindo did. For him, the effects of such a revolution could not affect Colombia for another hundred years. Yet this process had certain characteristics of inevitability. In fact, technological accumulation, in making the division of labor and class identification more complex matters, could only lead the bourgeois order to a critical point of disintegration.

The first symptom of social tension between classes apparently occurred in 1919 as a result of the First World War and the economic strain suffered by the country. The government of Don Marco Fidel Suárez (an illustrious writer of humble origins who was, however, coopted and assimilated by the oligarchies through educational and matrimonial relationships) had decided for example to acquire from abroad several hundred uniforms for the police. The garment workers of Bogotá and other craftsmen organized to solicit the President to buy only the cloth abroad and to have the uniforms made in Colombia, and decided to go to the streets to express their feelings. On Sunday, March 16, 1919, the police, unskilled in handling this type of action, attacked, and some were killed or wounded. These events increased the nation-wide dissatisfaction and gave impetus to the conflict between classes, and between workers and employers, for which the government found itself totally unprepared.

In addition, it was becoming increasingly clear that the benefits resulting from the United States indemnification for Panama after 1924 ("the dance of the millions") were being spread with no thought to equity. The benefits of this bonanza did not reach the less privileged groups except on a very limited scale, giving greater substance to the new class perspective and aggravating the situation of conflict.

The extensive construction of highways and railroads during these years tended to attract a large number of peasants who abandoned their plots and were employed in public works programs with (artificially) higher daily wages than they were accustomed to receiving. Agriculture suffered on all sides. Food products became more expensive, inflation developed, and the standard of living declined. People were restless in the cities but they did not return to the countryside. Day laborers from highway and railroad construction went to the incipient industries and became factory workers—the industrial proletariat—under conditions that were not satisfactory (Nieto Arteta 1962, 326–28; García 1955, 242).

On the other hand, the dominant groups, increasingly connected with foreign interests, continued to enrich themselves. They managed to exploit labor, oppressing the workers through submissive attitudes derived from the old ethos of caste urbanism. The arrogant and abusive tactics of management eventually invited a reaction by labor. The first strike by the oil workers employed by Tropical Oil Company in Barrancabermeja was repressed in 1927 and its promoters were killed. A worse massacre occurred at the end of 1928 in the banana-growing area of Santa Marta to end a strike by laborers of the United Fruit Company who wanted better working conditions. These conflicts served to underscore the critical point to which the social order had come and the instrumental nature of the subversion that it was fostering. Neither the government nor the bourgeoisie seemed to be ready to confront it, nor were they able to understand it.

Nonetheless, the true socio-economic development of the twentieth century began in Colombia at this time. The most authoritative observers have pinpointed 1925 and thereabouts as the period in which the process was most clearly observed, with almost immediate consequences shown in indices of economic development (Mesa 1965; Nieto Arteta 1962, 326; Ospina Vásquez 1955, 420; García Cadena 1943, 126, 130). Owing to the impulse from indemnification for Panama, between 1925 and 1929 the annual growth rate of the per capita gross national product was 5.2 per cent (CEPAL 1955, I, 27). The Sociedad Colombo-Alemana de Transportes Aéreos (SCADTA) began operations in 1919; its subsequent conversion into AVIANCA airlines had great positive effects on the bourgeois economy as well as on the processes of regional and national integration. The number of telephone lines increased from 5,095 in 1913 to 34,680 in 1927. The volume of mail became four times greater during the same period (Fluharty 1957, 16, 32; Currie 1950, 133ff.). By 1929 there were already 15,350 automobiles in the country. Between 1930 and 1933, 842 enterprises were established, including all the present basic Colombian industries. The industrial indices rose again between 1939 and 1948 from 100 to 243. Until 1953 the gross product of industries, transportation, electric power, and public services increased at annual rates varying from 7.8% to 9.1%. In 1953 the number of industrial workers rose to 200,000 and the value of the gross product of processing industries was 3,917 million pesos as compared with 641 million in 1945 (Mesa 1965, 9, 14). About this same time the first heavy industry (a steel mill) was founded in Colombia, the Siderúrgica de Paz de Río.

Meanwhile, agriculture remained almost stagnant because introduction of agricultural machines was very limited; only a few haciendas benefited from these innovations. However, during the decade from 1920 to 1930 some new elements such as chemical fertilizers and portable pump sprayers began to be adopted in the Andean region (Deutschmann and Fals Borda 1963, 46–50). The hacienda owners adopted them first; soon after, middle-sized farm owners followed suit and rented them to their *minifundium*-owning neighbors, thus leading, little by little, to an important transformation in agricultural techniques, perhaps the greatest since the rudimentary plow was introduced to the ayllic order in the colonial period. Factories manufacturing certain mechanical agricultural implements, such as the threshing machine, were successfully established (in Pasto). The peasants began to become accustomed to the periodic passing of these machines pulled by teams of oxen. About 1950 other innovations were introduced: chemical herbicides and new fungicides.

The rapid adoption of the agricultural tractor was very important. Its numbers rose from 3,821 in 1938 to 16,493 in 1956. The use of this apparatus extended from the haciendas to the minifundia (through rental arrangements) principally for the purpose of preparing fallow land. It presented a challenge to the work force, especially its younger members, whose aspirations turned from agriculture based on the hoe and direct physical effort to mechanized agriculture and the use of the new apparatuses. The consequences of this impact on agriculture (the disappearance of ox teams, for example) and on human behavior (the creation of new positions, roles, and expectations) were of strategic importance for stimulating disruption in the bourgeois order at the critical point (Fals Borda 1959a).

This pronounced tendency toward technology in Colombia was also demonstrated in other ways: modern and technological sciences started to displace law, theology, and philosophy in the country's universities; agricultural extension services began to be tried out; commercial agricultural enterprises prospered along with the first specialized institutes; the professions of agronomist and veterinarian acquired prestige; the first irrigated districts were experimented with in Tolima and the first large dams to control the Bogotá River were constructed; bus lines multiplied everywhere, fostering the creation of new markets and metropolitan economic units; and modern medicine began to enter the small towns and distant villages with convincing demonstrable effects.

All of these technical innovations had to affect the bourgeois order despite endeavors by the entrepreneurs to nullify the effects of these elements on the caste attitude. The convergence of technology and economic change on social organization at the same time that the traditional system of values was being attacked could only result in subversive induction. According to Mesa, "during the first post-war years, the development of the productive forces was of such nature that it already came into violent conflict with all the established relations of property ownership, the juridical system, the norms of society, and all levels of culture. The contradiction between the agrarian, semi-colonial country and the modern, predominantly bourgeois nation began to reach a climax" (Mesa 1965, 8).

The climax naturally led to a later frustration, for the subversion of the bourgeois order was not able to achieve culmination in the socialist order to which the instrumental challenge of the established values were leading. But efforts to neutralize the impact of modern technology and the nascent class consciousness were to no avail. The mere passing of the era of the wooden plow to that of mechanized agriculture implied a transformation in the attitudes and patterns of living of the people of the countryside. And the most ample diffusion of the factory also fostered change in the customs of the proletariat groups of the city who were now capable of confronting their employers. Only an ideology was lacking to induce the people to act in the pursuit of a new social order. It was expected that this order would be more satisfactory than the previous one.

The Socialist Challenge

Aníbal Galindo was profoundly mistaken concerning the rapidity with which his "economic revolution" was arriving. Not one hundred, but twenty-four, years after his prophecy, a member of his own class, General Rafael Uribe, deserted it in order to make the first formal attack on established values.

The declared purpose of General Uribe's iconoclastic attitude was to discover an ideology that could serve the liberal party that had emerged from the civil war of 1899–1902 exhausted and decimated. Uribe, who was one of the rebel leaders, had become a champion of peace in order to reconstruct the country after the painful secession of Panama. His meditations concerning the pertinent literature (and the example of certain reformers such as Gladstone) led him toward socialism as an ideology that could give the nation what it needed in this new era (Santa 1962, 411–23).

Uribe wanted the liberal party to be the champion of popular grievances and to take up the banner of syndicalism, social services, distributive justice, and agrarian and tax reform, all of which in his opinion could be accomplished only by an interventionist state. His ideas were presented in a speech in 1904 that, as was to be expected, traditional political leaders and dominant groups repudiated (Uribe 1904). Shortly after his return from a trip through South America, still defending his position, he was assassinated in the streets of Bogotá (October 15, 1914).

A small socialist group was organized, however, and its opportunities for growth, owing to the tensions that the bourgeois order was beginning to undergo, were elements that accelerated social change. About 1925, the year when the subversion could first be clearly seen, the rebel groups whose ideological affiliation led them to question the established order had already become visible. The first was a socialist group which constituted a counter-elite. It was composed mainly of university students between the ages of 20 and 25, of distinguished families of the upper and middle classes, young men who began to understand the meaning of the new age. Like those of the Republican School of 1850, these young men also reacted in a critical and revolutionary way, raising a cry of protest against the social inequalities and the moral incongruences and inconsistencies of the bourgeois order. Even though the Mexican Revolution was attractive for its dramatism and proximity, it was the Russian Revolution that inflamed their imaginations. They began to meet periodically in a new institution, "the Café" (coffee house) which had replaced the former tavern (*botellería*). Thus, in the Café Windsor in Bogotá the rebel group, *Los Nuevos* (The New Group) was formed in 1922. Among others who joined it were: Gabriel Turbay, Alberto Lleras Camargo, Juan and Carlos Lozano y Lozano, Germán Arciniégas, Moisés Prieto, Guillermo Hernández Rodríguez, Luis Tejada, and marginally, owing to his social origin, Jorge Eliécer Gaitán. He had distinguished himself with his haranguing during that bloody Sunday, March 16, 1919 and his doctoral thesis had dealt precisely with "Socialist Ideas in Colombia" (Osorio Lizarazo 1952, 64–65, 210, 255; Fluharty, 1957, 29). The group was stimulated by the entry of the important writer and journalist, Luis Cano, the former radical Antonio José Restrepo, and Gerardo Molina, Antonio García, Luis Carlos Pérez, Luis Rafael Robles, and others. The Socialist Revolutionary Party (PSR) was officially founded in 1926.

"The voice of the future in Colombia" was heard in the Windsor. The objectives of the Russian Revolution were discussed along with modern literary and artistic tendencies, and the banner of social change and the struggle against the "reactionary past" was waved. From these discussions seminal ideas developed which were soon widely disseminated concerning student organization and trade unions. These tendencies were fully realized toward the end of the decade with the creation of the first National Federation of Students, which had the additional incentive of the university autonomy movement of Córdoba, Argentina. The first trade unions were firmly established by the time the liberal party took over the government in 1930.

During the same years, a Russian dry cleaner and dyer named Savinsky (Sawadsky, according to some) arrived in Bogotá and joined *Los Nuevos*. At the request of the group, Savinsky expounded the principles of Marxist economics, exciting the enthusiasm of the young men. Thus some of them decided to found the first Communist cell in Colombia, in 1924, and proceeded to meet in secret in a church (probably Protestant) situated in the Las Nieves section of the city. This first cell was composed of the following members: Lleras, Turbay, Prieto, Tejada, and Hernández Rodríguez of the Windsor group as well as Alejandro Vallejo, José Mar, Diego

Mejía, and Luis Vidales (Rodríguez Garavito 1965, 60; Osorio Lizarazo 1952, 78, 90; Fluharty 1957, 29). These young men considered performing acts of terrorism, but the stimulus of these meetings was more of an intellectual and spiritual nature. Thus, for example, Tejada concluded that he owed to Lenin and Communism: "my acquiring an honest motivation for fighting, my reason for being and working, the strong, optimistic vision I have concerning the future, my sincere conviction that the world may become good and more just and that man will acquire an attitude of ennobled dignity" (quoted by Rodríguez Garavito 1965, 64). Turbay was attracted by "the myth of universal brotherhood, absolute equality among men, the disarmament of aggressors, the advent [of the distribution] of the world's riches among the humiliated and offended" (Rodríguez Garavito 1965, 66). Thus it was a group of visionary, enthusiastic young men determined to fight for the transformation of the country following the standards of the socialist utopia they were beginning to discover. They were anxious to adopt and disseminate those values because they considered them superior to those of the bourgeois order. The Colombian Communist Party (PCC) was formally organized and internationally recognized in 1930.

For reasons we shall study later on, the counter-elite of this era little by little disintegrated. But its members went through dispersion that was very similar to that undertaken by the *ladinos* and mestizos of the colonial era. Just as the seigniorial order and Christianity spread at the time, now there was an attempt to saturate the most important organisms of transition with socialism by means of the dispersion. Members of the counter-elite acted as reference groups to the trade unions and workers' groups whose organization was stimulated by Gaitán between 1927 and 1931. About 1929 they reached the peasants who were encouraged by the Communist group to invade hacienda lands, and in this they were partially successful. Between 1929 and 1936 they awakened university students whose federation (with Carlos Lleras Restrepo as president) was inclined toward socialism. In 1940 they installed Gerardo Molina as the rector of National University, and in this way gave vitality to the liberal party whose leadership coopted and assimilated the socialist rebels—who did not necessarily capitulate. The influence of the subversive reference group, be it through its own socialist party, which ultimately became well articulated with Antonio García at the head, or be it through the dispersion, turned it into a key group of the new subversion. This is why this movement will be called here the "socialist subversion."

It may be seen that the socialist counter-elite sowed its ideological seed at the precise moment at which the bourgeois order was reaching its critical point. The population was growing, the society was becoming differentiated by technological development, class conflicts were becoming apparent, and the incongruities of the society were becoming more visible. The subverters performed effectively and six years later came the decline of the conservative party and the initiation of the "Revolution on the March" of the resurrected liberal party.

The Diffusion of Secular Ideology

The introduction of instrumental secularism to Colombia as a challenge to caste urbanism should be differentiated as a social process from its exploitation as a slogan by the various political groups. We have said that instrumental secularism was the result of a combination of situations caused by sociocultural contact, population increase, technological accumulation, and the discovery of class consciousness, all of which pointed up the incongruities of the bourgeois society. The first socialist groups—that is, those that organized politically in order to impose their respective ideology and to achieve power—made the social situation a dynamic one: they were the catalysts who turned it into subversion. Therefore they became key groups. But the ideas, values, and norms making up the ethos of instrumental secularism were not the exclusive property of these socialist groups since some elements existed before these groups emerged. Some socialist ideas, upon being disseminated and adopted, also became the property of diverse political organizations that sought renewal and survival, especially of the liberal party. Later, instrumental secularism was partially extended to bourgeois groups that had to adapt themselves to the subversive élan in order to survive the change. Even the conservative party in power implemented projects that corresponded to the necessity for diffusion of these new ideas.

It is not difficult to cull from the documents the general intent of the subverters' goals, or the models they wished to follow, socialist as well as the reformed liberals. Analysis of those documents reveals, among other things, the adaptability of the socialist message to the necessities of immediate political action in different parts of the world and in different cultural contexts. Evidently, the utopia transmitted by Uribe and Savinsky, understood in all its emotional force by Tejada and Turbay, was one thing, and the translation of it to the conditions of daily struggle against the status quo was another. Thus, from a reading of Marx, Engels, Lenin, and the Fabians, the vanguard politicians derived formulas for proclamations in public plazas. There was talk of "integral revolutions," agrarian and tax reforms, "anti-imperialism," the necessity of achieving a truly national integration to confront the outside world, and the right of self-determination of peoples. In Latin America, the ideas of the socialist revolution were translated into the realities of the local scene through the work of intellectuals and politicians such as José Carlos Mariátegui, José Vasconcelos, José Ingenieros, Víctor Raúl Haya de la Torre, Vicente Lombardo Toledano, and Rómulo Betancourt. Later, in addition to socialism the following played a role in the articulation of the new instrumental goals: the organization of the Spanish Republic, Franklin D. Roosevelt's New Deal, Keynesian theory, and the posthumous discovery of the interest that Pope Leo XIII had shown in trade union reform during the last century.

There is little doubt that the socialists and their sympathizers represented change at this historical moment. They sought change in Colombian society, change so radical that its mere enunciation implied the opposite pole from that of the bourgeois order in many aspects. Their counter-values demolished colonial customs; their counter-norms destroyed the traditions of domination, and the previous economic structure. Had the compulsion to impose these counter-values and counter-norms as well as the unswerving direction of this new movement been maintained for more than one generation, organization of a radically different social order would have occurred. Even though the order that emerged was not the one sought by the subversives, they did produce a society in which there were clear signs of the retreat of the seigniorial and bourgeois forces.

In first place, the fundamental idea that stimulated the key groups of this subversive period—in harmony with the incipient secularist-instrumental movement—involved the desire to achieve the physical, intellectual, and spiritual freedom of man, especially that of the common man, the humble people, whose resources and talents had been wasted. It was necessary to give him a new sense of dignity. This was the grand plan for humanity, the great, new goal that broke down the traditional caste structure. There were to be no more Indians or servants of the glebe, or potentates whose prosperity was a consequence of the privations of the peasant and worker (García 1953). Human potentiality was to find outlets in constructive forms, leaving behind the chains that had subjected it to underdevelopment, injustice, poverty, ignorance, hunger, and disease.

For this reason and purpose it was necessary to encourage a secularism which legitimated the emerging counter-values and counter-norms. The new secularism wanted to free man from his old metaphysical presuppositions and his out-dated religion in order that he might live in the world and understand it as it really is. In this way dogma collapses and the possibility of choice among alternatives, all of which become institutionalized, is opened. Moreover, the possibility of variation and the autonomous responsibility of man to make his decisions are normatively accepted (De Vries 1961, Chap. 2).

The recognition of these goals led once again to thinking about the "instruments" with which to achieve them. These instruments were necessarily impersonal since they did not fit into the provincial world and primary relationships of the traditional order. The ethos of the new society was one of instrumental secularism. This instrumentalism expressed recognition of the interdependence of means and ends, and especially of the human capacity to change the surrounding environment through the development of personal self-control, technology, planning, and social invention (Mannheim 1941, 336–47; Mannheim 1958). These seem to be the human instruments with the greatest capacity for promoting the most profound transformation in social life.

The goals implicit in this ethos, and the necessities to be satisfied, demanded in addition that utility and efficiency be imposed as criteria on social and economic relations. This ethos also gave justification to state intervention. Intervention was felt to be a basic necessity once it was verified that the society does not develop harmoniously but rather allows lags in the advance according to the capacity of its institutions to respond to the process. There arise contradictions and tensions among the components of the social order (cf. Ogburn 1950; Hart 1959). The adequate functioning of the new order for this reason depends on the adoption of the ethos of instrumental secularism to indicate how to proceed in the allocation of resources and how to choose the means for achieving the ends of socio-economic change.

In short, this ethos implied a new type of social action that was much more impersonal and calculating to supplant the prescriptive action of the seigniorial order; it was elective action. A positive attitude toward change was institutionalized and the transition from habit to deliberate choice was socialized (Germani 1962, 71–75; Costa Pinto 1963, 174–75, 180–91).

As explained, the secularist-instrumental challenge was not limited to the individual level and national society; it also had international dimensions. The subversives spoke of the cause of the poor people of Colombia as one in common with the people of the rest of America, Africa, and Asia. The union of the workers of all nations was proclaimed. The similarity of the social problems affecting countries where indigenous groups were still important, such as Mexico, Guatemala, Ecuador, Peru, and Bolivia, was stressed. The myth of the mestizo "cosmic race" of all the Americas was invented (Vasconcelos 1930). Nationalism was not totally discarded, of course, but was considered a transitory stage in the achievement of a regional or supra-national social and economic integration by means of restructured society. The latent purpose of this supra-nationalism was to avoid the aberrations, absurd wars, wastes, and cultural and economic debacles experienced by Europe during the effervescent nationalist period since the end of the eighteenth century (cf. Toynbee 1947, 285–90). In this way, the state as it is classically conceived was looked upon as a traditionalist invention that made possible the perpetuation of the bourgeois order and its dominant groups. The latter benefited by the tensions and treaties between governments. The new loyalties were to be made with the human race in general, with Man. Such a system of counter-values weakened the related elements of the bourgeois order which promoted a nationalism of elites based on the perpetuation of seigniorial values. Consequently, bourgeois nationalism acquired an irrational image in the new context (cf. Mendes 1963).

The new ethos was also to modify the attitudes of the people toward nature. Until then, except for the initial changes imposed in the nineteenth century, the values of animism had sought an accommodation with nature, worshipping her and accepting her yoke. Now, instead, counter-values of technicism emerged with greater force. The aspiration was to dominate and transform the surrounding environment efficiently (Cottrell 1955).

In a similar way, the submissive otherworldliness and neo-Manicheism received the blow of instrumental secularism. There was no refuge in the opinion and wishes of the patrons and other members of the dominant groups. Such a practice had led to passivity among the people; whether through relations with political "bosses" (*gamonales*) or through the confessional. Now it was time to open the door to the perfectibility of man in order to "break the chains of monastic control" and create "truth, beauty, and goodness," aims to which the students of the University of Córdoba had referred in their manifesto of 1918. Therein derived the counter-values of the new humanism that gave value to human dignity and to the individual in community.

Only the values of family-centeredness remained from the bourgeois order. But now these values were reinterpreted so that they harmonized with the rest of the values. There was a desire to give them a sense of collectivity or communalism. It was unnecessary to conceive of the nuclear family as a significant unit of change. To the contrary, perhaps it was more than ever necessary to preserve

the sense of kinship and extend family and neighborhood cooperation in order to promote the transformations of the society as a
whole. Part of the attraction of the Peruvian APRA Party resided
precisely in its recovering from the ayllic order the familial values
of the Inca neighborhood group (particularly collectivist and socialist) in order to place them in the framework of modern political
action, giving them a communal meaning.

Finally, an acute confrontation was also observed with regard to
the normative framework. Deriving from the new ethos, the
counter-norms of the socialist subversion sought to eliminate the
seigniorial norms of prescriptive rigidity and acritical morality in a
way similar to that which occurred in 1850. Supported by the
counter-values already described, the counter-norms sought the dis-
solution of the caste structure with its discrimination according to
race, land ownership, wealth, occupation, education, and social position. Former norms concerning purity of blood, absolute private
property, *laissez faire*, and the rejection of manual labor became
incongruent. So did norms based on prescriptions, dogmas, and beliefs of seigniorial and bourgeois institutions which had served to
promote resignation, ignorance, and social inequality. In like manner
the counter-values of technicism (previously encouraged by the
bourgeoisie who did not anticipate all their consequences) and communalism imposed modifications in the meaning of traditional providence and stability in order to socialize persons disposed to accept
material and social innovations. In so doing they modified the old
conception of wealth and willingly accepted the implications of social mobility, egalitarianism, communication, and the broadening of
the prevailing *Weltanschauung*.

For these reasons, the instrumental counter-norms of the period
of the socialist subversion may be summarized within the following framework:

1. Mobility: counter-norms that led to broad social, economic,
and political participation and a form of egalitarian life in society,
whose structures should become more open.

2. Telic morality: counter-norms that sought efficiency in action according to the secular and instrumental goals proposed for

the new social order, and which facilitated progress as a planned activity of man (cf. Ward 1883, II, 108–09; Spencer 1911, 153–97; Mannheim 1950; Moore 1963, 43).

3. Technical control: counter-norms that led to the employment of elements that transformed or controlled the surrounding natural environment, such as those arising from empirical, technological, or scientific knowledge.

With these ideological goals, subverters and key groups worked until about 1925, scattering themselves among different levels of society. They conditioned the environment necessary for a profound transformation. Their first catalytic effects were felt in the cities among workers and students. In the countryside the process was slower, advancing only in certain parts of Cundinamarca and Tolima. But bases were amply provided for the interplay of the social compulsion and adjustment of the following years.

Evidently, the subverters involved in this transformation were unable to legitimize their conduct within the framework of the established social order whose norms and values they ideologically and morally rejected. They did so as visionaries, looking toward the future, legitimating their new attitudes only in the emerging social order, and seeking justification and encouragement among their own rebel reference groups.

Positive Cooptation and Violence

Few times in the history of Latin America has such an impetuous élan been registered as that of the socialist subversion in Colombia. The pioneer work of Rafael Uribe, the organization of socialist, communist, and neo-liberal cells as reference groups for workers, students, and peasants, and the diffusion of the new ideas among the proletariat, the peasantry, and the university student body, added to the ineptness of the conservative governments of the era, opened the way for the deep transformations of the social order.

The magnitude of the impact of this subversion may be easily understood if to these ideological ingredients there are added some factors deriving from the world economic and political situation that affected the country (the financial debacle of 1929–1931, the socialist consolidation in Russia, and the new revolutionary policy in Mexico).

An almost immediate consequence was the resurrection of the liberal party whose leaders, with General Benjamín Herrera at the head, propitiated the move toward the ideological left. With this move, positive cooptation of *Los Nuevos* was accomplished. Positive cooptation made it possible to attract the counter-elite and other subversive groups by means of granting positions by the dominant groups. In this manner the original rhythm of the subversion could be maintained for a time. This is the assimilative process followed in other countries in certain historical periods when a new social order has been achieved without incurring a total replacement of the former upper groups. In this process the subverters maintained control of the compulsion owing to their domination over factors such as moral argument and the coercive possibility of rebellion, and their superior or more efficient organization.

As a matter of fact, the pressure of *Los Nuevos* of the Windsor coffee house and other active groups began to have an unforeseen effect. Owing to this pressure and the calls of Uribe and Herrera, the political elite began to re-read the social encyclicals of Pope Leo XIII and found in them the thread for tying the Catholic tradition of the country to the secularist-instrumental movement. The liberal party called a convention in Ibagué in 1922 which adopted a platform with socialist tendencies. Two years later, in Medellín, the advantages of this movement could be more clearly seen and the new socialist orientation of the party was confirmed (Morales Benítez 1962, 1967; Ospina Vásquez 1955, 360). It was a wise play. Because of it, some of *Los Nuevos* began to return to the "glorious tents" of the liberal party.

But they did not return in capitulation. On the contrary, they continued to be convinced of the worth of their ideas and the justice of their cause, and proceeded to impose them within the regular party machinery. Herrera had to accept this situation until the time of his death (even though the traditionals called him a Communist) because its advantages were amply demonstrated. On the one hand the student movement was incorporated. Its intervention in the fall of President Reyes in 1909 and in the events of 1919 already described (and in those of June 7 and 8, 1929, when the government of President Abadía was seriously challenged) opened new perspectives for party action. On the other hand, worker-employer conflicts became more acute, with bloody repressions by the Minister of War, General Ignacio Rengifo, for whom any salary demands or the minimum sign of dissatisfaction was "proof" of Communist subversion (Osorio Lizarazo 1952, 103). In addition, the invasions of land began on the new communes of Viotá, southwest of the nation's capital.

There were of course differences of criteria between *Los Nuevos* and bourgeois defenders of the party, especially with the older ones called the "generation of the Centennial" (for the year 1910 in commemoration of Colombia's independence) or the "Notables," then in their fullness of life, who were alert to maintaining their control over party machinery. But *Los Nuevos* and other active groups knew how to take advantage of circumstances revealing the weakness of government, weaknesses complicated by the world economic depression that impinged upon the country. The impulse of the subversive group was such that at least at the beginning it managed to maintain its cohesion, making its influence felt in the acts of the first liberal governments, those of Enrique Olaya Herrera and Alfonso López Pumarejo. The class identification of *Los Nuevos*, who belonged to the emerging middle sector or identified with it, played an important role in this cohesion. They tended to lead the new proletariat groups of Bogotá in confrontations with the bourgeoisie.

The internal conflict of the party and the manner in which *Los Nuevos* exercised their compulsion to induce social change were well described in a letter written by the young leader, Don Alberto Lleras, to centennialist Armando Solano.

We are dissatisfied [declared Lleras at that time]. The Centennial generation did not have and does not have a feeling for the contemporary scene as ours has. In ideologies we have gone beyond that of Rojas Garrido and that of Aquileo Parra. We have not made our camp in the tranquil old parties comforted by the shade of traditions, without noise or turmoil. We have come with impetuosity. . . . We have not feared to dissociate ourselves with the past in order to soar toward the new movements (quoted by Rodríguez Garavito 1965, 175–76).

With this activist tone the liberal party took power in 1930, and the incumbents in government ceded to the subversives, offering them important positions without demanding radical concessions. The socialist group of Molina, García, Pérez, and Robles advanced through key positions in institutions of the state and of the university. Gaitán accepted ministries and mayoralties between 1936 and 1942 and became Second Vice-President of the Republic. Lleras Restrepo, the former president of the National Student Federation, became Comptroller General and Minister of Finance in 1938. Alberto Lleras, Gabriel Turbay, Carlos Lozano, Jorge Zalamea, Moisés Prieto, and other colleagues of this generation also became ministers, ambassadors, senators, and representatives to the House. Among them they organized the impressive "Revolution on the March" of President Alfonso López, a "centennialist" himself but willing to sponsor the positive cooptation of the counter-elite of the moment, which he cordially called "audacities under thirty (years of age)."

The "Revolution on the March" constituted the climax of the socialist subversion in the context of the governing liberal party. Under this hegemony, the "clerical and *godo*" Constitution issued by Nuñez and Caro in 1886 was revised. The revisionist of the moment was a brilliant lawyer from Tolima state, Dr. Darío Echandía, who found bases for his task in both the Constitution of the new Spanish Republic and in nationalist support ignited by the Leticia international conflict with Peru (Wood 1966, 169-251). The counter-norms of telic morality were incorporated into the Constitution through these revisions in 1936 when state intervention was approved and the bases were established for a future attempt at state planning. Mechanisms were established for making the state a welfare state. This was a real challenge to the old norms on providence that customarily left social problems such as old age and poverty to fate, the caprice of nature, or to Church charity. It was declared that "property ownership is a social function which implies obligations." Thus the principles for reforming the land tenure system and the bourgeois norms of *laissez-faire* were established. The separation of Church and state was proposed in a secular way that incurred the protests of the clergy. Furthermore, new tax rates, new social services for workers, and a minimum salary were adopted. National education, including that of university level, was reformed, the right to strike was recognized, and the organization of workers to confront employers was stimulated. In all of this there was a desire to encourage the diffusion of social mobility.

The cooptation of the counter-elite could have been carried further, perhaps, if it had not been for the ending of López's presidential term in 1938. The possibility of reversing the trends of change had begun to be visible to various groups: the "rightists" of the conservative party, the "centennialists" of the liberal party who wished to play into their hands, and the bourgeoisie (entrepreneurs) who began to prosper again owing to the protectionist measures introduced by the government. The interests of all of them were endangered by some of the "extremist" theses of the subversion. Moreover, the generational struggle produced an internal differentiation among López's followers. Thus those elements that were coopted in the positive way and whose élan left a profound mark on the governing party and on the country were distinguished from the others who submitted to reactionary cooptation. In fact, the pro-socialist group, with Gaitán at the head, led the rebellion and decided to maintain the initial compulsion. Gaitán went directly to the people to proclaim: "To the charge! For the moral restoration of the Republic!" The others, who nominated the well-known newspaper director, Don Eduardo Santos for the first magistracy, ceded to the centennialist, bourgeois, and employer interests in a way similar to that by which the illustrious members of the Republican School had been coopted in 1854 by the seigniorial elite.

With the election of President Santos, the interplay of adjustment between the opposing forces of socialist liberalism and the bourgeoisie began openly. The prior impulse was not totally contained since the Minister of Finance, Dr. Carlos Lleras Restrepo, promoted a policy of state intervention and state capitalism with the creation of various decentralized official institutes. Nonetheless, little by little, there was an arrest in development produced by the powerful oligarchical organization that was formed to destroy the reforms of the prior regime. Other factors played their roles: the polarization of forces due to the intensity and political-religious character of the Spanish Civil War; the tendency towards inertia produced by the institutionalization of innovations (trade unions, for example) made in prior years.

The reaction possessed characteristics similar to those of the reaction to the liberal subversion of the nineteenth century. There were a few isolated insurrections of conservative peasants in various parts of the country (some started by partisans of the conservatives, others caused by abuses of the liberals). In general, however, the bourgeois economic groups, defending the *status quo ante,* organized themselves to seek ways to repeal López's laws. They began by creating the National Employer's Economic Association (APEN), established in 1936 by latifundia owners and entrepreneurs. This organization outlined a strategy for the reaction, including the sabotage of Law 200 of 1936 concerning land tenure, a law which in fact became a boomerang for the peasantry. Soon after came the Union of Colombian Workers (UTC) sponsored by the Jesuit Fathers to counteract the "more leftist" Confederation of Colombian Workers (CTC); the National Association of Industrialists (ANDI); and the National Federation of Businessmen (FENALCO), new associations of employers. The venerable Society of Agriculturists of Colombia (SAC) also disclosed that it was made up of latifundia owners.

The bourgeois reaction continued to make a sweep during López's second term in the presidency and during the year in which Don Alberto Lleras Camargo was in office. The efforts to arrest the subversion revealed the fact that the strong social movements of previous years had been weakened by institutionalization and routine. For example, the labor movement lost momentum and autonomy and was unable to become firmly rooted among the people. For this reason it was relatively easy for President Lleras Camargo to subdue a labor strike on the Magdalena River; it meant the end of the Confederation of Colombian Workers as an effectively organized labor force (cf. Fluharty 1957).

With the bourgeois groups aligned against those who wanted change, a political complication was produced in the Liberal party when it divided into two factions that permitted the victory of the conservative party in 1946 with the election of the well-to-do entrepreneur, Don Mariano Ospina Pérez. The pressure of the upper bourgeoisie was maintained during Ospina's presidency and, in fact, important undertakings were promoted. But little was done to satisfy the deeper desires for secularist changes aroused in the liberal majorities by Gaitán. The remains of the subversive groups gathered around Gaitán soon after he captured control of the machinery of the liberal party and confirmed his struggle against "the plutocratic groups that behave as imperialists in external affairs and as oligarchs in internal matters" (Osorio Lizarazo 1952, 281–285).

The final confrontation was bloody. In the face of the serious threat of a decisive victory by Gaitán in the succeeding presidential election—which could at last effect the imposition of subversion so feared by "rightist" bourgeois groups in the government itself—the power elite played its last card: violent repression. Gaitán was assassinated on April 9, 1948.

This incident, a precipitant of change, like the discharge of a lightening bolt, immediately unleashed the repressed forces of development. Once again, at this moment, there occurred a revolution, the first one since 1854. The Gaitanist, socialist, leftist, liberal, communist, and other subversive organisms throughout the country spontaneously arose to take power and thus maintain the compulsion of development during this historical period. With the help of the national police, who took the rebels' side, they managed to occupy public buildings in many cities and towns. In some parts the presidency of the new leader of liberalism, Dr. Darío Echandía, was proclaimed. It was such a strong revolutionary movement that the fall of the central government of Dr. Ospina Pérez was taken for granted. At this moment the government no longer had the support of the majority of the people, nor did it have the moral sanction that legitimated state coercion.

But the liberal leadership held to the formulas of constitutional legality (perhaps because it was desirous of avoiding the embarrassment of a *coup d'état* before the Conference of Foreign Ministers that was meeting in Bogotá), and supported President Ospina to avoid his downfall. Exhausted and disillusioned, the revolutionary subverters were slowly placated, and they disarticulated the revolution at the end of April. The opportunity for the socialist subversion to reach its fulfillment had passed. There followed now the anticlimax of violence encouraged by the government itself. In this way the subversive élan was frustrated.

However, in a last effort at resistance, the liberals gathered around their new leader, Dr. Lleras Restrepo. They attempted to confront government repression with civil resistance, refusing to recognize the contrived election of Dr. Laureano Gómez as President of the Republic and rejecting his policies once he was installed in office. The inevitable outcome was *la Violencia*, which bled the country from 1949 to 1957.

This violence was not revolutionary: it did not directly contribute to the achievement of the valued goals of instrumental change. To the contrary, it was the greatest and most dramatic monument to the endeavor of the threatened champions of the seigniorial-bourgeois tradition to arrest the élan of the socialist subversion. Unfortunately, they discovered persons who would play their game at the level of rural communities within the old structure of political bossism. The process began with a political expedient of the conservative party (in its new Falangist stance) to keep liberals from voting since they were in the majority (López de Mesa 1962). The use of force on the part of the government, exercised through the police and armed party members, soon slipped out of the control of the leaders who had hoped to take advantage of the situation for their own purposes. Pandora's box of passions and vendettas of the little rural world was opened, and the creation of gangs, guerillas, and counter-guerillas was fostered. At first, there were several issues at stake: access to power and the national budget, the use and control of land, the defense of regional fiefs of political bosses, the traditional supremacy of the Church (which had received a hard blow on April 9); in short, the survival of vested interests having deep roots in the seigniorial past.

During Gaitán's lifetime, a great part of the people had supported change in social institutions, in harmony with the secularist-instrumental ethos. But once that charismatic leader disappeared, the energies that had accumulated and then been frustrated in their expectations became embittered and irrational, producing a wave of destruction. *La Violencia* was thus an outlet for the overflow of the frustrated revolutionary development of 1948.

Moreover, in the end, *la Violencia* was no more than a blind, leaderless conflict that undermined ancient customs of the peasant population, demolishing at the same time their yearnings for significant change and disorienting their angry reaction. It is improbable that this phenomenon was anticipated by the dominant groups, even with all the cunning at their disposal. But it undoubtedly served to alienate the people from the goal of their previous ideals. Even though there were efforts to channel and rationalize peasant violence and formally organize it, it escaped all bounds to the point of becoming a confused expression of predominately personal conflicts by peasants incapable of gauging the great transformation that might have been carried out. They could not seek the support of an ideology, and there was no national leader or any institution that might show them the way and redeem them from their deep tragedy.

It was only in the great eastern plains and the southern part of Tolima that the guerrillas and their followers achieved a certain formal stability and discipline, managing to dictate their own norms (counter-norms for the bourgeoisie). They issued laws that were extraordinary for their attempt to translate to legal form their local social institutions, giving them juridical life and supporting the autochthonous elements. In this sense, these norms recalled the former Spanish *fueros*. Nevertheless, lacking a clear ideology, the peasants fell back on their basic aggressiveness and returned to the sterile family, religious, and political struggles of the nineteenth century when liberal (*el rojo*) confronted *godo*, heretic fought fanatic, the condemned atheist punished the servile supporter of the clergy. These struggles also provided a pathway for the brutal rape of women, the stealing of land, the invasion of haciendas, the usurpation of management rights, and the expulsion of owners, tenants, and managers from their homes and neighborhoods, resulting in political homogeneity for certain regions. For this reason, with their energies wasted in such vendettas, sexual crimes, and forced barter of property, the peasants were unable to take the next step toward a true and complete revolution. This revolution was frustrated by the use, abuse, and ultimate routinization of brute violence. In this way the common people were led to identify their enemies among their own neighbors and relatives rather than among the members of the elite or dominant groups that had begun the whole tragedy (Fals Borda 1965b, 197–98; Guzmán *et al.* 1962, I, 367–81; 1964, II, Part I).

The spiritual condition of Colombian people during this period of intense conflict can well be imagined. It was recognized that there was an even worse "moral and religious crisis" than that of 1854 (Canal Ramírez and Posada 1955). This degree of anomie can be measured by two isolated, but highly significant events: one of the great liberal leaders, an initiator of the subversion of this period, Dr. Carlos Lozano y Lozano, committed suicide; another leader, Dr. Luis Ignacio Andrade of the conservative party, for reasons he kept to himself, entered a convent. Not even the short period of truce between 1953 and 1957 brought consolation. Its occurrence was facilitated by the *coup d'état* of General Gustavo Rojas Pinilla in 1953. But while he depended on a dual front of entrepreneurial and industrial groups, he gave no quarter either to "leftist" liberals or to conservatives who followed the deposed President Laureano Gómez. Even though conservatism discarded its Falangist dress and returned to its republican stance, under Rojas there was rather a return to the days of the all-pervading influence of the Catholic clergy and godo intransigents when the government adopted "Christ and Bolívar" as its patrons and the persecution of liberals and protestants was unleashed. The influence of Argentina's Perón soon led this government to adopt autocratic policies that alienated it from the traditional oligarchy.

Nevertheless, toward the end of the period the process of change was arrested, more easily seen in some institutions than in others, revealing the phenomenon of "cultural lag" (Obgurn 1950; Guzmán *et al.* 1962, I, Chap. 13). In Colombia it may be seen that some economic institutions moved forward in spite of *la Violencia* while the others, political and religious ones, became obstructions. In addition there were other conditioning factors to arrest subversive change at that time: the influence of the Cold War between East and West was felt during this period, uniting national leaders out of fear of Communism and for the related expedient of hemispheric defense, which fell into the hands of the United States as the dominant nation. Thus, with the implicit approval of the national leaders who were threatened by subversion, the United States became the principal support of the reactionaries.

Some Results of Development

Paradoxically (even though its social cost was high), socio-economic development did occur during the period of socialist subversion. It was impossible to turn back the clock of history because, on one side, the conservative bourgeois and liberal groups had fostered an important accumulation in the technological component and had sponsored instrumental innovations of great potentiality for bringing about change (middle-range and heavy industry, social security for example) whose own dynamics could not be restrained. On the other side, the subversive groups managed to apply the compulsive mechanisms of hegemonic domination and social diffusion already described during the climax of the subversion. The revolution and the bloody repression that followed turned precisely around the control of these mechanisms: attempt was made to slow the already inevitable march of the secularist development implicit in the subversion.

The transformation of Colombian society occurred haphazardly during this crucial period. The rural-urban equilibrium of the country was changed. Internal migrations to the cities that began in the years of development before 1925 were accelerated and multiplied with the establishment of new industries, the growth of commerce, the increase in state activities, the mechanization of agriculture, and a new, expulsive factor in the minifundium system. This tendency was additionally impelled by the dislocations of rural people caused by *la Violencia* and the very increase in the population, so that Colombia ceased to be a predominantly rural nation and moved into the category of semi-urban countries. The indices of this socio-economic development are significant, as was shown before.

The social and economic implications of this transition are known: the sense of primary loyalty and emotional affiliation of persons were changed, causing modifications in their personalities and in their conception of the world; new dimensions of life were discovered, especially those that were difficult to achieve earlier owing to the lack of equity and justice; and class consciousness was increased. Land ceased to be an enslaving element in itself and with the new self-image of the common people, old relations of subordination with employers, political bosses, and hacienda owners, with the priest and the mayor, and with political parties, were overturned in part. In this way, one of the subversive goals of this period was partially achieved: the mental and physical liberation of rural man, by conferring upon him a new sense of mobility and dignity.

Urban mobilization and the discovery of the new modes of civilization and nationhood changed the meaning of many cultural elements. Outstanding among these elements was education, to which was given the value formerly granted land within the naturalist framework and it was emphasized as a means for achieving non-seigniorial goals. In this process, the counter-norms of telic morality also became more accessible to the peasant. Prestige began to be acquired now through participation in events involving innovations, such as those connected with adoptions in mechanized agriculture, or through involvement in unusual occupations such as those of chauffeur, tractor-driver, salesman, or secretary of a consumer's cooperative. Prestige was no longer derived from meeting traditional standards like those required by the corn liquor (*chicha*) or beer-drinking rituals or by simple *machismo* (Fals Borda, 1955). Moreover, leaders emerged who were capable of working through impersonal channels not dominated by old political bosses. Communication and transportation were made increasingly available to the lower classes, destroying their sense of being bound to the land.

Thus, through all these means that emerged from the impact of instrumental secularism, technical development, and the increase and redistribution of the population, new social and economic perspectives were opened. There was a trend toward "modernization" of behavior, and unusual expectations in the improvement of the living standards of the people. Especially important was the discovery of a new dimension of the country, its human potentiality.

There are many studies that document this socio-economic development from "sandal and pigtails" to "shoes and textbook," from the humble servant of the glebe incapable of looking his employers in the face to the proud being with modern aspirations. It is only necessary to recall the studies made by the Technical Department of "Seguridad Social Campesina" (a government agency) (1956–1959); the analysis on coffee-growers (Guhl 1953); the monographs on the Santander tobacco zone (Pineda Giraldo 1955); those on the peasantry in general (Pérez Ramírez 1959); and those on the rural element affected by *la Violencia* (Torres 1963). Later studies about Barrancabermeja (Havens and Romieux 1966) and Candelaria (Parra Sandoval 1966) show the same tendencies. We are faced with a new peasantry and a new group of citizens and workers and we are discovering a country that has come a discernible way from the behavioral patterns of the seigniorial and bourgeois order.[1]

In summary, we may see the direction of the social process just studied. The group that initiated the subversion, of socialist or communist stamp, was eliminated or made marginal to the political process, and the liberal counter-elite that had in good faith attempted to work within the machinery of its own party in the positive mode of cooptation was frustrated. Those liberals who had capitulated to reactionary cooptation had repented and lost heart. There arrived a time in which there was no other option but *rapprochement* in order to achieve peace and rebuild the social order. The year of 1957 was approaching: thirty-five years had passed since those days of mysterious meetings in the Protestant church and the result of the national effort was heartbreaking. No longer was Colombia the first democracy of Latin America, nor could its capital any longer boast of the title "The Athens of South America."

The oligarchical groups attempted to retard social change but they were the ones most deceived. It is true that the new order sought by the subversion was not fully achieved, nor was the secularist-instrumental ethos totally adopted. But it was impossible to return to the bourgeois order with all its initial vitality. Neither neoliberalism nor conservatism achieved all its goals for arresting social change. *La Violencia* turned out to be, in a way unanticipated by the elites, a singular mechanism that broke open the monolith of the established order, revealing its various institutional cleavages and partly destroying it. Out of *la Violencia*, as the anti-climax of the socialist subversion, emerged a very different Colombia with a people that began to definitely leave behind the traditions that bound it to the seigniorial past (Torres 1963, 109–42).

Tired of fighting after a whole generation, psychologically and physically exhausted, the opposing factions facilitated among themselves the return to pacific adjustment and mutual tolerance. There was a desire to once again achieve relative stability and to arrive at what was more durable, at a topia. From this longing emerged in 1957 the present synthesis of the National Front, which is the political and governmental machinery of the new order, the liberal-bourgeois order, the general bases of which shall now be examined.

CHAPTER EIGHT

The Order of the National Front

ADDED TO the reformist compulsion deriving from the popular base was the ingredient of exhaustion produced by *la Violencia*. The result was the creation of the new liberal-bourgeois order represented by the government of the National Front.

This anomic exhaustion, with its negative effects on personality, was naturally more evident among the poor people who had suffered the impact of *la Violencia*, many of whom turned to the sanctuary of the city for refuge and to recuperate. The only empirical study concerning this particular, realized in Bogotá in 1962 under the auspices of the Faculty of Sociology of the National University, concludes that among many of those displaced by *la Violencia* there developed a defeatist attitude in which life lost its meaning:

The victim of *la Violencia* no longer looks toward the future but rather desires to take refuge in the past, in the time before *la Violencia*. The process has apparently made him incapable of controlling nature and his social environment becomes unpredictable and threatening. Furthermore, the old institutions, [especially] the government and the Church, to which he formerly turned in search of guidance now seem impotent to restrain *la Violencia* or to give its victim some support in the world of terror (Lipman and Havens 1965, 244).

The New Political Adjustment

The anomie produced by such a cruel, and to a certain point sterile, conflict impeded further subversive progress and propitiated a search for reconciliation and truce. As was earlier stated, it was necessary to reconcile the opponents and reach agreement on new rules for the political game in order to avoid the disintegration of the nation, the loss of international respect for the integrity and sovereignty of Colombia, and the routine preparation of chaos and anomie. These conditions were considered to be the culture medium of Communist subversion. Thus, in combining popular compulsion for transformation with the anomie of *la Violencia*, a synthesis that attempted to stabilize the inevitable changes was imposed, safeguarding vested interests to whatever degree possible. ("Plus ça change, plus c'est la même chose.")

The bourgeois groups set the rules of the game for General Rojas Pinilla. But they succumbed under the impact of certain instrumental norms and values promoted by the neo-liberals and retreated in matters pertaining to their relations with groups that had been subordinate within the seigniorial order. Thus instrumental and secular innovations such as social security, social services, apprenticeship opportunities for workers and unskilled laborers, the right to organize and the trade union system, laws concerning salaries and working conditions, stock-holding, controls on prices and imports, and so forth were adopted under the conservative government and the "necessary evil" of state planning and intervention was accepted. Some Colombian capitalists also adopted the humanitarian posture characteristic of their counterparts in more advanced countries. All these elements certainly fell within the sphere of domination of the bourgeois groups in power, but they essentially constituted adjustments to the secularist-instrumental compulsion that derived from the previous historical period when the neo-liberals governed.

The government of the National Front was the political mechanism conceived to achieve the relative stability of the new liberal-bourgeois order. Its goals, along with the most recent rules of the political game, derived from a pact made on March 20, 1957 by the representatives of the liberal and conservative parties growing out of agreements made earlier in the Spanish towns of Sitges and Benidorm by Lleras Camargo and Gómez.

This pact is not a revolutionary document. It does not seek to promote social change except in relation to the instrumental and popularly supported rhythm of development that was achieved in the first few years after the dreaded Communist order was averted. Its main purpose is to pose the necessity of a "democratic convalescence" in order to "restore" earlier institutions and "re-establish the Constitution." This is to be done by means of "understanding and joint action of the traditional parties with the purpose of presenting a civic resistance to the systematic destruction of the moral, institutional, and juridical patrimony of Colombia." The procedure to be followed was that of

creating a civilian government that acts in the name of both parties, representing each of them equally, in which both collaborate and which is sustained by a solid alliance that does not allow it to fail nor to permit the parties to tend toward hegemony; [that there be] an ordinance of permanent character that provides for equally-shared governments and permits alternation [of the two parties] in the supreme direction of the nation's course; [and that there be] equity in the representation of the parties [in the government] (Zalamea 1957).

These rules of adjustment were formally approved in the plebiscite of December 1, 1957, the articles of which partially modified the Constitutional amendments approved in 1936 and were clear evidence of the compromises between the parties. The liberal accepted the clerical declaration of Catholicism as the official religion; conservatism did not refuse to support the norms concerning state planning and allowing greater political participation of the people. However, in general, the agreements tended to prudently favor the conservative side, thus castrating neo-liberalism of the days of the subversion and causing the desertion and alienation of thousands of its members of all social levels. Apparently, a peculiar phenomenon was repeated: the conservatives were those that compelled and the liberals those who absorbed the adjustments, as occurred in the era of Caro and Núñez.

The fulfillment of these political compromises explains why the governments of Presidents Alberto Lleras Camargo and Guillermo León Valencia (1958–1966) were unable to promote any significant social change, but rather limited themselves to tranquilizing the nation with marginal development in order that it might better convalesce. Thus it can be understood why social movements with revolutionary potentials such as community action and agrarian reform sponsored by the National Front never really got started. Community action fell into the hands of party machinery or ineffectual entities that allowed its intentions for true popular involvement to be corrupted. Agrarian reform was defied with impunity by latifundia owners and local political bosses who perpetuated their seigniorial rule in the countryside and had to move largely in the direction of mere technical agricultural development. It can also be understood why university action and even urban guerrilla and terrorist action could have such notorious catalytic effects during the period of the socialist subversion (as also occurred between 1852 and 1854), while its effectiveness diminished when the same tactics were applied in the last years of return to the social order.

With a political mechanism such as the National Front, any civil servant may fall prisoner to the inflexibilities of the apparatus in which he happens to function. With this mechanism—by definition and by the original sin of its conception—it is extremely difficult to promote significant change in the country. Achieving development is a task for a giant, and perhaps half the civil servants of the government (by the rule of "parity") are doctrinally committed to maintaining the status quo or, at best, to tolerating the marginal development that follows subversion as a residue, and seeking that such development not be allowed to affect the interests of the national and foreign dominant groups.

The Role of Institutions

The economic and social homogeneity of the ruling class now formalized in the National Front is an advantage for imposing its inherent compromises. Such homogeneity assures that the social order will be maintained and that change will follow an "appropriate" course within the margin of tolerance. For this reason, the stabilizing factors of development socialization are applied; the legitimation of coercion in the new historical context is induced; the ideological persistence of the social order is encouraged by authorized persons in diverse institutions; and support for the status quo is fostered by the latest technology imported by industrialists and entrepreneurs. Thus there exists indeed a bourgeois compulsion to maintain the system.

It is evident that technological accumulation continues to favor the new dominant groups. It still has negative effects on the rate of creation of new jobs and it increases the concentration of income (cf. Furtado 1956, 389). Thus, in promoting the importation and adoption of new elements of modern science (super-fertilizers, super-combines, citadels of mechanized silos, and so forth, in addition to electronics and automation), the dominant groups make themselves even more powerful and wealthy. The adverse effect which these innovations—completely useful for other purposes—may have on the people do not seem to concern them; especially acute is the impact of such innovations on the increase in unemployment and general poverty. On the other hand, the transistor radio is spread among the consumer masses and it is consequently in control of the people's behavior because the radio stations are mainly in the hands of the friends of the *status quo*. Yet this may in the long run be a boomerang because it broadens the *Weltanschauung* of the lower classes and takes them closer to a new critical point brought about by technological accumulation.

This compulsion for dominion over the social order by means of modern technology has another support in the national defense complex. Weapons were a positive element in the imposition of the seigniorial order and played a role in the last two subversions, especially in implementing the revolution of 1854. They were largely ineffective for dominating the guerrillas of *la Violencia* because they do not fulfill an ideological, educational, economic, or religious function. In this case what humanity periodically has learned and forgotten since time immemorial was demonstrated: that in the long run, ideas are more powerful than weapons. But when modern technology is more rapidly applied to the military establishment while a new social order is being sought, the armed forces lose their former autonomy, surrender the subversive potential that they have historically utilized, and become a supporting element for the conservative key groups.

This compulsion of the key groups caused the officers to become more bourgeois, especially those in upper echelons. They were separated from the popular classes and became obligated to defend the social order even to the point of breaking norms derived from formal democracy. This manner of sanctioning situations that do not harmonize with the classic legal structure of the country with incongruous repressive norms is what Umaña Luna has called "juridical disorder" (1966). "Juridical disorder" within the social order has led the army to take unpopular positions through not being allowed to perceive the real significance of movements that representatives of this order or agents of the Cold War have induced it to repress.

Furthermore, a series of *ad hoc* interpretations in military penal jurisdiction have led the armed forces to take the side of a political party against the subversives. In this manner accommodated politicians "win electoral grace with military Ave Marias" (Anonymous, 1965). Fortunately, the newly promoted officers, sub-officers, and soldiers who have been socialized in the secularist ethos have open attitudes toward social problems and therefore understand the self-defeating implications of that anti-popular position. One group has attempted to link itself to "national transformation" through civic action in order to change the public image of the army and make it a more active agent of social and economic change. Even though this effort is no more than a palliative, as is recognized by North American investigators Barber and Ronning (1966, 233, 236), it does not cease to be symptomatic of the concern felt by those officers regarding the situation of the people. However, the weight of the armed forces as an institution placed on one side of the scale makes its total effect today as counter-insurgency support of the liberal-bourgeois order.

Reviving the classic Suárez concept of the sixteenth century regarding absolute tyranny, it is seen that the Cardinal Primate of the Colombian Catholic Church also played the role of a central support for the maintainance of the status quo. The Church withdraws from social debate and takes refuge only in truth which is eternal (*El Tiempo* 1965). "Truth" is used here as a euphemism that includes the defense of the established order. This is understandable if the historical role played by the Church in Colombia as an ally of the

state since colonial times is evoked and if it is furthermore recalled
that the social composition of the ecclesiastical hierarchy is an intrinsic part of high society, be it through family ties or through
cooptation or cultural assimilation (Torres 1963, 129). Thus the
bourgeois peace is blessed by the sacred hierarchical hand of the established order, and the Church with all its creative potential retires
to the convents, parish houses, belfries, and episcopal palaces to
await the arrival of the "absolute tyrant" and then awake for social
action.

The bourgeoisie also have another important support in their international or "imperialist" connections. There is a supra-national
economic alliance of national and foreign groups that benefit from
the present situation and whose influence goes a long way back. As
it has been seen (in Chapter Six), in Colombia the relations of
dependence with dominant countries had a firm beginning as a consequence of the liberal subversion when the *nouveaux riches* became
hallucinated with the exploitation of tobacco, indigo, cinchona, rubber, and coffee. One of them, Florentino González, went so far as to
propose the annexation of Colombia to the United States in 1858
(Vega 1913, 214–15). Of course, nothing could be more "Herodian"
(cf. Toynbee 1947, 280–90). The present oligarchy does not have to
go to such extremes because the modern technology it manages
allows it to arrive at the same goals of local exploitation and control
by more subtle and effective means. It is also their members who
take advantage of the Cold War to strengthen their position.

One consequence of the stabilizing factors mentioned and the
mutual support of the political, military, religious, and economic
elements of the present order is the formalization of the National
Front as a one-party government, representing bourgeois interests
to carry it beyond 1974 when it will constitutionally end. A natural
tendency of the two parties to converge can be perceived in the
move toward this point. There are now no very radical differences
between the liberals and conservatives who take turns in government and share the sock of the national budget. The existence of
only one party is possible because the majority of those who benefit
from power are committed to keeping the country in its comfort-
able period of convalescence, giving it only palliatives for its weak-

ened condition, combatting the vestiges of prior subversion, and strengthening themselves to confront the next one. The symptoms are alarming: there are liberals who think, write, and act like conservatives in a way reminiscent of what Núñez himself described with regard to the parties of his day; and there are conservatives who have moved toward classic liberalism. But almost no one has really moved toward the people with an altruistic zeal to examine their great necessities and to provide them with opportunities for advancement and improvement.

Significance of the Present Transition

Although the social order of the National Front may last a long time (as ocurred with the previous three orders), it bears implicitly within it the potential elements for its eventual subversion because it continues to frustrate the desire of the people for progress and for achieving the goals of economic and social justice.

The disillusionment with the system within this framework of physical and moral exhaustion until now has not shown any but nihilistic escapes. There has been a drift to the side of General Rojas Pinilla, the new symbol of protest. Other expressions have been to some degree masochistic in the face of successive currency devaluations, or the search for scapegoats such as university activist groups, or the perennial Communists. The people are perplexed. But they already see the system as an imposition that does not represent their urgent needs and yearnings. For this reason the tendencies that have been observed among the people indicate that they are not going to be passive much longer, especially if they nourish themselves ideologically with reformist visions as they do now. Until now, owing to the diffusion of the secularist ethos, the people have manifested their dissatisfaction with the system through electoral abstention, which has increased each year since 1958 (cf. Weiss, 1968), and with the vote or local action in favor of rebel groups. These indicators are eloquent because they demonstrate the existence of an important fissure in the present society.

Thus, the incongruities of the social order, the normative inconsistencies, the moral contradictions, the great differences between economic groups, the lack of equity in the control over and benefits derived from technology, all have become visible once again, and their offensive reality spurs the desire for and formulation of a new subversion. The speed which characterizes the modern world can produce variations in the stabilizing factors of a social order (which factors are already fully active in support of the present order) that lead to another crisis of serious proportions. The liberal-bourgeois order, which does represent an important recession of seigniorial forces from the historical perspective, may disintegrate as previous orders have done. The Colombian people have not yet forgotten the goals toward which the last generation of subverters was leading them, because many of the counter-values were adopted, and have already begun to be values, owing to the diffusion of the ethos of instrumental secularism. This is clear in the reiterations of the socialist utopia, now with a more rooted or indigenous accent, that have erupted in recent times to challenge once again the status quo.

CHAPTER NINE

Reiteration of the Utopia

IN CONTRAST to previous historical situations, the beginning of the liberal-bourgeois order in 1957 has been accompanied by various events that make it possible to anticipate an unusual outcome. Be it because of the continued accumulation in the technological component, the increased "social scale," the wider popular participation, the secularist-instrumental advance, or the changing nature of the international balance of power in the hemisphere and outside it, little time passed after the inception of the new order when in 1965 another utopia made its dramatic appearance.

At this time there was heard the cry of protest of a young contingent that until this time had been marginal. The members of these protest groups, born in or after 1925, had not known any other world than that of the socialist subversion. It was the generation of *la Violencia*, which grew up in an environment of terror, seeing its impressive deformities, suffering its intolerances and injustices, and participating in its miseries. It was the victim youth that could morally flog its progenitors for having brought about that great carnage, for having induced the national tragedy. It was youth that placed the oligarchical groups and traditional elites against the wall and accused them of the crime of *lesa patria*. It is youth, without responsibility for the original implementation of *la Violencia*, which now emerges to leave its mark on history.

At the critical moment of the presidential campaign of 1965, the generation of *la Violencia* found a champion in a Catholic priest and sociologist who was influenced by the ecumenical environment of Western Europe and whose message and example were to become more vibrant day by day. He was Father Camilo Torres Restrepo, creator of the political organization of the United Front which expresses an utopia of its own: pluralism. This utopia has new ingredients derived from religious convictions and the study of the realities of contemporary Latin American revolutions, especially that of Cuba. But it is essentially a reiteration of socialist ideals in response to the secularist-instrumental challenge of the people and the times.

Understood in this way, the pluralist utopia of Father Torres has had not only national but also international repercussion. His orientation is of a type that in transcending reality and moving to the level of practice tends to profoundly modify the existing order, producing social and personal crises, leading society to self-examination, and promoting subversive change. This impact is not lessened by the inquisitorial zeal of agents of traditional political and religious institutions who wish to bury such ideas in the ground or answer them with bullets. Thus Father Torres has become the paradigm of the generation of *la Violencia* and the spokesman for their repressed protest, injecting vitality into the ideological confrontation. His utopian platform may initiate a fourth subversion in Colombia, the neo-socialist one.

In contrast with what occurred in previous local subversions when the effect of the utopias on their champions and on the society were felt only after several decades, the present case saw almost immediate consequences. The pluralist utopia was decanted and twisted by realities almost immediately, and Father Torres was killed eleven months after having expounded it. But the influence and determination of his rebellious group, with the support of the secularized population, stimulated diverse political groups, gave support to protest movements against the "system," made possible a counter-elite in university circles, and encouraged assistance to guerrillas and similar rebel organisms. Therefore there already exist the minimum ideological and organizational elements to initiate a new cycle of subversive development in Colombia that will lead to another order, the fifth of the historical series.

The Birth of Utopian Pluralism

It should be clarified at the outset that the following analysis is based on very recent documents and experiences, to which it is therefore difficult to attribute a definitive value. Many aspects of the events related or analyzed are still obscure and it is possible that the interpretation proffered here will have to be revised in the light of new evidence. It has been decided to make an early interpretation here in order to present the pluralism of Camilo Torres according to what is presently known, because the life and thought of this leader in the history of Colombia will not be overlooked and can much less be ignored within the analytical framework of this book.

In his Platform for a Movement of Popular Unity (March 17, 1965), prepared in a simple form for the masses, Father Torres declared that one of the objectives of the United Front "is the structuring of a pluralist political apparatus, not a new party, that is capable of seizing power" (Torres 1966, 24–25). He gives the details of this apparatus in the eighth point of this platform: "The political structure to be organized would be of pluralistic character, taking maximum advantage of the support of new parties, dissatisfied sectors of the traditional parties, non-political organizations, and the masses in general" (Torres 1966, 18).

The pluralism of Camilo Torres constitutes the essentially utopian element of his thought and should be studied as such for the effects it had on the first steps of his United Front movement. In order to understand it, one ought to place himself within the political and religious context from which the author derived it and from which there also spring its differences from similar contemporary formulations.

The purpose of this pluralism is not to sanction the policy of tolerance, of "live and let live," that has characterized other societies. The result of this is to better reinforce and cement the status quo around which the diverse groups turn and in which they are accommodated and do co-exist. In fact, this type of pluralism could be discerned in the political system of the National Front, in which liberal and conservative divergencies are legally respected. It could also be found in the present political system of countries like the United States, France, and Chile where there is tolerance of divergent points of view, provided they follow rules designed to preserve a social order that is considered to be basically functional. This is the ideology of the democratic consensus that appears in political and ecclesiastical circles, where social pluralism is defined as "a system in which all social classes and functional interest groups, more or less on the basis of equal opportunities, may compete for what the nation offers" (D'Antonio and Pike 1964, 7, 260; cf. Frei Montalva 1964; Silva Solar and Chonchol 1965). This is not the pluralism of Camilo Torres, even though such ideas may become part of the instrumental norms.

The utopian conception of Father Torres is more dynamic: pluralism is not a system within the social order, nor does it follow present rules. It is rather a tool for joining diverse groups to make them move in the same direction. It is designed as a strategy that seeks to change the rules and in doing so to transform the social order in which it is implemented. But its final goal is socio-economic revolutionary development conceived as the creation, resolution, and advancement of a neo-socialist subversion. This subversion, in turn, should result in a society in which the diverse progressive movements work in mutual understanding.

If there is an insistence on analogies, it may be conceded that something similar may have occurred in the colonial inception of the United States when the diverse religious sects decided to live and work together for the sake of the higher goals for rebuilding their society on the American soil. And the idea had its immediate antecedents in Colombia in attempts to "unite the lefts" in organizations such as the United Front for Revolutionary Action (FUAR) and the Worker-Student-Peasant Movement (MOEC) that has attempted to carry out revolutionary political action in recent years.

Like other utopias, the pluralist utopia of Camilo Torres embodied an implicit criticism of the prevailing culture and civilization. It attempted to discover the potentiality of existing institutions that would facilitate the advent of a new social order. But this utopia does not produce the authoritarian conception, or monolithic discipline, that Mumford notes in the majority of the classical utopias: an inflexible and dogmatic social order is created, with a Big Brother system of government that is centralized and absolute (1962, 4). A closed society that frustrates or excessively binds the free development of humanity does not appear as a goal in Father Torres's utopian pluralism. Rather there is a society in which diverse tendencies meet whose valued goals may principally be those derived from the secularist-instrumental ethos. With this purpose in mind, the tendencies all unite in a common creative effort. They are presented with several alternatives to choose among, and base their action on modern rationality.

With heterogeneous political apparatus to make it function, the pluralist utopia is made more complex by the religious element involved. The very concept of pluralism has been more current in ecclesiastical circles where its meaning has been limited to recognizing the value of coexistence of different faiths in the same area. Father Torres acquired this idea during his time as a student at the University of Louvain where there is a vanguard of creative Catholic thinkers. He also derived it from his contact with the European environment that was at the same time secular and religious, making possible heterodox experiences such as that of the worker priests (that fostered the rapprochement with Marxism) and the common worship of Catholics and Protestants. This pluralism has an important support in the modern ecumenical movement (cf. Van Leeuwen 1966, 294–95). It finds outstanding champions such as Richard Niebuhr in the Protestant bulwark and Father François Houtart in the Catholic camp (Houtart was a professor and friend of Father Torres).[1]

The pluralist conception, at the same time Christian and political (the initial basis of the personal and public action of Camilo Torres), is found in the crucial document of his career, the declaration of June 24, 1965 in which he requested release from his clerical duties. In this document he contends that "the highest measure of human decisions should be charity, should be supernatural love," and consequently, he joined a just revolution "in order to be able to give food to the hungry, drink to the thirsty, dress the naked, and bring about the well-being of the majority of our people. I believe that the revolutionary struggle is a Christian and priestly struggle. It is only through this struggle, in the concrete circumstances of our country, that we can love in the way that men should love their neighbors" (Inquietudes 1965, 41). As he had previously maintained that he had arrived at this decision also as a sociologist ("in analyzing Colombian society"), the three principles of the pluralism postulated by Verghese were embodied in him.

Once the utopian bases of Camilo Torres's thought are understood, the two central sociological concepts upon which he constructs his neo-socialist ideology fall into proper perspective. They are the concept of dignity based on the existential values of contemporary humanism, and that of counter-violence, or the just rebellion, that is based on telic morality.

The meaning of dignity for Torres is essentially a recapitulation of the secularist ethos. He speaks of dignity with emphasis in his last proclamation "from the mountains" (Torres 1966, 102), and the platform proposed in March, 1965 is aimed almost exclusively at pointing out the elements that make it possible to give the people, "the popular majorities," their true value. He underlines the symptoms that lead to the liberation of the common man, in the countryside as well as in the city (Torres 1966, 54–56, 97–98). He elaborates the moral significance that this task has for the redemption of the people and for national progress.

Connected with this goal of giving new status and worth to the human being are the other elements of the ethos of instrumental secularism. Supra-nationalism is expressed in the platform through support of the ideal of Latin American integration (Torres 1966, 21) and in the proposition that Colombia maintain relations with all the countries in the world (p. 23). He conditions these values to the adequate promotion of nationalism, especially economic nationalism, for which the people need "concrete objectives of socioeconomic development" (p. 98) and through declaring independence from the oligarchical interests that maintain the country subordinate to the United States. For this reason, pluralism must necessarily be "anti-imperialist" and condemn surrender to United States interests by national groups.

Technicism—and the norms derived from technical control—is emphasized by Camilo Torres in numerous ways, especially in his desire to create "unity on technical and rational bases" by means of the application of the social and economic sciences made relevant to the Colombian reality. This would be accomplished by "leaders who are able to abandon every sentimental and traditional element that is not justified by techniques, dispensing with imported theoretical schemes . . . in order to seek Colombian paths" (Torres 1966, 98–99). His platform proposes, moreover, planning and state intervention, with the nationalization of various institutions, free and obligatory public education, and university autonomy.

Communalism had a decided defender in Torres. The agrarian and urban reforms proposed by the platform are based on one or another type of collective action. It cites "communal action" as the "basis for democratic planning," supports cooperation and seeks greater participation by the workers in decision-making of enterprises and in sharing the end products (Torres 1966, 18–22, 59–60).

Moreover, Father Torres supports the rediscovery of the worth of the human being with the idea of the moral justification of rebellion or counter-violence. This also leads him to postulate the antinomy, people-antipeople. His thought is set forth in four of his "Messages": those directed to Christians, to peasants, to the oligarchy, and to political prisoners. He postulates first of all that "the oligarchy has a double standard by which, for example, it condemns revolutionary violence while it itself assassinates and imprisons the defenders and representatives of the popular classes" (Torres 1966, 80, 83–86); or it divides the people in groups that artificially oppose each other and fight among themselves over academic matters such as the immortality of the soul, while being distracted from making radical discoveries such as "hunger, yes, is mortal." He says further that "we must seek effective means to achieve the well-being of the masses . . . [which] privileged minorities in power are not going to seek for us . . . [and] therefore it is necessary to take away their power . . . in order to give it to the poor majority. The revolution may be peaceful if the minorities do not resist violently" (pp. 33–

34). And since this revolution seeks justice and bread for all groups, participation in it is "not only permissible but obligatory for Christians" (p. 34).

It is impossible to enter here into the polemic over the justification of the use of violence, which has been going on for several centuries, and in which very distinguished theologians and philosophers are involved today (cf. Shaull 1966; Wendland 1966). Nor is it necessary to turn to the classical thesis of Saint Thomas Aquinas concerning the just war, even though it is important to recall the way in which it was revived in the sixteenth century to legitimate the Spanish conquest and the Christian subversion. At that time a justification was sought for the use of violence to subvert the ayllic order. This order represented a morally autonomous pattern of norms that the Spanish sought to supplant with a Christian one which they considered superior. Translated to present situations of internal conflict in which the control of the social order is fought over, the same positive argument for the use of subversive violence appears. Of course, this violence is not legitimated by the established social order, but rather by the emerging one. It is based on another normative framework, the subversive one of telic morality, and for this reason it is counter-violence. The idea is similar to the distinction that Lenin makes between "revolutionary violence" and "reactionary violence" ("The Proletarian Revolution and the Renegade Kautsky," 1934–1938, VII, 175) when he refers to its use by modern socialist movements.

Evidently, as Ortega y Gasset has said, violence becomes "exasperated reason," the *ultima ratio;* for Marx, it is "the midwife of history." The problem is not so much in its absolute justification as in the conditions and limitations of its use. The use of violence entails problems of strategy: it may serve as a catalyst for the masses just as it may alienate them. The strategy depends on the historical and social circumstances; it is according to the immediate and long range goals set by the subverters during periods of development (cf. Torres 1966, 58). In any case, it is strategy that evokes the Hobbesian certainty that there exists latent or manifest violence to maintain the status quo and that it is expressed in many forms of coercion, some legitimate and others illegitimate (Míguez Bonino 1966; Weber 1922). Torres maintains that this violence is immoral when it is directed against the people and that it becomes tyrannical when the masses do not support the government (Torres 1966, 34; cf. Johnson 1966, 91). Counter-violence confronts it to the degree and intensity to which the anti-people or the minorities in power take action against the community, thus placing on themselves the grave moral responsibility of unleashing a bloody revolution.

Finally, Torres declared that there are two indices by which the efficacy of the revolutionary mystique may be measured: poverty and persecution (Torres 1966, 65, 74, 81). The mystique, of course, is maintained by the subverters. Besides the guerrilla, the most important groups are those composed of workers and students (p. 53, 63–66), precisely those who supported the United Front.

This is the pluralist utopia that Camilo Torres presented to Colombia in terms of goals for adopting "a system oriented by brotherly love" (Torres 1966, 35). It may be seen that it synthesizes and simplifies some of the instrumental tendencies of the modern world through reiterating prior socialist ideals, pouring them into Colombian cultural molds, and seeking local authenticity. It is not a clerical utopia: it was exactly the clerical structure of the Colombian Church that Father Torres had to leave in order to be able to spread his ideal and fight for it, even though none of his theses contradicts the teachings of the Church. It is neither a liberal nor a conservative platform because the political dynamics of today have surpassed the ideological framework in which those parties have functioned, parties to which Camilo Torres never belonged. Nor is it even a servile copy of ideological formulations conceived by European philosophers, nor is it a translation of constitutions or precepts of more advanced countries, as it has been the habit of Colombian politicans and intellectuals to make. It is rather the vision of a completely open society in which differences of opinion, belief, or attitude are respected for the higher purpose of achieving as a commonwealth progress within a just structure.

The Decantation of the Pluralist Utopia

Inevitably, as in the case of other historical utopias, the process of decantation that affects absolute utopias to make them relative is carried out with respect to pluralism. Perhaps such demanding and idealistic goals are beyond comprehension either by activist groups or by simple spectators.

Among the first to show a lack of understanding of this utopia were a number of priests and bishops of the Colombian Catholic Church who began to abandon Father Torres and even to attack him, declaring that his doctrines were "erroneous and pernicious" (Inquietudes 1965, 35). The "Camilo Torres case" pointed up some present anachronisms and incongruities in the Church, especially in the post-Vatican Council era. Here is a Church whose most representative groups, in the face of the drama of the human and social injustice plaguing its people, prefers to close its eyes and avoid self-criticism, in order to sustain a social order that is objectively unjust (Inquietudes 1965, 44–59). For an enlightened priest like Father Torres there could be no other way than to separate himself from the clerical structure of that institution that, paradoxically, alienated him from God and His work in history. In the document of June 24 not only did he confirm his pluralist ideal, but he also put his brothers and superiors in the faith to a test of sincerity. Thus, even after his death in the mountains of Santander, on February 15, 1966, another Colombian priest attempted to dismiss the event by sustaining that Father Torres had been a victim not of the social and religious order against which he fought, but of the defects and immaturity of his own personality and his lack of intellectual preparation that only at this time became evident (Andrade Valderrama 1966, 177–81).

Not only was there desertion and misunderstanding on the part of many of Father Torres's brothers in the faith, but difficulties in the application of the utopia were experienced by its very author. In the prior cases of decantation there was a certain prolonged period of discussion and diffusion and even a determined effort to try out the innovations as occurred in Hispaniola, Cumaná, and Michoacán under the leadership of Las Casas and Quiroga. This time the utopia was conditioned by local realities and factors within eight months.

The study of this decantation merits the attention of sociologists. Presently it is known only that the pluralist apparatus did not achieve results in practice and that at the communal and neighborhood level the diverse commandos of the movement (from the

Christian Democratic ones to the Communist ones), instead of manifesting the expected tolerance, turned the subversion into a Tower of Babel. This seems to have been a tactical error that caused the United Front to disband. Its nucleus was reduced to "unaligned" members, that is, persons who did not formally belong to any political group and whose tendencies as decided friends of revolutionary change were kept active.

There are indications that just before joining the guerrillas, Camilo Torres had begun to reorganize his movement, basing it on the "unaligned" participants, which would have allowed him to make his group more homogeneous and to really create a new political party. With this, however, the pluralist basis of the movement would have been conditioned and the decantation of the utopia would have become formalized. The utopia, then, would have remained in essence an ideology similar to that introduced earlier in the 1920s, but more clear and indigenous and more committed than the earlier one to revolutionary action.

In logically anticipating events through the study of history, it is realistic to expect that the impact of the pluralist utopia which leads to revolutionary neo-socialism will take time to incubate. It will be felt again with all its renewing, subversive force in achieving the refraction of the order of the National Front.

CHAPTER TEN

Alternatives for Prediction

WITH the reiteration of the socialist utopia, the incongruities of the established order have made themselves felt once more and the people have again discovered the existing normative inconsistencies, contradictions, and injustices. According to the framework we are using, a refraction of the liberal-bourgeois order may now be anticipated, with the creation of appropriate subversive groups that are constantly dispersed to take the new message of counter-values and counter-norms to all levels of society. This recent challenge places in check the agents of tradition once again.

The process of disintegration of the social order should be clear by now. The study of Colombian history showing the behavior of past leaders and groups should have made it rather easy to understand. Such behavior has indicated some mechanisms of compulsion that make it possible to give direction to economic and social development. Such behavior has pointed out some stabilizing factors that provide minimum durability for the valued elements gained in new social orders. Further, it has provided clarification concerning the mechanisms of adjustment by which subversions are frustrated or promoted through the cooptation of counter-elites, control over technology and the economy, and the use of violence and political hegemony.

It would be unfortunate if with these lessons learned from the nation's history it were not possible to prepare this fourth subversion, the one that would make possible the achievement of goals that Colombian society has been pursuing for such a long time.

Before discussing the alternatives predicted for the next social order, the fifth one of the series, it is necessary to remember the limitations of the "self-fulfilling prophecy" to which reference is made in Appendix C. When the scientist anticipates or foresees, he proceeds on the basis of observed trends and on the existence of repetitive factors whose effects will probably be manifested in the future. He has no other recourse on the basis of which he can make a serious judgment. This practice, which is so common in the exact sciences, becomes complicated in the field of the social sciences owing to the effects that public exposition of the results of sociological investigation may have on subsequent events related to it. This phenomenon may be inevitable in the present case, which should lead equally well to the anticipation of its consequences in order to make the necessary empirical distinctions later. It would thus be necessary to discriminate between the divergencies with the prediction itself and that part of the change (or its frustration) conditioned by the exposition and discussion of the study in question.

It should be remembered that there are differences between the classical socialism introduced in the 1920s and that of today. The present movement has a more indigenous temper. The essence of this Latin socialism is revolutionary; that is to say, it does not hesitate to recognize the important need for the just rebellion and it rationally includes counter-violence within plans and projects as part of its political strategy. For this reason, present neo-socialism, committed as it is to integral change, is distinct from the socialism adopted by groups tending toward reformist or evolutionary policies. Only this revolutionary movement would provide the key groups necessary for the next historical transition.

The Bases for the Prediction of Development

There are two general points of reference to be considered in relation to the alternatives of middle and long range prediction for the subversion that may be taking shape in Colombia today, facts which have obvious social, economic, and political consequences: (1) in moving into the semi-urban category, for various reasons the country has reached a greater level of regional and national integration, and the city has begun to play a major role in the behavior of the Colombian people; this regional integration affects party organization and calls for radical changes of tactics. (2) The population increase during the previous subversive period, subject to a new ethos, has produced a great mass, especially of young people, that has been socialized in the counter-values of secularism. These are persons who do not feel strongly attached to tradition, who act indifferently toward the traditional parties, and who do not vote for their candidates because they may be expecting new patterns for political action (cf. Weiss 1968).

Several sociological factors play a negative role in this general situation: (1) the increase in social scale that impinges on the forms of interaction in communities has not led to greater opportunities for socio-economic advancement but, on the contrary, has produced a worsening of the level of living for a majority of the population; (2) the uneven accumulation of technology that affects industry, defense, transportation, medicine, agriculture, and so forth has continued to produce incongruities and tensions that dramatize the present injustices, as occurred in the second half of the nineteenth century and at the beginning of the present one. To these factors other dynamic elements are now added. The subversive groups of the generation of *la Violencia* have the advantage of moral compulsion over their elders, whose efforts were frustrated; and the valued goals are much more clearly delineated now in relation to the elements that they should complement or supplant.

Moreover, the traditional groups against which the subversion would be principally directed are likewise more visible: the landowners, local political chiefs, and intermediaries who exploit the peasantry; the entrepreneurs, industrialists, and bankers who monopolize the resources at their disposal, ignoring the needs of the poor; the members of the clerical hierarchy who continue to identify with aristocracy, wealth, and government; the military, politicians, intellectuals, and journalists who are subject to neo-colonialism, who would yield to the demands of foreign entities today incompatible with the goals of regional development; and other similar sectors of the traditional oligarchy.

There are specific factors operating on these general bases that intervene in short-term prediction: (1) the effect of the Cold War between East and West that has led the country more and more into a relation of dependence within the sphere of influence and action of the dominant United States, to the point of turning a section of the Colombian ruling classes into consuls of the "American way of life" and turning Latin American countries into satellites (Jaguaribe 1966); (2) the conversion of the National Front to the party of "national transformation" under the presidency of one of the most outstanding leaders of the liberal party, Dr. Carlos Lleras Restrepo; (3) the appearance of potential counter-elites in or outside the traditional political parties; and (4) the intensification of popular protest movements in cities and in the countryside which are a response to the mounting tensions produced by the incongruities of the system.

The three specific national factors that affect short-term prediction are described now. (The Cold War dependency implications were mentioned earlier.)

The presidential campaign of Dr. Lleras Restrepo, baptized as the campaign for "national transformation" to placate national discontent, let Colombians know that the new government would fight for a more just society, providing equal opportunities for all, opening educational institutions to all the people, guaranteeing the population easy access to medical and hospital services, speeding up agrarian reform and promoting change in the structure of peasant society, adopting new forms of social capitalization that imply a gradual modification of the capitalist system, modifying the institutions that foster the increasing concentration of wealth and income, attending especially to the marginal classes for the purpose of fully incorporating them into the life of the community, giving labor participation in the planning of economic and social development—in addition to the other equally important aspects regarding improvement in the functioning of the state (Anonymous 1966, 43).

Undoubtedly, such an ambitious plan requires great determination in order to overcome the intrinsic difficulties presented by the political-economic system of the National Front in which the President must act. The system will not allow him to form a homogeneous governing team and the National Congress is often hindered by its own rules. But President Lleras, during the period since he took

office (August 7, 1966), has shown himself to be a man of persever-
ance and also that his efforts may promote marginal change in important sectors.

Obviously, if the government orients itself toward genuine
change, it cannot count on the support of the oligarchical and traditionalist persons and groups whose interests are affected. Such an
orientation is unlikely, simply because the constitutional system im-
pedes profound and significant change. Therefore, the failure of the
National Front is clearly foreseeable.

Anticipating this failure and reflecting popular pressure for
change, in the last few years some key groups of young politicians
and intellectuals have appeared which might have become ideological counter-elites. Great hopes were held for a while for the extremist and rebel wing of the liberal party, the "Movimiento Revolu-
cionario Liberal" (MRL), headed by Dr. Alfonso Lopez Michelsen.
Once representing deep-rooted popular dissent, the MRL leaders
slowly lost their fervor for significant or revolutionary change and
let themselves be assimilated by the regular party machinery. As
expected, with such wavering a great portion of its following deserted the party and remained aloof from any other, abstaining from
voting in all subsequent elections (the proportion of abstention in
these elections has gone up to 75 percent of electors). By the end of
1967 the MRL had been coopted, except for a small group of stal-
warts still faithful to the original subversive ideals. The MRL surrendered its iconoclasm and forgot its rebellious platforms through
acceptance of important posts in the National Front government
and by negotiating the approval of government-sponsored laws in
the Congress.

Another hopeful counter-elite was one organized in the Antioquian town of La Ceja in August, 1966. The main advocates of this
group mouthed almost all the elements of the pluro-socialist ethos,
perhaps because they had gone through the first impact of the pluralist utopia and were impressed by the quick response of the people to
the United Front. However, it turned out to be a short-lived, marginal rebellion bent more on attracting the former MRL subversives
than on actually forming an ideological counter-elite with all its
social and economic consequences. The La Ceja group quickly fell

into line when its peers and the leaders in the regular party pulled the strings to impede the group from going too far. Today its members are also in the government and no longer constitute a challenge to the social order.

To date no other counter-elites with true commitment for significant change have appeared in Colombia. Prospects for fundamental transformations in the immediate future therefore are limited, and the people may now attempt to form and develop their own leadership, independent of tradition and precedent, as a sort of "popular counter-elite": indeed, this may be one of the most decisive acts of the neo-socialist subversion. Only the guerrillas, a few student groups, and some political and intellectual circles are keeping alive the embers of subversion. This may continue to be so until objective conditions for revolt are created.

Indeed, our analysis tends to show that genuinely popular movements may in the end hold the only solution for significant change to coalesce in Colombia. Those that have been recorded lately demonstrate the vitality of the changes that have occurred among the Colombian people. It seems that unlike earlier historical periods, today holds youth and adult masses, and masses of peasants and workers, who have declared their total or partial mental or psychic independence by means of the new ethos. But they have not mobilized themselves politically even though they knew how to respond to the stimulus of the short campaign of Camilo Torres in 1965. There is a lack of decided leadership. Evidently, the masses are there, in the country as well as in the city, waiting to be "motivated" and led to constitute adequate subversive organisms.

The only political leader who has been able to approach the masses up until now, has been General Rojas Pinilla, director of the Popular National Alliance (ANAPO). His strategy illustrates the way in which the themes of the secularist-ethos may be used in political activity. As a matter of fact, it may be perceived that the popular support achieved by ANAPO derives not only from its role as a symbol of protest, but also from its adoption of secular goals dressed with a certain measure of class struggle. The latest speeches and writings of the leaders of this movement are sprinkled with watchwords such as those of the national revolution and nationalism and the struggle against ignorance, the latifundia system, economic inequality, electoral fraud, imperialism, and the power of monopolies. It is sought that "a new order—more just, more human, and more Christian" arise from the national revolution by means of a planning-oriented technological state that promotes "the take-off of our country toward development." The immediate goal is to break the mold of the National Front by creating a third party composed of liberals and conservatives of popular origins that commands respect in rallies and that may carry its leader to the Presidency of the Republic for a second time (Anonymous 1967).

Popular action and involvement, dramatized today by ANAPO, cannot be ignored as long as the National Front exists and identifies itself with the incongruities, weaknesses, and injustices of the established social order. It may open the way to true subversion.

The Strategy of the Subversion

The potentiality of the movement for change that is taking shape in Colombia and that should eventually lead to the topia of the fifth order can be well appreciated. This possibility invites the potential key groups of the period to consider the mechanisms and factors already studied, for the purpose of adopting a short and long range strategy for advancing the neo-socialist subversion and starting it from its beginning as demanded by present historical circumstances. The prior analysis makes it possible to anticipate the following developments at least.

1. *Hegemony.* Obviously, the devices for this are several: goal of the key groups in periods of subversion has been and is the hegemonic control of the power mechanisms. It has already been observed that the present system of shared control of the National Front government produces "rigidities and limitations to political action for the purpose of carrying out the transformation the country requires" (Agudelo Villa 1966). There is a legal time limit of 1974 for the system; but the incongruities of the liberal-bourgeois order, underscored by election abstention and the repeated economic and political crisis, may accumulate so rapidly that they demand a total

revision in political rules before then, as has periodically occurred in Colombia (1886, 1910, 1936, 1957).

The acceleration of change, with the sense of insecurity and indecision that accompanies all subversion, may lead the oligarchy to experience what Chalmers Johnson calls the power vacuum, one of the symptoms of near revolution, that is, the advent of social change in its violent form (Johnson 1966, 91). The result of the existence of a power vacuum can be anticipated. When there is no other hope left for the dominant classes except the support of armed force, the people-antipeople confrontation is produced. The power vacuum leads the popular masses, headed by new iconoclastic leaders, to consider illegitimate the use of institutionalized violence and to proclaim the necessity of just rebellion or counter-violence.

This conflict would have definite characteristics of a class struggle: the National Front order has weakened the traditional bipartisan and multi-classist polarity, identifying with greater clarity the oligarchy. To this popular discovery is added the incidence of *la Violencia* which this time is interpreted by the people in terms of class. The outcome of such a conflict might be a complete replacement of the present elite and upper class, the fall of their repressive regimes. In fact, such a conflict would not help the dominant groups or the morality of their position, which is ever more untenable. Their fading economic and *caudillo*-oriented ethos of the nineteenth century and their Herodian tendencies that orient them toward the foreign may not assist them. To sacrifice the lives of one hundred thousand peasants in Colombia in order to frustrate the last subversion was immoral and criminal. For the power elite to repeat this deed in order to frustrate the new impulse toward change would be intolerable.

The real possibility of using violent conflict to gain control of power leads to the study of the role of the revolutionary operations that Johnson calls "accelerators" of conflict (1966, 98–99; cf. Smelser 1962; MacIver 1942, 163–64). If the thesis of Father Torres is accepted, that use of counter-violence would depend on employment of repression by the elite to defend the social order that is considered unjust, then it follows that the subverters can justifiably obtain the necessary elements to respond in kind. In fact, these elements would constitute the equivalent of the coercion at the disposal of the established order, the use of which is normally anticipated. Thus, there may be more groups that demand total commitment to the cause of change (to the point of revolution) such as guerrilla fighters, urban cadres, organized intellectuals and students, aroused peasantry and clandestine cells. Such committed groups have played a crucial role as "accelerators" of change deployed at strategic times and places in the 1950s, as well as during the climax years of the previous socialist subversion and during the climax of the liberal subversion around 1850. There already exist nuclei of such groups in Santander and Sinú (The Army of National Liberation, ELN) and in Huila and Meta (The Revolutionary Armed Forces of Colombia, FARC); there is no reason why other such groups identified with changing the system are not also being formed.

2. *Direction.* The strategy that would lead to hegemonic dominion must give adequate direction to the subversion. The second compulsion factor, *sine qua non*, leadership ability, implies above all articulating or forming groups or cadres capable of overcoming the obstacles created by opposing organisms. In so doing an attempt is made to maintain the initiative in action and stress the moral superiority of their revolutionary position. One of the key groups has been and continues to be the university counter-elite that played an essential role in the subversions of 1848, 1925, and later years. Young people have the right to know the reality of the nation and to play a role in the solutions outlined through serious analysis and study of that reality. To complement education with the ideology of subversive development has proved to be a good beginning for achieving this goal. Struggles may be anticipated for a true, autonomous university with adequate resources that can prepare its students in every way, one in which there is room to maintain constructive zeal for achieving the new social order, and which enables them to defend themselves against the cooptation and conformity that assaults them when they leave the university.

The appearance of rebel groups in the ranks of the oligarchy recall the significance that counter-elites have had at certain historical moments (the Republican School of 1850, *Los Nuevos* of 1922). It may be another favorable symptom of the refraction of the social order. However the dual course that such groups may follow in the future can be anticipated. On the one hand, they may introduce positive cooptation and thus break their own ideological mold at the proper moment, making it possible for the country to advance toward the new social order. Or they may eventually produce a reactionary cooptation with the established parties, which would be cause for a new national frustration. These indecisions are less likely in popular groups like guerrillas, the committed urban groups, and the clandestine cells whose leadership is more convinced of the need of revolutionary change.

Last of all, it may be seen that leadership ability counter-balances the stabilizing effect of ideological persistence exercised by agents of the established order on society. As a general rule, these agents have control of the means of communication and, in part, of the confessional and the pulpit. But the force of moral conviction does not aid them and a tenacious effort on the part of the rebel groups cannot but create uneasiness among them.

3. *Diffusion.* An appropriate acceleration is anticipated with regard to the other mechanism of compulsion, diffusion of subversive development, especially at the community, neighborhood, and family level, in order to carry the counter-values and counter-norms of the neo-socialist subversion. This would be accomplished by means of an effective social organization such as those of earlier successful cases since the Spanish conquest. This is the real field for the battle with tradition, which has in its favor the regular socialization process. What will happen there depends on how well subversive movement resists becoming simple "populism" or demagogery and thus frustrating itself, as has occurred before in Colombia and in other Latin American countries.

The renewing influence of the Church, with its enlightened bishops, parish priests, and ministers who may actively support a new order and who would work shoulder to shoulder with the subverters, can also be predicted. Fortunately, there are already to be found priests and ministers inspired by the *aggiornamento*, capable of confronting the injustices of the prevailing systems, and able to stand fast in the face of insult. (In Donmatias, state of Antioquia, in Jan-

uary 1967, such men were referred to as "Satan's hands.") These
priests may become the prophetic voices of Christianity—like new
Amos and Hosea—and thus concomitantly save the Colombian
Church that it might recover its institutional functionality.

4. *Technology*. It is vital to have control over technology, not
only for the sake of imposing the subversion, but also for maintaining its direction and stabilizing the subsequent order. In this respect
the lesson of history has been especially clear from the periods of
the Christian subversion and the adjustment of the nineteenth century. Today there exist more advanced means of communication, of
production, electronics, automation, advanced medicine, and so
forth, that could be placed at the service of subversion. In addition,
the means of military defense of the social order are considered
especially important. In view of the bourgeois orientation of the
higher officers, previous cases of indoctrination and infiltration in
the armed forces by progressive groups may form a basis for anticipating an adequate course. In the long run it would be difficult for
the armed forces not to fraternize with the people in just rebellion
because they are part of this people. It would be especially difficult
for the young officers, sub-officers, and soldiers, who have been secularized and who have adopted an open mind with regard to social
problems, to remain outside the efforts of their own friends and
relatives to achieve the goals of all. Sooner or later they would have
to respect the struggle that these efforts imply.

In addition to the indoctrinating efforts within the armed forces,
the utilization of the knowledge of modern science to advance a
creative task stands out among the endeavors to bring about a new
social order. An effort so gigantic as the reconstruction of a society
requires the greatest inventiveness and keenest ingeniousness of its
members to produce the technical elements necessary to development. The university is again outstanding; but the people themselves, with some encouragement, can also produce technical solutions (cf. Fals Borda 1958, 39–42).

5. *World support for subversion*. Finally, as part of the broader
strategy that can be predicted for profound social change in Colombia, there is discerned the need of an international alliance of
subversive groups to counteract the old and powerful international

conspiracy of the friends of the status quo. Until now the advantage has been on the side of the latter because they have been supported by governments and private entities coordinated by imperialist interests that do not respect national boundaries. One last maneuver of this group has been the capture of the Alliance for Progress for the purpose of changing the potentially subversive elements that it has into a reinforcement for decadent political systems. In like manner the rebel groups may organize themselves on an international scale.

There are subversive groups in advanced countries that have been historically connected with Colombia such as the United States, Great Britain, Germany, France, Belgium, and Italy. These groups understand the situation and sympathize with the Colombian rebels. They may be under attack in their respective countries today, but they may well catalyze there important social and political movements that could topple the factors of power, leaving the Herodian groups of the dependent nations without their necessary outside support. Such activist groups may well be the young workers who want a greater participation in decision-making and who fight the capitalist tradition; the Negroes who battle for dignity and social justice; the students and intellectuals who reach for creativity in order to apply it to obsolete structures and propitiate the renovation of society. The assistance of these rebel groups from advanced countries may not be negligible; but they would also receive stimulation from their companions in revolt from the less advanced countries.

This groping across national boundaries to identify strategic rebel groups working for similar goals in different countries—especially in the "Third World"—opens the way to understanding Cuba's role in the immediate future. International assistance to subversion has been institutionalized through the Latin American Organization for Solidarity (OLAS) with headquarters in Havana. This is a new and important fact that recognizes the true dimensions of the revolutionary struggle in Latin America. Could it be that the true integration of this region, that which would liberate Latin America from its old colonial dependence, would be gained instead through that subversion that unites the rebels of all our countries? This possibility exists. The realization of this ideal would be immensely creative because it would be genuinely Latin American. It would merit universal respect.

In conclusion, the principal utopian elements, social mechanisms, and factors that enter into the present interplay between compulsion and adjustment in Colombia may be apprehended. It is on the counterpoint of these processes that the disintegration of the liberal-bourgeois order and the reconstruction of another, superior order will depend.

The period that follows is a crucial one. Once the utopia succeeds in refracting the order of the National Front there will be revealed once more that the young generations have received a doubtful heritage. Their elders have not been able to resolve the old problems posed by the search for identity and collective progress of the Colombian nation; on the contrary, they have permitted the successive accumulation of social incongruities. Those of today come from the cumbersome bourgeois apparatus filled with democratic myths, all moving in the decrepit feudal mold. Today's heritage is the accumulation of three frustrations: the Christian, the liberal, and the bourgeois. This is sufficient cause for concern for the oncoming crisis and for the need to have a clear understanding of its meaning.

The neo-socialist subversion may foster a movement of great importance to carry Colombian society into a better world. Success will depend on how the key groups are able to control the mechanisms and factors of the strategy of compulsion. If we still can learn from history, the arrival of the fifth order should not be a catastrophe. It may be the time when Colombia finds itself.

Some Typologies of Societies in Transition

THE phenomenon of accelerated social change has recently produced certain classifications and new concepts in sociology that merit a short resumé. One of the most meritorious is Alvin Boskoff's concept of "social indecision" (1959), postulated in terms of "dysfunction" and the necessity to restore anterior stability. Another is that of Jacques Lambert, who refers to "dual societies" (1960, 27–50) in which ways of life of different "times" and "technologies" coexist, thus producing maladjustments and "asynchronies" (Germani 1962) in underdeveloped countries.

In reality, this is a very old idea (similar references are found in classical literature), whose principal immediate antecedents are the dichotomy of Tönnies and the distinction made by Durkheim in relation to social solidarity. It may be equally well applied to situations of the past, and to the contemporary process of "development." These dichotomies open the door to a series of polarized typologies: the folk-urban one of Redfield (more that of his followers, for the author did not conceive it in this way), the sacred-secular one of Becker, that of status-contract of Maine—all difficult to confirm in the field. This occurs because reality presents intermediate characteristics or combinations of polar types that makes its reconciliation with the typology difficult (Moore 1963, 66–68). Furthermore, logically a polarity cannot be transposed to reality as a continuum (Martindale, 1960, 93); for this reason it blocks the second step toward the analysis of the social elements of a period of transition, especially when it contains ideological and utopian ingredients.

Howard Becker's concept of a "pronormless" society (Becker 1957, 160–61, 171–74) includes a similar occurrence. It should be distinguished from deviant subcultures such as those of the delinquent group that have been studied more adequately. From its analysis there have arisen theories such as that of normative tension and the conflict of values. Unfortunately, with Becker's documentation, it is only possible to generalize in relation to contemporary situations; thus his propositions concerning the causality of the phenomenon lose some of their force, and the comparative and predictive possibilities of the concept are weakened. Specifically, his paradigm of the pronormless society has the following aspects that are not found in the case of the transition of the sixteenth century that is studied in this book: (1) stabilized crystallization of prior norms; (2) stimulus to the formation of values that produce a fluid situation without obstacles; (3) social mobility and the loss of differences between social classes in a search for equality; (4) tolerance and open-mindedness; (5) sensibility for scientific developments; and (6) futurism.

Evidently, Becker was thinking more about events that occur today in developing countries than in similar processes of the past when transition depended on different cultural elements. The concept ought to have wider and more thorough application. The difference between what occurs today and what occurred in the second half of the sixteenth century in the Andean region of Colombia—a phenomenon similar in many aspects to the present one of accelerated social change and one which proceeds at nearly the same speeds—the difference, we say, is to be found in at least three factors whose theoretical importance cannot be underestimated and which are studied at length in this book: (1) the nature of the cultural contact; for the societies whose values and norms entered into contact with each other in the sixteenth century led toward an order in which social action of the prescriptive type prevailed; (2) the nature and role of the key groups involved in situations of contact at a subcultural level after the Spanish conquest because they fostered the adoption of a different way of life, with a seigniorial *Weltanschauung;* and (3) the function of technology in each historical period.

The periods of historical transition in Colombia present other, distinct, pronormless societies: at least one in the revolutionary movement of the nineteenth century, one in the period following the Second World War in the twentieth century, and another that is developing in present trends toward change. One explanation for the differences among them may be found in the factors mentioned. For this reason, in our search for the integrative concept of "subversion," it has seemed useful to broaden the conceptual framework of Becker's pronormless society, in order to take the direction of change, which Becker only suggests for this type of society, into greater account.

Definitions of Sociological Concepts

Section I. Components of the Social Order

The components of the social order employed in this book are: values, norms, social organization, and techniques. They are defined as follows:

1. *Values* are general beliefs and conceptions and existential or cognitive and affective judgments of people that have the most saturating and profound effects on the social order. Values are conceived of in two ways: (*a*) according to action oriented toward fundamental problems of life, such as that concerning the nature of man, his relations with the universe and the surrounding environment, his idea of time, his preferred type of activity, and his patterns of relations with other persons (Kluckhohn and Strodtbeck 1961, 4–12); and (*b*) according to the goals and rules set by groups to define the legitimacy of the action (Smelser 1962, 9). Values are analogically integrated and distributed in ranks or according to priorities (for example, the "central" values of Thompson 1956, 73). The ethos of a society is determined by identifying its dominant values; this is what Redfield calls a "world view" (1957, 86–108) and certain German authors call *Weltanschauung*.

Basic psychological sources of values are "attitudes," defined as "predispositions . . . toward an *evaluative* response" (underscore of the author—Osgood et al. 1957, 189–91). Therein resides the individual participation in social action based on psychic states, on characteristics of the basic personality and temperament, and on socio-psychological tendencies that permit the person to make evaluations of his own reality and of that of others. In any case, these evaluations and attitudes are articulated under certain circumstances and mutually support each other in order to develop social values, organize them analogically, and establish those which are dominant.

For the purposes of this study, the value component is studied in two ways: (*a*) through the ethos and certain dominant values that summarize essential characteristics of the respective society and culture, according to participants or authorized observers; and (*b*) through the expression of divergent ideas that arise owing to the contradictory dynamics of the social order or through contact with ideas of other societies.

Because they are essentially psychic, existential, or affective phenomena, values are expressed verbally and not necessarily through acts; the latter are rather evidences of norms, which are in any case related to values.

2. *Norms* are the many rules of behavior that are derived from values and that are applied in certain contexts, varying according to the degree of coercion and acceptance or according to the meaning of the value orientation (Parsons and Smelser 1956, 102). Thus norms are directly observable in the reality of behavior. On the individual level, norms vary from simple practices to habits; on the group level, from customs to mores (Lee 1945). The third, or societal, level proposed by Lee has been eliminated because it becomes confused with the value system as it has been defined here. In order to simplify analysis, in this book norms are clustered in large groups according to affinity, constituting what we indicated with the designation "normative framework."

The normative framework also includes norms of political or juridical character such as laws, jurisprudence, and doctrines that reflect concrete social performances and precedents derived from the values, customs, and mores such as the Anglo-Saxon social law. Nevertheless it is possible to measure the distance among values, customs, and laws when these are dictated as ideal propositions or goals to be achieved, as frequently occurs in Latin American (French) tradition of law (cf. Umaña Luna 1967). The normative framework encompasses both the rules and decrees derived from

values having to do with the use of political power and the legitimation of coercion by the state apart from the specific social organization that activates such norms.

3. *Social organization* reflects the formation of groups, institutions, and status roles (personal positions and the behavior inherent
in them) as mechanisms that embody and translate values and norms
into the practice of everyday life (Linton 1936). The institution,
the community, and the political apparatus should be stressed among
these mechanisms. Institutions are concrete manifestations, in a new
dimension, of norms related to one specific necessity or purpose;
their operativeness depends upon the manner in which the groups
employing such norms are organized and oriented. Institutional
organization gives margin to variations in the performance of roles
and in the resulting expectations in order to produce: (*a*) diverse
types of social stratification; (*b*) various kinds of economic groups;
(*c*) diverse types of prescriptive, elective (Germani 1962), or conditioned action. On the other hand, the unit in which culture is
created, transmitted, or modified, the person is socialized, and the
primary necessities of individuals are fulfilled is the community,
understood as a social group that is integrated within a given region
and at a certain ecological level (Emerson 1956, 150; Arensberg
1961). The community tends to reorganize itself at ever broader
and more complex levels of integration that incorporate ever greater
numbers of persons in interaction and larger territory (Sahlins and
Service 1960; Wilson and Wilson 1945).

The political apparatus includes those groups, entities, and persons
that establish relations of domination and dependence based on values and norms implied in the use or in the seeking of state or world
power (Weber 1964). It is strategic to examine the role of groups
such as the elite and its relations to the masses, and the effect of
such groups on the processes of participation, representation, and
institutionalization that lead to the formation of regional, national,
or international political entities (cf. Jaguaribe 1966). In the strict
sense, "social organization" as it is used here is synonymous with
"social structure." However, many sociologists extend this concept
to include value and normative systems, a confusing procedure that
we have not adopted here.

These three components of the social order have a characteristic that differentiates them from the technological one: their tendency to shape changes that are multi-causal; once produced, they are multi-directional and do not necessarily lead to an accumulation of culture or to significant changes in behavior. These components present greater possibilities for regression or detention than the technological component and allow changes of form without the content being affected. For this reason they seem to benefit from certain regenerative attributes through repetition, in different molds of the substance and traits of prior entities.

4. *Techniques,* on the other hand, include a series of elements and innovations that are cumulative and uni-directional and have a certain autonomy from the rest of the social order. Therefore they can produce changes that may or may not have significant consequences in life patterns; or their autonomous development may have auxiliary or supportive consequences for social organization such as reinforcement of the existing power structure or its transformation into a technocracy. Expressed in another way, technology may produce economic advancement without promoting social development (cf. Parra 1966, 123–28). It includes the cultural elements, knowledge, abilities, and tools that permit man to transform the environment in which he lives or to determine the conditions under which he exercises his activity. Therein arise the agricultural techniques, patterns for the use of land and energy, cultural complexes related to medicine, industry, transportation, defense, communication, and similar activities that go along with the diverse social orders (Smith 1953, 332ff; Cottrell 1955; Erasmus 1961).

Section II. The Elements of Subversion

The elements that are dialectically articulated in the social condition of subversion, when the social order is refracted with a utopian impact, are by necessity replications of the elements included in the four components of the social order, those that become integrated in the condition of tradition. Placed in broad categories, the elements of subversion are: counter-values, counter-norms, disorgans, and technological innovations that are defined in the following way.

1. With the beginning of the period of transition, ideas appear in the form of statements of valued utopian goals or distinct collective purposes. They may originate within or without the society, in conquest or rebellion, in an individual or in a group. They do not necessarily originate with an intellectual elite; there have been cases in which goals or watchwords have arisen from the people themselves (Mexico, Bolivia). These new values confront those of tradition, attempting to substitute for those that are incompatible or to add and assimilate those that are compatible. But as long as they are not definitively adopted by the majority of the society and its dominant groups, they remain as *counter-values* of the established order within the period of subversion. Thus the two groups of values exist together in conflict, becoming gradually adjusted to one another until one of the two imposes itself upon the other by means of the component of social organization. Meanwhile, the values of a reform, conquering, or rebel group will be the counter-values of another that is conservative or reactionary and tends to maintain the status quo. One as much as the other will be an objective reality and represent an alternative morality. The legitimation of the counter-values, of course, is not found in the established social order but rather in the emerging one. And the effectiveness of the change may be measured to the degree that the reformist groups become reference groups within the framework of the emerging social order and finally become dominant groups therein. This occurs because traditional values at this time begin to be displaced or assimilated by the new counter-values that are legitimated now not by local traditional groups but by the reference groups representing change.

The existence of counter-values may be logically derived from the theory of conflict, but some sociologists see not the positive but only the negative aspect of the phenomenon. Becker infers it by relating the counter-value to the distance between generations, the conflict between internal norms of the same society, and the intrusion of innovations (Becker 1960, 808). Counter-values are more clearly formulated by J. Milton Yinger as those that "a person holds in opposition to the values of the surrounding society"; he calls them "inverse" or "counter-values" and the resulting normative system the "counter-culture" (Yinger 1960, 627). However, Yinger limits this concept to groups exhibiting socio-pathological behavior which is unacceptable in the framework of social change we are following. Parsons states the matter in a similar manner: for him the culture of a deviant group, such as the gang, is a "counter-culture" (Parsons 1951, 522); and he approaches the concept of the counter-value, calling it "counter-ideology" when he defines the latter as "opposition to the system of values and ideology of the larger society" (Parsons 1951, 355). Although he views the phenomenon in an opposite way, Luis E. Nieto Arteta also refers to the "counter-value of sociological thought in 1850" to contrast it with that of the "regeneration" of 1886 (when conservative ideas were set into the present Colombian constitution). The idea is basically the same (Nieto Arteta 1962, 224). The point of reference for counter-values is not so much the established social order as the collection of ideas with which it is hoped to shape a new collective state.

On the other hand, it is essential to understand the role played in this concept (and in those of the counter-norm and disorgan) by the reference group, generally defined as that external group whose influence determines the behavior, judgments, and attitudes of a person. First of all, Robert K. Merton (1957a, 357–68) makes a distinction between "non-conformist behavior" and "deviant behavior" in order to differentiate the "rebel" type of individual adaptation to anomie from the merely criminal or delinquent type. The non-conformist rebel "seeks a modified social structure" (Merton 1957a, 155). He does so with open determination, often altruistically, rejecting the legitimacy of prevailing norms and expectations for the sake of creating or imposing new ones with a different moral basis. Thereby he contradicts the behavior of the common criminal, in spite of society's insistence to the contrary.

Now the criminal as well as the rebel has reference groups that are determining factors of behavior. But the rebel as a "radical" has recourse to "values, norms, and practices that have not yet been institutionalized but that are considered to shape the normative system of future reference groups" (Merton 1957a, 360). Since these concepts support the interpretation given earlier it is not superfluous to emphasize that the futuristic meaning embodied in Merton's definition of "radicalism" (and his tendency to place rebellion outside the social structure, 1957a, 155) does not seem to fit the reality of the situation of subversion. This is so because in this situation the reference groups that determine the rebel or iconoclastic conduct of other persons are actualities and they exercise their activity within the context of the actual society they combat; they are not of the "future." Nevertheless, by using Merton's framework it may be seen that the rebel type refers to non-conformist individual behavior within the overall diachronic situation of subversion as conceived herein.

Another mode of interpretation is to situate the concept of reference groups within the theory of role conflict as done by Parsons (1951, 281–83); in this case the way out is to acknowledge "significant alters" that support conflicting expectations. Eisenstadt (1954, 175–85) applies the concept of "level of aspiration" to explain the behavior of the individual in relation to his reference group and to postulate the theoretical existence of orientations toward "deviant reference groups." This is close to the formulation presented here although the tendency to view the subject negatively is not shared. It must be remembered that counter-values are concretely applied at certain levels of integration (such as the community, the neighborhood, and the family) by means of reference groups situated at other levels that are identified with the emerging society. These groups combat the present topias.

2. The theoretical formulations we have followed indicate that values are translated as concrete norms of everyday behavior or as those of juridical or political nature. In the same manner, when the social order starts to disintegrate, the counter-values then breed counter-norms of the established order as long as it exists and the next one is not achieved. The counter-norm is a pattern of behavior that is sanctioned negatively in a given context whether it be by tradition or by law or by any other reason for social control derived from the prevailing social order. But at the same time it becomes positively sanctioned whenever it is viewed in relation to a reference group of divergent, rebel, or subversive conduct and that as a general rule is situated at a different (higher) level of integration. Like the counter-value, the counter-norm is legitimated only by these reference groups and not by the traditional groups of primary rela-

tions or established institutions. It is a device that guarantees the reformulation of modes of acting, perceiving, and valuing. It changes the social self-image in a given environment until, little by little, through the socialization of a larger number of persons, it becomes the usual norm.

In sociological literature there is a short tradition that postulates the existence of counter-norms but as undesirable. Harold D. Lasswell first defined "countermores" as "cultural patterns that are principally supported by the id" and that are found among "revolutionaries, prostitutes, prisoners, obscene and subversive persons" (Lasswell 1935, 64). Later the same author defined them as "cultural traits symbolized by the group as deviations from the mores and that even so are expected to occur" (Lasswell 1950, 49), giving emphasis to the usual normative expectation and not allowing room for the creative innovation that is the essence of the theory we are following. Lee's "variant mores" refer to the same phenomenon (Lee 1945, 488). Becker limits his "counter-norms" to the norms of groups of persons that are "not human" owing to their low mode of living, thus eliminating the possibility that counter-norms may be positive or become norms acceptable to society (Becker 1960, 806). Yinger's concept of "counter-culture" already mentioned includes the element of the counter-norm that is called the "emergent norm" (Yinger 1960, 627). This type of norm results in cases of frustration or conflict between a group and the larger society (or the established order). By broadening these concepts and eliminating the obvious biases embodied in them the objective reality of the counter-norm becomes clear and its effects on the processes of social change are understood.

3. *Disorgans* are those innovating groups or institutions that challenge the established order and emergent status roles, that sustain heterodox, rebel, or iconoclastic activity for the purpose of producing, disseminating, or imposing counter-values and counter-norms. The word "disorgans" is an abbreviated formula for referring to the elements described as a whole, that is, a nominal definition (Bierstedt 1959). The prefix is from the Latin *dis-*, meaning separated or contrary, and not from the Greek *dys-*, meaning imperfect or bad. Another alternative, but awkward to use, is "counter-institution."

Disorgans, especially political ones, do not always present complete internal homogeneity. Subversive groups may have dissensions within themselves caused by independent attempts to impose different ideologies, which naturally weaken their action in the face of traditional institutions. However, the most effective are those that, consistent with their valued goals, direct their activity against the crucial elements of tradition without allowing themselves to become disoriented by chameleonic political processes or social cooptation or by internal jealousies and sabotage of a tactical nature. The initiation and success or frustration of subversions (developments, movements, and revolutions that are initiated or restrained in certain historical periods and circumstances) seem to depend on this organizing component. It is only when the disorgans achieve optimum effectiveness in compulsion, are rationally and homogeneously articulated, and institutionalize their contacts with the rest of society that they may achieve the goals they have set for themselves.

Reference groups such as the counter-elite that arise from dominant political, economic, and cultural milieux (military men, intellectuals, or university students) are strategic when they maintain the rhythm of refracted action, and through it reach the basic levels of society. Groups that attain self-awareness and seek change in the established order, that is, political parties, counter-elites, guerrillas, rebel bands, and groups such as juntas, trade unions, and fraternities that challenge vested interests, all constitute disorgans. Equally important are the institutions that impose themselves following a conquest when there is an intention to change the way of life of the conquered people. In this case the disintegration of whole institutions is engineered by disorgans of different kinds.

Stemming from the master process of adjustment and compulsion there also appear new status-roles because the old ones are incongruous with the action required by the new circumstances of subversion and the emerging order; furthermore, the patterns of domination and dependence are changed. The new roles exist alongside old ones in the personality. Thus, in affected regions persons are found who are conservative in certain matters (such as religion) while in others (such as in occupations) they seek and accept change.

Sociological literature about tension, disorganization, and conflict that includes these points of view, such as the psychology of role strain, is so extensive and well-known that it need not be repeated here even in its general details. However, it should be re-read in order to correct the biases it may contain about rebel, nonconformist, or heterodox groups as they confront prevailing social orders for the purpose of achieving utopias or valued goals (cf. Dahrendorf 1958, 176). Obviously, an "extremist group" is not necessarily alienated from society and therefore "hostile to the political order" (Shils 1956, 231) but rather it is hostile to the prevailing order because it wishes to supplant it with another it believes to be superior. This positive interpretation of change (generally absent in current so-called "neutral" functionalist studies) is indispensable for understanding subversion in its real context.

4. In harmony with the general framework of the social order in that which relates to the technological component (its autonomy and uni-direction orientation), special significance is proposed for *technical innovations*. In first place, the term "innovation" is used in the sense of "any thought, behavior, or thing that is new because it is qualitatively different from existing forms" (Barnett 1953, 7). By developing the distinctions made by Barnett in regard to the "cultural inventory" that is found at the disposition of innovators, it may be clearly understood that innovations are made in the field of ideas, things, and techniques as much as behavior and social organization. Many disorgans are innovations as well as the adjustments and changes they foster in traditional institutions. Nevertheless, in the case of the category we are studying, it is deemed advisable to limit the meaning of the concept "technological innovation" to the material, applied or natural aspects of culture. The purpose for this is to take into account the relations and mutual influences the new developments have in agricultural techniques, patterns of using land and energy, and the cultural complexes and goods related to medicine, industry, transportation, defense, communication, and similar activities with the three kinds of elements of subversion.

This position results from the recognition that the technological component may have its own dynamic. However, the cumulative progression of technology and science may reach such a critical point that it precipitates and requires important changes in values, norms, and social organization. This thesis broadened to apply to the economic field in general is similar to the materialist interpretation of history (Marx [1859], 1911a, 11–12); it recognizes the importance of these material factors and their tendency to create or maintain an ideological superstructure. Nevertheless, it implies acceptance of the limitations of technological accumulation in certain historical periods when far from promoting change it reinforces the traditional social and economic structure. For this reason this kind of technical element is considered to be supportive of the others: it may have a positive role in the subversion of the order or it may also obstruct reformist or revolutionary movements.

Section III. Counter-elites and the Cooptation Process

There is little systematization of the concept of "counter-elite" in sociological literature, and as far as the author is aware, no thorough description of this social group is available to date, in spite of the fact that it has undeniable political and social importance. The practical difficulties and even dangers of these undertakings are also clear.

However, the concept itself does appear in well-regarded treatises. Harold D. Lasswell, for example, defines the counter-elite as a group of individuals "perceived as adherents of a counter-ideology" who nevertheless "are recognized and exercising a significant influence over important decisions . . . [and who] inhibit, or otherwise modify, the established elite" (Lasswell and Lerner 1965, 16–17). S. N. Eisenstadt claims that counter-elites sponsor "general rebellion" within society aimed "at the disruption of social continuity and the establishment of a new secular social order," and sees an element of youth in them (Eisenstadt 1964, 314–15). Chalmers Johnson refers to counter-elites as "status protesters" who have two courses of action: either to recast the existing status hierarchy, or to restore the old status hierarchy (Johnson 1966, 106). And in one of the latest pertinent analyses, counter-elites are identified as "challenging elites" by Robert E. Scott, underlining their "turncoat" characteristics (Scott 1967, 126–27).

Evidently there should be an element of fact in this concept, discernible by the observer who scrutinizes history within a socio-logical framework and appreciates the more widely accepted phe-nomenon of Pareto's "circulation." Up to a certain point, the heuristic value of the concept "counter-elite" is tied up with that of "elite," defined loosely as the dominant power and prestige hold-ers in a society. Therefore it is also subject to the ambiguities that have affected this more general concept, especially those related to the social origin and composition of dominant groups. But this should not be necessarily so, and further research may be produc-tive in this regard.

In short, as "elites" express themselves under different historical and social circumstances, so do the groups that challenge them. When this challenge comes from a peer group bent on varying the rules and the power structure of society, especially in its higher echelons, the basic and most general requisites for a counter-elite are met. Essentially, therefore, a counter-elite may be defined as that group of persons of high prestige status who turn against the dom-inant groups to wrest political power from them.

The scientific productivity of this definition hinges on the inde-pendent variable "high prestige status" as well as on the characteris-tics of the conflict between elite and counter-elite. By "high pres-tige status" is meant the composite of positions occupied by persons who have valued symbols ascribed to them, or who have achieved them, especially in relation to knowledge and education, political and ecclesiastical power, wealth, and administrative or patronizing activities. This sub-definition allows us to include in the analysis of counter-elites strategic groups of different social origins, like intel-lectuals, university students and professors, religious, military, and labor leaders, and politicians who in a given moment may form an opposition to a regime, even though they may not belong to the upper or aristocratic classes.

To understand the real nature of the conflict between elite and counter-elite is just as crucial as an alertness to the social origin and composition of the members. Political action is paramount in this respect, because the social power base is at stake, with all its eco-nomic and ideological ramifications. As far as research results allow us to proceed, two types of conflict appear to be important in this regard: that which is mainly *generational*, and that which is mainly *ideological*.

Generational counter-elites seem to be a regular or permanent feature of society, produced by built-in deviations in socialization and other differentiating mechanisms, like aging, marriage and the family, education, and so forth that do not threaten the value foundations of the social order. Divergent perspectives on norms and organization and different ways of sharing or distributing prestige symbols and advantages may appear between the older and early-adult generations, or between those in power and those outside, that stimulate inter-personal conflict on the political level. Conflicts may be so acute that civil war is a possible outcome. But these divergencies, even though potentially destructive, do not undermine profoundly the rules of the game. On the contrary, the resolution of this type of conflict usually does not weaken the status quo. In Latin America the right to armed revolt was among the rules, since it was sanctioned during the wars of independence. Thus a circulation of elites is effected in this manner without changing the social order. In these circumstances the generational counter-elites perform a positive function of preserving the traditional structures of society and of serving as a renewal mechanism for the elites. The whole process can be viewed more in the order of adaptation than of definitive substitution.

Ideological counter-elites spring from generational ones in certain critical historical periods. This occurs when members of the counter-elite—usually the younger and the intellectual—are capable of articulating an ideology based on newly observed incongruities and inconsistencies in their society or on the felt need of redistributing power and prestige symbols and advantages to deprived and marginal groups. When they succeed in organizing themselves and in spreading their revolt to other collectivities with a vested interest in change, the ideological counter-elites have a profound effect in the transformation of society, and in fact are instrumental in achieving a new social order. They become then a key element in initiating subversion, that is, they turn into a type of "disorgan" (see above).

In these circumstances, the ideological counter-elites appear to have the following functions:

1. To initiate the creation and diffusion of counter-values and counter-norms of the established social order.

2. To serve as a reference group to other rebel collectivities located at different levels or strata in society.

3. To challenge the dominant groups from the inside by using their own weapons and devices.

Counter-elites are seen to be important for the *initiation* of subversion, although not so effective for maintaining the pressure of the subversive élan. For this onerous task the burden lies with more determined and constant disorgans. This is so because counter-elites, even during subversive periods, appear to undergo a metamorphosis in two stages, one of which permits a cooptation process to set in that tends to arrest the revolutionary impulse. These stages are:

1. The iconoclastic stage, during which the schism with the elite is real, with active criticism and protest. When newly observed incongruities and inconsistencies in the social order receive ideological support, and commitment toward change is maintained, this stage converges into subversion.

2. The assimilative stage, by which the counter-elite institutionalizes itself and either crystallizes into a new elite once the old one is totally or partially supplanted; or its members are coopted in succession by the traditional dominant groups as these undertake maneuvers of survival. This process of cooptation takes two forms: (*a*) a positive one, whereby the elite agrees to share and redistribute power and prestige symbols and advantages and to open new possibilities of social and political action (cases of England, Sweden, Mexico, Japan); and (*b*) a reactionary one, whereby the rebels are subjected, and give in, to enticements by means of positions or prerogatives in the Establishment, gifts, social sanctions, and the like, or are jailed, exiled, or killed when they do not submit.

All of the sociologists cited above agree that the cooptation process is a regular feature affecting the counter-elite. Therefore, it may be concluded that the counter-elite is a group that has the same conservative tendencies of self-perpetuation and institutionalization enjoyed by other social groups. This seems especially true of the generational type, and of the ideological type after the initiation of subversive action. However, the fact of the appearance of the ideological type in recent subversive periods and the martyrdom that its rebelliousness has brought on some of its members in several countries may point toward its great potentiality as a factor for social change. In theory, counter-elites may be potent elements for revolution when they are not coopted. The effort to forestall cooptation or, at least, the effort to recognize the dangers of cooptation, especially of the reactionary type, appears to be paramount in reassuring the efficacy of counter-elites in transforming societies. This is evident when studies are made of actual historical cases.

Consequently, efficacy in changing the social order seems to be related to the degree of commitment to subversion. Of course, the outcome of the conflict does not depend on the counter-elite alone (this would be a highly simplified and erroneous uni-causal explanation), but on the combination of social and economic factors and conditions present during the subversive period (counter-values, counter-norms, political and other disorgans, and technological innovations). If the counter-elite and other rebel groups remain faithful to the original goals of subversion, including their utopian elements, and if they succeed in compelling the rhythm of the transformation and creating the objective conditions for revolt, a new social order is achieved that may be revolutionarily different from the previous one.

Section IV. Marginal and Significant Change

In order to understand the marginal and significant types of social change, we usually begin with a general view of traditional society as it was in a given historical period. As a start to systematizing observations, we can analyze traditional society through the four components making up the social order of the times: (1) the system of social values; (2) the normative structure; (3) the social organization; and (4) the technological support elements, as usually defined in sociological treatises (see above). The historical and cultural expressions of these components constitute a given social order developed and imposed over time. The constitutive elements mutually support and reinforce each other in such manner that a cultural monolith, extremely resilient, is in the making. One great source of resistance to change in the social order stems from the strength of the value system, especially when it has not been seriously challenged either directly or through action in other components, particularly the technological.

As a general rule, to use modifications in the value structure as a measuring stick to determine the significance of social change appears to be acceptable procedure. This is so because of the saturating effects that the value component has on other elements of the social order, and also on account of the cause and effect relationship that exists between values, techniques, and economic development. Moreover, the sense of direction and drive toward aims or collective goals perceived in a social order, or whenever a social order transforms itself, is registered most genuinely in the value system, and more specifically in dominant or core values. (Sorokin 1957; Smelser 1962; Ellul 1964; Cooley 1909, 328).

Significant change seems to occur when variations in the components of the social order call for adjustments in the existing patterns of value dominance and collective aims of society. When these adjustments are sufficiently profound, especially if their impact is felt coherently on the total structure of society, a new social order may emerge that is an adaptation of, or revolutionarily different from, the previous one. In these processes, strategic key groups and variations in the technological elements that furnish support to the existing socio-economic order are extremely important.

Concurrently, *marginal change* occurs when modifications in the components of the social order are either partial or minor, so that the value system is not inherently in question and no measurable consequences are felt in social or economic organization that would bring about a new social order. This is the specific type of change that has been hypothesized as having occurred during such periods as that of the wars of independence in Latin America.

Of course, what is partial, minor, or profound is open to debate, in spite of having the value system and collective goals of the social order as measuring rods. Empty debate could be avoided by study-

ing the actual historical record and comparing the effect of pertinent events on systems of beliefs and ways of behavior of the people
involved. In order to achieve this end, the sociologist has no other
recourse but to go to archives and primary sources (often very rich
and untapped) and to rely on observations recorded by participants,
informed travellers, chroniclers, and other writers of authority and
responsibility.

APPENDIX C

Conceptual Bases of Projective Research

To STUDY Colombia and Latin America today implies entering into the whirl of an extremely dynamic society whose spiral of change, in spite of current theory, is not finding its equilibrium as it progresses. It is a fluid, contradictory society that is difficult to understand and to systematize. Anyone who would submerge himself in the tumult of this type of society and remain conscious of himself and his role as an investigator should cast aside limited frameworks and be prepared to deal with what is apparently illogical. If the conceptual tools with which he is working are inadequate—which is probable—he should begin to formulate those that can correspond to the most basic of necessities. Furthermore, he should adopt attitudes and formulate techniques that on the surface do not seem very orthodox.

In fact, one way to begin might be to employ the Diltheyan technique of the "understanding grasp," which permits an initial freedom of action and thought in relation to the elusive problems under observation. This is necessary because if the rules of field work are maintained immaculate, if complete emotional or intellectual independence is sought in relation to the processes studied, in the majority of cases these problems will not be understood. For example, it does not seem possible to study violence and its effects on Colombian society in a profound way, using the intellectual equivalents of prophylactic gloves and face mask, or to arrive at the strategic arenas of change in urban slums or in humble peasant communities with the august, aloof attitude of the scientist who thinks only in terms of accumulation of knowledge.

And even though he might wish to stay in this removed position, the mental tension of the social scientist would be such that he would have to formulate new techniques of research in order to study in depth the issues he perceives. On one hand he would find it difficult to understand clearly that which he has not lived, if he has paid heed to the teachings of Cooley (1909) on "sympathetic intro-spection." On the other hand, his understanding would be hampered if he did not wish to apply even the "understanding grasp" or empathy in critical situations of social change. For this reason it is considered essential to be committed to the process of changing the society and to be identified with its goals of economic, social, and cultural advancement. In this way, the nature and characteristics of social processes may be better understood.

Commitment is in no way a matter of rebellion against classical scientific method because basic principles of inference are observed and the control of intervening factors and elements is sought. Objectivity is also maintained, within adequate bounds. The divergencies with the purists (and certain functionalists) are more those of orientation, thereby creating a different set of priorities regarding the relation between theory and practice. Thus the personal value framework of the committed investigator is expressed largely in the choice of themes of research and in the working hypotheses that guide inquiry in the field. These themes and hypotheses may have merits similar to those that an "uncommitted scientist" would have chosen even though the latter's decision be also conditioned by his own scale of values, which places high value on social equilibrium. In this context the students of change gain the advantage of partici-pating empathetically in the processes of change because they seek such transformations along with the rest of society and as human beings desire that changes should occur. They are able to understand them at first hand and in this way to control variables and attributes that are strategic and essential.

The primary reason for a scientist to adopt this position of com-mitment to social change and identification with the processes of socio-economic development of a country is to be found in the verification that these processes have a purpose or *telos* whose transcendence and meaning may be understood only through active participation in them.

As a consequence, the feasibility of a method of research that may be called telic, projective, or anticipatory is logically established. The present function and nature of social institutions and cultural elements are examined through telic research relating them to subsequent or future necessities and to models and goals valued but not yet achieved by the society. The present is studied, but in the reflection of the future and with a view to consciously shaping it. The advantage of this method is in its ability to anticipate which elements of the present order of affairs have the potential to produce incongruities in the new one, given the goals set by society. It may have not only investigative merit for better understanding the present as related to future necessities, but also a practical value for anticipating greater conflicts and dislocations.

This method harmonizes with present tendencies toward a planned society and may depend on the advantages of the great development of statistics and other technical systems of information accumulation and utilization. Furthermore, it has the benefit of historical experience. The capacity to deduce laws from this experience has not been achieved, as desired by John Stuart Mill, but it is possible to derive general propositions that aid in anticipating situations and in determining the degree of congruity of various social orders.

In fact, it is relatively easy to note the institutions that in the past produced serious internal conflicts when the transition was made from one social order to another. One, for example, was slavery, once the societies in which it was practiced adopted the liberal-democratic ideology as a guide line. Clearly, maintaining the institution of slavery within the new framework could only produce serious social tensions. The solution demanded a much more serious effort to approximate the liberal utopia and to put its ideal principles into practice. In an equal way, it would not be difficult to determine which institutions of the present social order would be incongruent if the transition to a different one were completed. History and experience might teach us to be more consistent and more clear in our decisions. In fact, it would only be necessary to establish models and defined collective purposes, goals toward which the society would advance consciously and rationally.

The scientists committed to historical transitions of this type, today as in the past, tend to ask themselves, as did many of their predecessors, "What purpose does the knowledge gained serve?" The answer is not science *per se* but its concrete application, even though science itself is as a general rule also enriched during the process. The tradition of the scientific question "what purpose" (in addition to the classic "why") has a very respectable origin in sociology. It was in essence the attitude of thinkers and scientists to whom we owe much today, men motivated by high aims (often "subversive") who were inspired by an ideal or had a missionary sense about life: Malthus, Comte, Ward, Ortega, and many others, such as Durkheim, who is presented in the academies as the standard bearer of strict sociological method. Even this champion of orthodoxy ends his classic work on suicide with a chapter on practical consequences. Tönnies was inspired to study the problems of the laborers of Hamburg after a stormy strike; the *verstehen* of Max Weber himself opens similar possibilities for teletic prediction; Marx alludes to the necessity for completing the esoteric knowledge of philosophy with a sense of urgency to change the world, in one of his *Theses on Feurbach;* Freud is above all a rebel clinical psychologist with a great sense of the practical implications of his transcendental theories; Mannheim pleads for a new sense of objectivity adjusted to realities and elaborates his ideas concerning democratic planning along these lines; Cooley, Park, Myrdal, Wirth, Mills, Redfield all stated clear points of view that reinforce the telic position and projective investigation. All asked themselves not only "why" but also "for what purpose" knowledge, and thus conditioned social science. Moreover, a similar type of projective method is used in such disciplines as agricultural economics and industrial psychology in order to anticipate results within a system (the "quickening" of systems research).

However, there is a limitation to this method that should be mentioned in order to be able to equally anticipate its efforts. It is true that the projections made are based on facts studied and documented with the evidences of social processes. And for this reason, as in all scientific prediction, projections are limited to the conditions from which they depart and are subject to repetitive factors and to others that may be unforeseeable in prior analysis; this is common to all empirical investigation. Nevertheless, as Merton maintained, the projections derived from the use of telic research in sociology may come to have the characteristics of a "prophecy" that conditions or engenders its own implementation. This phenomenon of self-fulfillment is not experienced outside the world of the super-organic and constitutes a real factor that may impinge upon forecasts made. To establish further, through inquiry and well-controlled special work, the divergencies between the actual prediction and its implementation, in addition to discovering what part is conditioned by the publication of the results, could be a task of great scientific interest in the sociological field.

In any case, the use of this method, even with the dangers of its self-determination, would reduce the total amount of oversight to manageable proportions and would open the possibility of leading collective action toward previously established goals in a conscious manner.

A Graph Showing Social Change in the

Components of the Social Order	Ayllic Order (1)	Christian Subversion	Seigniorial (2)
Years	1493 1537	1595	1794
Values	Missional Utopia Tolerant sacralism: 1. Animism 2. Family-centeredness 3. Nature 4. Future	[Assimilated counter-values]	Liberal Caste Urbanism: 1. Animism 2. Family-centeredness 3. Nature 4. Otherworldliness 5. Neo-Manicheism
Norms	1. Communal stability 2. Providence	[Assimilated counter-norms]	1. Communal stability 2. Providence 3. Prescriptive rigidity 4. Acritical morality
Social Organization (Key Groups and Institutions)	Neighborhood (sybyn)	Ladino counter-elite Reservation Doctrine	Señores Encomienda Hacienda Clergy
(Integration) (Strata)	Neighborhood Semi-closed	Neighborhood Closed	Communal Closed
Techniques (Accumulative)	1. Digging stick and hoe 2. Row crop culture 3. Crafts 4. Manual defense	5. Wooden plow 6. Iron implements 7. Wheel and harness 8. Mounted defense 9. Gunpowder	

History of Colombia (from 1493 to 1968)

	Bourgeois Order (3)		Liberal-Bourgeois Order (4) (National Front)	Order (5)
Liberal Subversion		Socialist Subversion		Neo-socialist Subversion

1848	1867	1904	1925	1957	1965

		Socialist Utopia		Pluralist Utopia	
[Unassimilated counter-values] Mechanicism Entrepreneurial ethic Nationalism	Seigniorial and liberal values	Instrumental Secularism: 1. Supranationalism 2. Technicism 3. Humanism 4. Communality	[Partially assimilated instrumentalist values]	[Secular values reiterated]
[Unassimilated counter-norms] Laissez-faire Formal democracy	Seigniorial and liberal norms	1. Mobility 2. Teletic morality 3. Technical control	[Partially assimilated instrumentalist norms]	[Secular norms reiterated]
Liberal counter-elite "Democratic Society" Caudillos Guerrillas Bourgeoisie I	Bourgeoisie II Settlers Political parties	Socialist counter-elite University students Trade unions Guerrillas	Entrepreneurs Technocracy Middle class	Neo-socialist counter-elites Students Workers Peasants Guerrilla groups, juntas, commandos, etc.
Communal Closed	Communal Closed	Regional Semi-open	Metropolitan Semi-open	Metropolitan Open
10. Commerce 11. Steam 12. Slope cultivation (tobacco)	13. Industry 14. Railroad 15. Communication 16. Slope cultivation (coffee, etc.)	17. Heavy industry 18. Combustion engine 19. Air transport 20. Mechanized agriculture	21. Advanced modern science 22. Transistor 23. Automation 24. Modern technical defense	

Notes

Chapter Two. The Refraction of the Social Order

1. Smelser formulates his "theory of collective behavior" within the framework of the theory of social action in a manner parallel to that realized here. However, he recognizes that the "components of social action" constitute a hierarchy according to "their importance in the integration of the *social order*" (my italics). On the other hand, the theory of social action leads to the use of the concept of social system that Smelser follows and that is avoided in this book because of the monistic dangers and the closed circuit that it incurs, apart from being based on dubious units that complicate projective explanations of society. This has given rise to polemics and scientific disorientation (cf. Moore 1966; Cahnman and Boskoff 1964, 10).

For this reason, the theoretical framework of the concept of social order has been preferred here to that of "structure" or "society" because both these concepts have specific references in modern sociological literature, tending to be employed in the more restricted context of the social system. Also, concepts related to social order such as "civilization" and "culture" have been discarded because they denote even more general entities than social orders as they are conceived here. Thus, within the same context of Western civilization or culture, three social orders have been experienced in Colombia since the Spanish conquest until today.

2. The elements that form subversion are responses to the opposite condition and are therefore grouped in four categories that correspond to those of tradition. This does not imply that there exists a dual reality or dichotomy that gives rise to the well-known polar typologies. Within the refraction of the social order it is possible to conceive of different degrees of acuteness of the subversion, and even the case of assimilation or cooption of groups by one side or the other, ideologi-

cal adjustments, or similar phenomena. However, for the purposes of analysis of the phenomenon of social change in Colombia and in Latin America in general, especially today, paying direct attention to the concrete extreme of subversion makes it possible to locate, isolate, and examine the most pertinent social facts. Future investigations may probe the refraction of the social order that lies between the two extremes which clearly oppose each other in a subversion.

3. The search for evidence on this phenomenon in other historical periods and in diverse countries, using the same framework, gives an answer to the just criticism of Blumer (1966) who observes the near lack of seriousness of some monographs that pretend to study "development," the meaning of which evades them because their authors do not study its historical background. Thus, this concept should not be made synonymous with modernization even though the step toward a concrete type of modernization, following a capitalist or socialist model or a model indigenous to Latin America, may be one of the goals of many contemporary societies or of the designs prepared by the ideologues and planners of our times.

4. The systematic study by the author of the phenomenon of socioeconomic change in Colombia covers the period from 1955 to the date of writing. During this period empirical studies were carried out (individually or in collaboration with others) in various places, some of which gave origin to publications. In Colombia they were: the central municipalities of Boyacá; Buga and Siloé (Valle); San José de Albán and Consacá (Nariño); Líbano, Cunday, and Villarrica (Tolima); Yarumal and Piedrasblancas (Antioquia); Tolú (Córdoba); Sucre (Bolívar); the central municipalities of Chocó; Candelaria, Manatí, and El Bosque (Atlántico); San Pedro de Arimena (Meta); Leticia (Amazonas); Fómeque, Manta, Machetá, and Chocontá (Cundinamarca).

The author has maintained contact with the community of Chocontá and its neighborhood, Saucío in Cundinamarca, since 1950 when he first studied them. (The reports of that first contact with the rural reality were published in 1955 and 1961.) Three complete surveys were made in Saucío (1958, 1961, and 1964) in a search for data and measurements concerning the phenomenon of social change, and the author participated actively in the processes of change in an effort to direct them toward development goals. There are partial reports (Fals Borda 1959, 1961b, 1965a) published. The last study of the series (1965a) presents the counter-norm theme for the first time and analyzes statistically the change in attitudes among rural workers by groups according to their land-tenure relationships. Subsequent reports, based on the data gathered on the site, are concretely related to the frame of reference presented in this book (which was not developed to its final form until 1966) and will test the hypotheses derived from it.

5. Owing to the importance that utopias originating in Europe have had for the transformation of the social orders of Colombia, the present work inevitably stresses the exogenous factors of change. This does not mean to say that the elements of internal change are not important, and in fact it may be observed that, even though the ideological source of the change may be found abroad, the local mechanisms that autonomously translate those ideas to the national context with their own endogenous dynamic are analyzed as well. The processes are different in other countries of the Americas and merit special treatment.

6. This was the first integral, modern study of the Colombian nation to combine history with sociology, economics, and social psychology. Similar later studies (such as those of Nieto Arteta, Montaña Cuéllar, García, Liévano Aguirre, Hernández Rodríguez, Gómez Hurtado, Jaramillo Uribe, and so forth) are less ambitious although equally important (see bibliography).

Chapter Three. The Rise and Decline of the Chibchas

1. The word *sybyn* is found in: *Gramática, vocabulario, catecismo y confesionario de la Lengua Chibcha*, compiled on the basis of the original by Padre Bernardo de Lugo by Ezequiel Uricoechea (1871, 127). It means "captain" and, by extension, *capitanía* as used by the Spanish to designate a large extension of land under the control of a "captain."

2. It is desirable to avoid using the terms "Indian," "native," "primitive," and "tribal" to designate this order because these have connotations which are negative or which imply inferiority in relation to other orders. This is unproductive theoretically and does not reflect the reality of specific aspects of the societies under study. Furthermore, it would not respect the rule of seeing history insofar as possible from the viewpoint of the common people, in this case from the perspective of the conquered race.

Use of the term "Chibcha" does not seem to be justified for denoting a culture or social organization, the prevalence of which was critical for the order with which we are concerned. It would be as if the term "Western" were employed to refer to the seigniorial order, which would thereby become lost in the ocean of meanings of this complex cultural entity.

Chapter Four. Formation of the Seigniorial Order

1. This is a component of "cultural inertia" or of the intrinsic tendency to preserve and observe customs merely because they exist. Therefore it involves a certain "non-rational" sense from the secularist point of view. In reality it is a rationality conceived in terms of the

seigniorial order, which is prescriptive; Becker calls it "prescriptive rationality" (1957, 136–47, 156). Note that behavior may also be rational in other normative, organizational, or technological aspects within the seigniorial order.

2. On the other hand, perhaps owing to the nature of the land and the quality of the seeds, the use of the scythe for reaping grain was not successful; this task was limited to the small sickle. But historical data to prove this statement have not been encountered. However, the fact is that even today the more efficient scythe is hardly used (Fals Borda 1958).

Chapter Five. Subversion and Frustration in the Nineteenth Century

1. The author was unable to verify the existence of the book that the most well-known historians allege to be the work of Montjoie, *Historia de la Asamblea Constituyente de Francia* (Henao and Arrubla 1952, 311). According to the presentation of Montjoie in the English edition of his *History of the Conspiracy of Maximilian Robespierre* (1796, A-2), he wrote only *L'ami du Roi* and *Les causes et commencement de la Revolution* during the early days of the French Revolution, *History of the Conspiracy of Orleans*, and the books written about the royal couple years later. Nariño himself never specified his source for the Declaration (Posada and Ibáñez 1903, 51–110).

Chapter Seven. Subversion and Frustration in the Twentieth Century

1. Owing to his contacts since 1950 with the rural neighborhood of Saucío in the Cundinamarca-Boyaca altiplano, the author has attempted to document this trend of the seigniorial order toward instrumentalism. He tried to measure it statistically on the basis of synchronic value scales applied in different years. The preliminary study entitled "Pautas conservadoras en el salto a propietario," presented in the Seminar on Agrarian Problems of Latin America under the auspices of the National Center of Scientific Research (Paris, October 11–17, 1965), includes the results of that measuring which used agrarian land-holding groups. The twelve variables employed in the statistical analysis were conceived within the instrumental normative framework presented in this book.

According to this study, the neighborhood of Saucío was still predominately seigniorial-bourgeois in 1950, with an index of instrumentalism of 0.30 (which confirms the anthropological and sociological study carried out at that time). The index rose to 0.55 in 1961 and to 0.58 in 1964. The 1950 index tells us how slowly the changes were produced in the Colombian countryside until then, since the first clear impacts of instrumentalism had been felt in the country since the beginning of the century. This demonstrates an organizational failure in the subversive diffusion of 1925 since the political movements begun were unable to reach the peasantry with all their effectiveness. But the trend was already defined and the direction was toward greater instrumentalism, as the higher indices of 1961 and 1964 demonstrate. This trend becomes even clearer if the neighborhood is analyzed according to land-holding sub-groups. The sub-group of young proprietors who were beginning their entrepreneurial cycle, be it through inheritance or through purchase of land, had an index of instrumentalism of 0.67 in 1964. There were significant differences between them and other sub-groups according to the Q test of association and the Chi square test. This figure is interesting because it represents the attitudes of the sub-group that is taking or has taken the positions of authority in the locality. They reveal themselves to be a group that has radically departed from the patterns of the seigniorial-bourgeois order, reflected in their improved agricultural practices and in a new type of socialization.

Other studies by the author which document or describe the transition of the peasantry toward instrumental secularism are those of 1956 (on passivity), 1959a (on theory and facts), 1959b (on Nariño), and 1960 (on agrarian reform).

Chapter Nine. Reiteration of the Utopia

1. The idea on which this secular pluralism is based has its origins in the concept of *koinonia* (community), the result of a "pact between the Deity and Man" such as that which emerged from Moses' subversion in Egypt. Once the idea of the community was broadened until it embraced all races, nations, and tongues. Later, it was the Christian apostles who made this teletic conception of the original idea of "community" their own, applying it in practice through overcoming the barriers between Jew and gentile, man and woman, Greek and barbarian, as an anticipation of the unity of all men (Castillo 1967). Today *koinonia* seeks to promote a sense of ecumenism or universal brotherhood (cf. Visser't Hooft 1966) and, for such purpose, the "pluralistic community" has three principles: love, freedom (justice), and wisdom, which become a "theophany" or "temple of God" (Verghese 1966, 373–81). This is a goal toward which Christians should move, as well as the believers of other faiths (Houtart 1964). It is the visionary goal that indirectly led Father Torres to take a defined ideological position in relation to the country and the society, as we shall see. This is true even though, paradoxically, he himself was moving toward anti-pluralist attitudes required by the necessity of organizing an independent homogeneous party. He became aware of the unrealizable quality of his utopia shortly before joining the guerrilla group of the Army of National Liberation (ELN) in Santander in late October, 1965 (Guzmán 1967).

Bibliography

Aguado, Pedro de, 1906, *Recopilación historial*. Bogotá: Imprenta Nacional.

Agudelo Villa, Hernando, 1966. "Hacia una revolución por consentimiento," *El Espectador* (August 20th).

Ancízar, Manuel, 1942. *Peregrinación de Alpha*. Bogotá: Editorial ABC.

Andrade Valderrama, Vicente, 1966. "Quién es responsable de la tragedia de Camilo Torres?" *Revista Javeriana*, 65, pp. 177–81.

André Edouard, 1884. "América equinoccial (Colombia-Ecuador)," in *América pintoresca: descripción de viajes al Nuevo Continente*. Barcelona: Montaner y Simón, Editores.

Anonymous, 1965. *La Nueva Prensa*, No. 134 (July 19), pp. 22–23.

Anonymous, 1966. *Acción Liberal*.

Anonymous, 1967. *Somatén*. Bogotá, No. 2 (February 1967).

Arboleda, Gustavo, 1933. *Historia contemporánea de Colombia*, vol. I. Cali: Editorial América.

Arcila Farías, Eduardo, 1946. *Economía colonial de Venezuela*. México: Fondo de Cultura Económica.

Arensberg, Conrad M., 1961. "The Community as Object and as Sample," *American Authropologist*, 63, No. 2, pp. 241–64.

Athayde, Tristão de, 1966. "Exponentes de la nueva cristiandad," *Tercer Mundo*. Bogotá. Nos. 29–30 (September-October), p. 13.

Ballesteros y Beretta, Antonio, 1944. *Historia de España y su influencia en la historia universal*. Barcelona: Salvat Editores.

Barber, Willard F. and C. Neale Ronning, 1966. *Internal Security and Military Power: Counterinsurgency and Civic Action in Latin America*. Columbus: Ohio State University Press.

Barnes, Harry Elmer, 1952. *Society in Transition*. Englewood Cliffs, New Jersey: Prentice-Hall, Inc.

Barnett, H. G., 1953. *Innovation: the Basis of Cultural Change*. New York: McGraw-Hill Book Company.

Bateson, Gregory, 1958. *Naven: A Survey of the Problems Suggested by a Composite Picture of the Culture of a New Guinea Tribe.* Stanford: Stanford University Press.

Becker, Howard, 1957. "Current Sacred-Secular Theory and Its Development," in H. Becker and A. Boskoff (eds.), *Modern Sociological Theory.* New York: The Dryden Press, pp. 133–85.

Becker, Howard, 1960. "Normative Reactions to Normlessness," *American Sociological Review*, 25, No. 6, pp. 803–10.

Bendix, Reinhard and Bennett Berger, 1959. "Images of Society and Problems of Concept Formation in Sociology," in L. Gross (ed.), *Symposium on Sociological Theory.* Evanston: Row, Peterson and Company, pp. 92–118.

Bergson, Henri, 1930. *L'evolution créatrice.* Paris: Librerie Félix Alcan.

Bierstedt, Robert, 1959. "Nominal and Real Definitions in Sociological Theory," in L. Gross (ed.), *Symposium on Sociological Theory.* Evanston: Row, Peterson and Company, pp. 121–44.

Bishko, Charles J., 1952. "The Peninsular Background of Latin American Cattle Ranching," *Hispanic American Historical Review*, 32, pp. 509–16.

Blumer, Herbert, 1966. "The Idea of Social Development," *Studies in Comparative International Development*, II, No. 1.

Boskoff, Alvin, 1953. "Postponement of Social Decision in Transitional Society," *Social Forces*, 31, No. 3, pp. 229–34.

Boskoff, Alvin, 1959. "Social Indecision: A Dysfunctional Focus of Transitional Society," *Social Forces*, 37, No. 4, pp. 305–11.

Boskoff, Alvin, 1964a. "Recent Theories of Social Changes," in W. J. Cahnman and A. Boskoff (eds.), *Sociology and History.* New York: Free Press of Glencoe, pp. 140–57.

Boskoff, Alvin, 1964b. "Social Indecision in Two Classical Societies," in W. J. Cahnman and A. Boskoff (eds.), *Sociology and History.* New York: Free Press of Glencoe, pp. 246–57.

Bottomore, T. B., 1964. *Elites and Society.* New York: Basic Books, Inc.

Briceño, Manuel, 1878. "La Revolución 1876–1877," *Recuerdos para la historia.* Bogotá: Imprenta Nueva.

Brinton, Crane, 1952. *The Anatomy of Revolution.* Englewood Cliffs, New Jersey: Prentice-Hall, Inc.

Broadbent, Silvia M., 1964a. *Los Chibchas: Organización socio-política.* Bogotá: Facultad de Sociología.

Broadbent, Silvia M., 1964b. "Agricultural Terraces in Chibcha Territory, Colombia," *American Antiquity*, 29, No. 4, pp. 501–04.

Bushnell, David, 1966. *El Régimen de Santander en la Gran Colombia.* Bogotá: Facultad de Sociología.

Cahnman, Werner J. and Alvin Boskoff, 1964. "Sociology and History: Reunion and Rapprochement," in Cahnman & Boskoff (eds.), *Sociol-*

ogy and History: Theory and Research. New York: Free Press of Glencoe, pp. 1–18.

Camacho Roldán, Salvador, 1889. "Prólogo," in *Manuela* by Eugenio Díaz, I, pp. i–xv. Paris: Garnier Hermanos.

Camacho Roldán, Salvador, 1892. *Escritos varios*. Bogotá: Librería Colombiana.

Camacho Roldán, Salvador, 1893. *Escritos varios*. Second Series. Bogotá: Librería Colombiana.

Camacho Roldán, Salvador, 1923. *Memorias*. Bogotá: Librería Colombiana.

Camus, Albert, 1951. *L'homme révolté*. Paris: Gallimard.

Canal Ramírez, Gonzalo and Jaime Posada, 1955. *La crisis moral colombiana*. Bogotá: Editorial Antares.

Cané, Miguel, 1907. *Notas de viaje sobre Venezuela y Colombia*. Bogotá: Imprenta de la Luz.

Casas, Bartolomé de las, 1929. *Historia de las Indias*. Barcelona.

Castellanos, Juan de, 1886. *Historia del Nuevo Reino de Granada*. Madrid: A. Pérez Dubrull.

Castillo, Gonzalo, 1967. Letter to the author (January 17th).

CEPAL, 1955. "The Economic Development of Colombia." Bogotá (mimeographed edition).

Comte, Auguste, 1851–1854. *Systéme de politique positive, ou traité de sociologie instituant la religion de l'humanité*. Paris: L. Mathias.

Cooley, Charles Horton, 1902. *Human Nature and the Social Order*. New York: Charles Scribner's Sons.

Cooley, Charles Horton, 1909. *Social Organization*. New York: Charles Scribner's Sons.

Coser, Lewis F., 1956. *The Functions of Social Conflict*. New York: The Free Press of Glencoe.

Costa Pinto, L. A., 1963. *La sociología del cambio y el cambio de la sociología*. Buenos Aires: Eudeba.

Cottrell, Fred, 1955. *Energy and Society*. New York: McGraw-Hill, Inc.

Cuervo, Angel and Rufino José Cuervo, 1954. "Vida de Rufino Cuervo y noticias de su época," in *Obras de Rufino José Cuervo*. Bogotá Instituto Caro y Cuervo.

Cuervo, Rufino José, 1914. *Apuntaciones críticas al lenguaje bogotano*. Paris: R. Roger & F. Chernoviz.

Currie, Lauchlin, 1950. *The Basis of a Development Program for Colombia: Report of a Mission*. Washington: International Bank for Reconstruction and Development.

Dahrendorf, Ralf, 1958. "Toward a Theory of Social Conflict," *The Journal of Conflict Resolution*, II, No. 2, pp. 170–83.

Dahrendorf, Ralf, 1959. *Class and Class Conflict in Industrial Society*. Stanford: University Press.

D'Antonio, William V. and Frederick B. Pike, 1964. *Religion, Revolution and Reform: New Forces for Change in Latin America*. New York: Frederick A. Praeger.

Departamento Técnico de Seguridad Social Campesina, 1956. *Caldas: Estudio de su situación geográfica, económica y social*. Bogotá: Empresa Nacional de Publicaciones.

Deutschmann, Paul J. and Orlando Fals Borda, 1963. *Communication and Adoption Patterns in an Andean Village*. San José: Programa Interamericano de Información Popular.

Devanandan, P. D. and M. M. Thomas (eds.), 1960. *Christian Participation in Nation Building*. Bangalore: Christian Institute for the Study of Religion and Society.

De Vries, Egbert, 1961. *Man in Rapid Social Change*. Geneva: World Council of Churches.

Díaz, Eugenio, 1889. *Manuela*. 2 volumes. Paris: Garnier Hermanos.

Díaz del Castillo, Bernal, 1943. *Historia verdadera de la conquista de la Nueva España*. Mexico.

Dilthey, Wilhelm, 1922. "Einleitung in die Geisteswissenschaften. Versuch einer Grundlegung für das Studium der Gesellschaft u. der Geschichte," in *Gesammelte Schriften*. I. Leipzig, Berlin.

Duque Gómez, Luis, 1963. *Reseña Arqueológica de San Agustín*. Bogotá: Imprenta Nacional.

Durkheim, Emile, 1897. *Le Suicide*. Paris, F. Alcan.

Edel, Abraham, 1959. "The Concept of Levels in Social Theory," in L. Gross (ed.), *Symposium on Sociological Theory*. Evanston: Row, Peterson & Company, pp. 167–95.

Eder, Phanor V., 1959. *El Fundador, Santiago M. Eder*. Bogotá: Editorial Antares.

Eisenstadt, S. N., 1954. "Reference Group Behavior and Social Integration: An Explorative Study," *American Sociological Review*, 19, No. 2, pp. 175–85.

Eisenstadt, S. N., 1964. *From Generation to Generation: Age Groups and Social Structure*. New York: The Free Press of Glencoe.

Ellul, Jacques, 1964. *The Technological Society*. London: Jonathan Cape.

Emerson, Alfred E., 1956. "Homeostasis and Comparison of Systems," in R. R. Grinker (ed.), *Toward a Unified Theory of Human Behavior*. New York: Basic Books, Inc., pp. 147–63.

Engels, Friedrich, 1885. "History of the Communist League," in Engels, *Germany: Revolution and Counter-Revolution*. New York: International Publishers, Appendix I, pp. 120–31.

Engels, Friedrich, 1925. "Introduction" to Karl Marx, *The Class Struggles in France (1848–50)*. New York: International Publishers, pp. 9–30.

Engels, Friedrich, 1933. *Germany: Revolution and Counter-Revolution.* New York: International Publishers.

Erasmus, Charles J., 1961. *Man Takes Control: Cultural Development and American Aid.* Minneapolis: University of Minnesota Press.

Etzioni, Amitai and Eva Etzioni (eds.), 1964. *Social Change: Sources, Patterns and Consequences.* New York: Basic Books, Inc.

Fals Borda, Orlando, 1953. "Notas sobre la evolución del vestido campesino en la Colombia central," *Revista Colombiana de Folklore,* Segunda Epoca, No. 2, pp. 139–47.

Fals Borda, Orlando, 1955. *Peasant Society in the Colombian Andes.* Gainesville: University of Florida Press, 2nd. ed., 1962.

Fals Borda, Orlando, 1956. "El campesino cundi-boyacense: conceptos sobre su pasividad," *Revista de Psicología,* I, No. 1, pp. 74–83.

Fals Borda, Orlando, 1957. *El hombre y la tierra en Boyacá.* Bogotá: Editorial Antares.

Fals Borda, Orlando, 1958. "La introducción de nuevas herramientas agrícolas en Colombia: resultados de varios experimentos agrosociológicos," *Agricultura Tropical,* 14, No. 1, pp. 23–44.

Fals Borda, Orlando, 1959a. *La teoría y la realidad del cambio sociocultural en un sistema social rural.* Bogotá: Facultad de Sociología, Monografía No. 2.

Fals Borda, Orlando, 1959b. "El vínculo con la tierra y su evolución en el Departamento de Nariño," *Revista de la Academia Colombiana de Ciencias Exactas, Fisicas y Naturales,* 10, No. 41.

Fals Borda, Orlando, 1960. "La Reforma Agraria," *Revista de la Academia Colombiana de Ciencias Exactas, Fisicas y Naturales,* 11, No. 42.

Fals Borda, Orlando, 1961a. *Campesinos de los Andes.* Bogotá: Editorial Iqueima.

Fals Borda, Orlando, 1961b. *Acción comunal en una vereda colombiana.* Bogotá: Facultad de Sociología, Monografía No. 4.

Fals Borda, Orlando, 1962. *La Educación en Colombia.* Bogotá: Facultad de Sociología.

Fals Borda, Orlando, 1965a. "La esencia de la transformación rural: Estudio de una comunidad." Bogotá: Facultad de Sociología (mimeographed).

Fals Borda, Orlando, 1965b. "Violence and the Break-Up of Tradition in Colombia," in Claudio Veliz (ed.), *Obstacles to Change in Latin America.* London: Oxford University Press, pp. 188–205.

Fernandes, Florestan, 1960. "Atitudes e motivações desfavoráveis ao desenvolvimento," in Centro Latinoamericano de Pesquisas em Ciências Sociais, *Resistências à mudança: fatôres que impedem ou dificultam o desenvolvimento.* Rio de Janeiro: Editôra Lioro S.A., pp. 219–59.

Fluharty, Vernon Lee, 1957. *Dance of the Millions.* Pittsburgh: University of Pittsburgh Press.

Franco-Isaza, Eduardo, 1957. *Las guerrillas del llano.* Caracas.

Foster, George M., 1960. *Culture and Conquest: America's Spanish Heritage.* New York: Werner-Gren Foundation for Anthropological Research.

Foster, George M., 1962. *Traditional Cultures: and the Impact of Technological Change.* New York: Harper & Brothers.

Frank, Lawrence K., 1956. "Social Systems and Culture," in Roy R. Grinker (ed.), *Toward a Unified Theory of Human Behavior.* New York: Basic Books, Inc., pp. 201–22.

Frei Montalva, Eduardo, 1964. "Paternalism, Pluralism, and Christian Democratic Reform Movements in Latin America," in William V. D'Antonio & Frederick B. Pike (eds.), *Religion, Revolution and Reform: New Forces for Change in Latin America.* New York: Frederick A. Praeger, pp. 25–40.

Friede, Juan, 1944. *El Indio en lucha por la tierra.* Bogotá: Ediciones Espiral Colombia.

Furtado, Celso, 1959. *Formação econômica do Brasil.* Rio de Janeiro: Editôra Fundo de Cultura.

Furtado, Celso, 1961. *Desenvolvimento e subdesenvolvimento.* Rio de Janeiro. Editôra Fundo de Cultura.

Furtado, Celso, 1965. "Development and Stagnation in Latin America: A Structuralist Approach," *Studies in Comparative International Development,* I, No. 11.

Furtado, Celso, 1966. "Hacia una ideología del desarrollo," *El Trimestre Económico.* Mexico, 33, No. 131.

Fussel, G. E., 1952. *The Farmers Tools, 1500–1900: The History of British Farm Implements, Tools and Machinery Before the Tractor Came.* London: Andrew Melrose.

Galindo, Aníbal, 1880. *Estudios económicos y fiscales.* Bogotá: Imprenta a cargo de H. Andrade.

Galindo, Aníbal, 1900. *Recuerdos históricos: 1840 a 1895.* Bogotá: Imprenta de la Luz.

Ganivet, Angel, 1923. *Idearium Español.* Madrid: Suárez.

García, Antonio, 1953. *La revolución de los pueblos débiles.* Bogotá: Fondo Socialista de Publicaciones.

García, Antonio, 1955. *Gaitán y el problema de la revolución colombiana.* Bogotá: Cooperativa de Artes Gráficas.

García, Antonio, 1961. "Colombia: esquema de una república señorial," *Cuadernos Americanos,* México, 20, No. 119, pp. 76–133.

García, Genaro, 1907. *El clero de México durante la dominación española.* México: Vda. de C. Bouret.

García Cadena, Alfredo, 1943. *Unas ideas elementales sobre problemas colombianos.* Bogotá.

Geertz, Clifford, 1963. *Peddlers and Princes: Social Change and Eco-*

nomic Modernization in Two Indonesian Towns. Chicago: University of Chicago Press.

Gellner, Ernest, 1965. *Thought and Change.* Chicago: University of Chicago Press.

Germani, Gino, 1962. *Política y sociedad en una época de transición.* Buenos Aires: Editorial Paidós.

Gilmore, Robert Louis, 1956. "New Granada's Socialist Mirage," *Hispanic American Historical Review*, 36, pp. 192–203.

Gómez Hurtado, Alvaro, 1958. *La revolución en América.* Barcelona: Editorial AHR.

Goode, William J., 1960. "A Theory of Role Strain," *American Sociological Review*, 25, No. 4, pp. 483–96.

Goodenough, Ward Hunt, 1963. *Cooperation in Change.* New York: Russell Sage Foundation.

Groot, José Manuel, 1889. *Historia eclesiástica y civil de Nueva Granada.* Bogotá: M. Rivas y Cía.

Guhl, Ernesto, 1953. "El aspecto económico-social del cultivo del café en Antioquia." *Revista Colombiana de Antropología*, I, No. 1, pp. 197–257.

Gutiérrez, José, 1961. *De la pseudo-aristocracia a la autenticidad: psicología social colombiana.* México: Imprenta Laura.

Gutiérrez, José, 1962. *La rebeldía colombiana.* Bogotá: Ediciones Tercer Mundo.

Guzmán, Germán, Orlando Fals Borda and Eduardo Umaña Luna, 1962 and 1964. *La Violencia en Colombia.* Bogotá: Facultad de Sociología & Ediciones Tercer Mundo, 2 volumes.

Guzmán, Germán, 1967. *Camilo: Presencia y destino.* Bogotá: Ediciones Tercer Mundo.

Hagen, Everett E., 1962. *On the Theory of Social Change.* Homewood, Illinois: The Dorsey Press, Inc.

Hanke, Lewis, 1935. *The First Social Experiments in America.* Cambridge: Harvard University Press.

Hanke, Lewis, 1949. *The Spanish Struggle for Justice in the Conquest of America.* Philadelphia: University of Pennsylvania Press.

Harrison, John P., 1952. "The Evolution of the Colombian Tobacco Trade, to 1875," *Hispanic American Historical Review*, 32, p. 167.

Hart, Hornell, 1959. "Social Theory and Social Change," in L. Gross (ed.), *Symposium on Sociological Theory.* Evanston: Row, Peterson & Company, pp. 196–238.

Havens, A. Eugene, 1966. *Támesis: estructura y cambio. Estudio de una comunidad antioqueña.* Bogotá: Facultad de Sociología.

Havens, A. Eugene and Michel Romieux, 1966. *Barrancabermeja: conflictos sociales en torno a un centro petrolero.* Bogotá: Facultad de Sociología and Tercer Mundo.

Hegel, George Wilhelm Friedrich, 1896. *The Philosophy of Right.* London: George Bell.

Heilbroner, Robert L., 1963. *The Great Ascent: The Struggle for Economic Development in Our Time.* New York: Harper and Row.

Heinrich, Max, 1964. "The Use of Time in the Study of Social Change," *American Sociological Review,* 29, No. 3, pp. 386–97.

Hempel, Carl G. "The Logic of Functional Analysis," in L. Gross (ed.), *Symposium on Sociological Theory.* Evanston: Row, Peterson & Company, pp. 271–307.

Henao, Jesús Maria and Gerardo Arrubla, 1952. *Historia de Colombia.* Bogotá: Librería Voluntad.

Hernández Rodríguez, Guillermo, 1949. *De los Chibchas a la colonia y a la república.* Bogotá: Universidad Nacional.

Herrera Carrizosa, Guillermo, 1966. *El Espectador* (November 20th).

Hinojosa, Eduardo de, 1905. *El régimen señorial y la cuestión agraria en Cataluña durante la Edad Media.* Madrid: Victoriano Suárez.

Hirschman, Albert O., 1963. *Journeys Toward Progress.* New York: Twentieth Century Fund, Inc.

Hobbes, Thomas, 1950. *Leviathan,* New York: E. R. Dutton and Company, Inc.

Hobsbawm, Eric J., 1959. *Primitive Rebels: Studies in the Archaic Forms of Social Movements in the 19th and 20th Centuries.* Manchester, England: Manchester University Press.

Hoenigsberg, Julio, 1940. *Santander, el clero y Bentham.* Bogotá.

Höffner, Joseph, 1957. *La ética colonial española del Siglo de Oro: cristianismo y dignidad humana.* Madrid: Ediciones Cultura Hispánica.

Horowitz, Irving L., 1966. *Three Worlds of Development: The Theory and Practice of International Stratification.* New York: Oxford University Press.

Houtart, François, 1964. *The Challenge to Change: The Church Confronts the Future.* New York: Sheed and Ward.

Ingenieros, José, 1922. *Por la unión Latino Americana* (Speech made on October 11th at a banquet given by Argentine writers in honor of José Vasconcelos). Buenos Aires: L. J. Kosso & Cía.

Inquietudes, 1965. *El "caso" del Padre Camilo Torres.* Bogotá: Tercer Mundo.

Jaguaribe, Helio, 1966. "Political Models and National Development in Latin America." Study presented at the VI Congreso Interamericano de Planificación, Caracas, Venezuela.

Jaramillo Uribe, Jaime, 1964. *El pensamiento colombiano en el siglo XIX.* Bogotá: Editorial Temis.

Johnson, Chalmers, 1966. *Revolutionary Change.* Boston: Little, Brown and Company.

Jovellanos, Gaspar Melchor de, 1887. *Obras escogidas.* Paris: Garnier Hermanos.

Kluckhohn, Florence, 1956. "Value Orientations," in R. R. Grinker (ed.), *Toward a Unified Theory of Human Behavior.* New York: Basic Books, Inc., pp. 83–93.

Kluckhohn, Florence and Fred L. Strodtbeck, 1961. *Variations in Value Orientations.* Evanston: Row, Peterson & Company.

Kolb, W. L., 1957. "The Changing Prominence of Values in Modern Sociological Theory," in Howard Becker & Alvin Boskoff (eds.), *Modern Sociological Theory.* New York: Dryden Press, pp. 93–132.

Kubler, George, 1946. "The Quechua in the Colonial World," in *Handbook of South American Indians.* Washington: United States Government Printing Office, II, pp. 321–75.

Lambert, Jacques, 1960. "Les obstacles au développment provenant de la formation d'une société dualiste," in Centro Latino-Americano de Pesquisas em Ciências Sociais, *Resistências à mudança.* Rio de Janeiro, pp. 27–50.

Landauer, Gustav, 1919. *Die Revolution.* Frankfurt am Main: Literarische Anstalt Rütten Loening.

La Piere, Richard T., 1965. *Social Change.* New York: McGraw-Hill Book Company.

Lasswell, Harold D., 1935. *World Politics and Personal Insecurity.* New York: McGraw-Hill, Inc.

Lasswell, Harold D., 1950. *Power and Society.* New Haven: Yale University Press.

Lasswell, Harold D. and Daniel Lerner, 1965. *World Revolutionary Elites: Studies in Coercive Ideological Movements.* Cambridge, Massachusetts, The M.I.T. Press.

Lee, Alfred M., 1945. "Levels of Culture as Levels of Social Generalization." *American Sociological Review,* 10, pp. 485–95.

Lehmann, Paul J., 1963. *Ethics in a Christian Context.* New York: Harper & Row.

Lema, Marqués de, 1927. *De la Revolución a la Restauración.* Madrid: Editorial Voluntad.

Lenin, V. I. U., 1934–1938. "The Proletarian Revolution and the Renegade Kautsky," in *Selected Works.* New York: International Publishers, VII.

Liévano Aguirre, Indalecio, 1946. *Rafael Núñez.* Bogotá: Libreria Siglo XX.

Liévano Aguirre, Indalecio, 1963. *Los grandes conflictos sociales y económicos de nuestra historia.* Bogotá: Ediciones Nueva Prensa.

Liévano Aguirre, Indalecio, 1966. *El juicio de Mosquera ante el Senado.* Bogotá: Editorial Revista Colombiana.

Lleras Restrepo, Carlos, 1966a. *El Espectador* (November 30th).

Lleras Restrepo, Carlos, 1966b. *El Tiempo* (December 13th).

Lleras Restrepo, Carlos, 1967. *El Tiempo* (January 15th).

Linton, Ralph, 1936. *The Study of Man.* New York: D. Appleton-Century.

Lipman, Aaron and A. Eugene Havens, 1965. "The Colombian Violencia: An Ex Post Facto Experiment," *Social Forces,* 44, No. 2, pp. 238–45.

Lipset, S. M. and A. Solari, (eds.), 1967. *Elites in Latin America.* New York: Oxford University Press.

Loomis, Charles P., 1960. *Social Systems: Essays on their Persistence and Change.* Princeton: D. Van Nostrand Company, Inc.

López, Alejandro, 1927. *Problemas colombianos.* Paris: Editorial Paris-América.

López de Mesa, Luis, 1934. *De cómo se ha formado la nación colombiana.* Bogotá: Libreria Colombiana.

López de Mesa, Luis, 1956. *Escrutinio sociológico de la historia colombiana.* Bogotá: Academia Colombiana de Historia.

López de Mesa, Luis, 1962. "Un historial de la violencia." *El Tiempo* (September 30th).

López Michelsen, Alfonso, 1955. *Cuestiones colombianas. (Ensayos).* México: Impresiones Modernas, S.A.

Lozano y Lozano, Carlos and Fernando de la Vega, 1939. *Quién fue Núñez?* Cartagena.

Mackay, John A., 1933. *The Other Spanish Christ.* New York: The Macmillan Company.

MacIver, Robert M., 1942. *Social Causation.* Boston: Ginn & Co.

MacIver, Robert M., 1947. *The Web of Government.* New York: The Macmillan Company.

Malthus, Thomas R., 1894. *Essay on the Principle of Population.* New York: The Macmillan Company.

Mannheim, Karl, 1941. *Ideología y Utopía.* México: Fondo de Cultura Económica.

Mannheim, Karl, 1943. *Diagnosis of our Time: Wartime Essays of a Sociologist.* London: Routledge & Kegan Paul Ltd.

Mannheim, Karl, 1950. *Freedom, Power and Democratic Planning.* New York: Oxford University Press.

Mannheim, Karl, 1958. *El hombre y la sociedad en la época de crisis.* Buenos Aires: Ediciones Leviatán.

Marías, Julián, 1949. *El método histórico de las generaciones.* Madrid: Revista de Occidente.

Mariátegui, José Carlos, 1934. *Siete ensayos de interpretación de la realidad peruana.* Lima: Librería Peruana.

Martín, Guillermo E., 1887. *Campaña del ejército del Norte en 1885.* Bogotá: Imprenta de La Luz.

Martindale, Don, 1960. *The Nature and Types of Sociological Theory.* Boston: Houghton, Mifflin Company.

Marx, Karl, 1911a. *A Contribution to the Critique of Political Economy.* Translation by N. I. Stone. Chicago: Charles H. Kerr & Company.

Marx, Karl, 1911b. "Introduction to the Critique of Political Economy," in K. Marx, *A Contribution to the Critique of Political Economy.* Chicago: Charles H. Kerr & Company, Appendix, pp. 265–312.

Marx, Karl, 1928. *The Class Struggles in France (1848–1850).* Translation by C. P. Dutt). New York: International Publishers.

Mendes de Almeida, Cándido, 1963. *Nacionalismo e desenvolvimento.* Rio de Janeiro: Instituto Brasileiro de Estudos Afro-Asiáticos.

Mendieta y Núñez, Lucio, 1959. *Teoría de la revolución.* México: Instituto de Investigaciones Sociales, Universidad Nacional.

Merton, Robert K., 1957a. *Social Theory and Social Structure.* Glencoe: The Free Press.

Merton, Robert K., 1957b. "The Role-Set: Problems in Sociological Theory," *British Journal of Sociology,* 8, No. 2, pp. 106–20.

Mesa, Darío, 1965. *Treinta años de nuestra historia.* Bogotá: Facultad de Sociología, Lectura No. 161 (mimeographed).

Míguez Bonino, José, 1966. "Christians and the Political Revolution," *Motive,* 27, No. 3, pp. 37–40.

Mill, John Stuart, 1843. *A System of Logic, Ratiocinative and Inductive.* London: J. W. Parker.

Mills, C. Wright, 1959. *The Sociological Imagination.* New York: Oxford University Press.

Misión "Economía y Humanismo," 1958. *Estudio sobre las condiciones del desarrollo de Colombia.* Bogotá: Aedita Editores.

Mojica Silva, José (ed.), 1948. *Relación de visitas coloniales.* Tunja: Imprenta Oficial.

Montaña Cuéllar, Diego, 1963. *Colombia: país formal y país real.* Buenos Aires: Editorial Platina.

Montjoie, Christophe Félix de la Touloubre (Galart), 1789. *Les causes et commencement de la Revolution.* Paris.

Montjoie, Christophe Félix de la Touloubre (Galart), 1796. *History of the Conspiracy of Maximilian Robespierre.* London: T. Egerton, Whitehall.

Moore, Wilbert E., 1963. *Social Change.* Englewood Cliffs, New Jersey: Prentice-Hall, Inc.

Moore, Wilbert E., 1966. "Social Structure and Behavior," in G. Lindzey & E. Aronson, *Handbook of Social Psychology.* Reading, Massachusetts: Addison-Wesley Publishing Company.

Morales Benítez, Otto, 1951. *Testimonio de un pueblo*. Bogotá: Antares.

Morales Benítez, Otto, 1957. *Revolución y caudillos*. Medellín: Editorial Horizonte.

Morales Benítez, Otto, 1962. *Muchedumbres y banderas*. Bogotá: Ediciones Tercer Mundo.

Mosquera, Manuel José, 1858. *Documentos para la biografía e historia del episcopado, defensa de la Iglesia*. Paris: Tipografía de Adriano Le Clere, II.

Mumford, Lewis, 1962. *The Story of Utopias*. New York: The Viking Press.

Munch, Peter A., 1956. *A Study of Cultural Change: Rural-Urban Conflicts in Norway*. Oslo: H. Aschehong & Company.

Myrdal, Gunnar, 1953. "The Relation Between Social Theory and Social Policy," *British Journal of Sociology*, 23.

Nichols, Theodore E., 1954. "The Rise of Barranquilla," *Hispanic American Historical Review*, 34, pp. 158–74.

Nieto Arteta, Luis E., 1962. *Economía y cultura en la historia de Colombia*. Bogotá: Tercer Mundo.

Novikoff, Alex B., 1945. "The Concept of Integrative Levels and Biology," *Science*, 101, pp. 209–15.

Núñez, Rafael, 1885. *La Reforma política en Colombia: colección de artículos publicados en "La Luz" de Bogotá y "El Porvenir" de Cartagena, de 1881 & 1884*. Bogotá: Imprenta de La Luz.

Ogburn, William F., 1950. *Social Change with Respect to Culture and Original Nature*. Rev. ed., New York: The Viking Press (First edition, 1922).

Ortega, Alfredo, 1932. *Ferrocarriles colombianos*. Bogotá: Imprenta Nacional.

Ortega y Gasset, José, 1923. *El tema de nuestro tiempo*. Madrid: Calpe.

Ortega y Gasset, José, 1933. *En torno a Galileo*. Madrid: Calpe.

Ortíz, Juan Francisco, 1907. *Reminiscencias (Opúsculo autobiográfico, 1808–1861)*. Bogotá: Librería Americana.

Ortíz, Venancio, 1855. *Historia de la revolución del 17 de abril de 1854*. Bogotá: Imprenta de Francisco Torres Amaya.

Osgood, Charles E., George J. Suci, and Percy H. Tannenbaum, 1957. *The Measurement of Meaning*. Urbana: University of Illinois Press.

Osorio Lazarazo, J. A., 1952. *Gaitán: vida, muerte, y permanente presencia*. Buenos Aires: Ediciones López Negri.

Ospina Vásquez, Luis, 1955. *Industria y protección en Colombia*. Medellín: E.S.F.

Ots Capdequí, José María, 1946. *El régimen de la tierra en la América Española*. Ciudad Trujillo: Editora Montalvo.

Oviedo y Valdés, Gonzalo Fernández de, 1852. *Historia general y natural de las Indias*. Madrid: Real Academia de la Historia.

Park, Robert E., 1925. *The City*. Chicago: University of Chicago Press.

Park, Robert E., 1952. *Human Communities*. Glencoe: Free Press.

Parra, Aquileo, 1912. *Memorias*. Bogotá: Imprenta de La Luz.

Parra Sandoval, Rodrigo, 1966. *El caso de Candelaria, Valle*. Bogotá: Facultad de Filosofía and Tercer Mundo.

Parsons, James J., 1949. *Antioqueño Colonization in Western Colombia*. Berkeley: University of California Press.

Parsons, Talcott, 1951. *The Social System*. Glencoe: The Free Press.

Parsons, Talcott, 1956. "The Relation Between the Small Group and the Larger Social System," in R. R. Grinker (ed.), *Toward a Unified Theory of Human Behavior*. New York: Basic Books, Inc., pp. 190–200.

Parsons, Talcott, 1956. "The Social System: A General Theory of Action," in R. R. Grinker (ed.), *Toward a Unified Theory of Human Behavior*. New York: Basic Books, Inc., pp. 55–69.

Parsons, Talcott and Neil J. Smelser, 1956. *Economy and Society*. Glencoe: Free Press.

Pérez de Barradas, José, 1950–1951. *Los Muiscas antes de la conquista española*. Madrid: Instituto Bernardino de Sahagún.

Pérez Ramírez, Gustavo, 1959. El campesinado colombiano. *Un problema de estructura*. Bogotá: Editorial Iqueima.

Piedrahita, Lucas Fernández de, 1942. *Historia general de las conquistas del Nuevo Reino de Granada*. Bogotá: Editorial ABC.

Pineda Giraldo, Roberto, 1955. *Seguridad Social Campesina: Estudio de la zona tabacalera santandereana*. Bogotá: Ministerio del Trabajo.

Posada, Eduardo, 1933. *La esclavitud en Colombia*. Bogotá.

Posada, Eduardo and Pedro M. Ibáñez (eds.), 1903. *El Precursor: Documentos sobre la vida pública y privada del General Antonio Nariño*. Bogotá: Imprenta Nacional.

Posada Gutiérrez, Joaquín, 1929. *Memorias histórico-políticas*. Bogotá: Imprenta Nacional.

Rapoport, Anatol, 1956. "Homeostasis Reconsidered," in Roy R. Grinker (ed.), *Toward a Unified Theory of Human Behavior*. New York: Basic Books, Inc., pp. 225–46.

Redfield, Robert, 1956. *Peasant Society and Culture: An Anthropological Approach to Civilization*. Chicago: University of Chicago Press.

Redfield, Robert, 1957. *The Primitive World and its Transformations*. Ithaca: Cornell University Press.

Restrepo, José Manuel, 1849. "Ensayo sobre la geografía, producciones, industria i población de la provincia de Antioquia en el Nuevo Reino de Granada," in the *Semanario de la Nueva Granada*. Paris: Libreria Castellana.

Restrepo, José Manuel, 1858. *Historia de la revolución de la República de Colombia*. Besanzon: José Jacquin.

Restrepo, José Manuel, 1952. *Historia de la Nueva Granada*, I. Bogotá: Editorial Cromos.

Restrepo, José Manuel, 1963. *Historia de la Nueva Granada*, II. Bogotá: Editorial El Catolicismo.

Restrepo, Vicente, 1895. *Los Chibchas antes de la conquista española*. Bogotá: Imprenta de La Luz.

Restrepo Sáenz, José María and Raimundo Rivas, 1928. *Genealogías de Santa Fe de Bogotá*. Bogotá: Librería Colombiana.

Ríos, Fernando de los, 1927. *Religión y estado en la España del siglo XVI*. New York: Instituto de las Españas en los Estados Unidos.

Rippy, J. Fred, 1943. "Dawn of the Railway Era in Colombia," *Hispanic American Historical Review*, 23, No. 4, pp. 650–63.

Rivas, Medardo, 1946. *Los trabajadores de tierra caliente*. Bogotá: Universidad Nacional.

Rivera y Garrido, Luciano, 1897. *Impresiones y recuerdos*. Bogotá: Librería Nueva.

Rodríguez Garavito, Agustín, 1965. *Gabriel Turbay, un solitario de la grandeza: Biografía de una generación infortunada*. Bogotá: Internacional de Publicaciones, S.A.

Rodríguez Piñeres, Eduardo, 1950. *El Olimpo Radical: ensayos conocidos e inéditos sobre su época, 1864–1884*. Bogotá: Talleres Editoriales de Librería Voluntad.

Rodríguez Plata, Horacio, 1958. *José María Obando, íntimo*. Bogotá: Editorial Sucre Ltda.

Rojas, Ricardo, 1928. *El Cristo invisible*. Buenos Aires: Libreria La Facultad.

Ryan, Bryce, 1964. "Social Values and Social Change in Ceylon," in W. J. Cahnman & A. Boskoff, *Sociology and History*. New York: Free Press of Glencoe, pp. 197–205.

Ryan, Bryce, 1965. "The Resuscitation of Social Change," *Social Forces*, 44, No. 1, pp. 1–7.

Sahlins, Marshall D. and Elman R. Service (eds.), 1960. *Evolution and Culture*. Ann Arbor: University of Michigan Press.

Samper, José María, 1861. *Ensayo sobre las revoluciones políticas y la condición social de las repúblicas colombianas*. Paris: E. Thunot & Cía.

Samper, José María, 1873. *Los partidos en Colombia*. Bogotá: Imprenta de Echeverría Hermanos.

Samper, José María, 1886. *Derecho público interno de Colombia*. Bogotá: Imprenta de La Luz.

Samper, José María, 1946–1948. *Historia de un alma*. Bogotá: Editorial Kelly.

Samper, Miguel, 1898. *Escritos político-económicos*. Bogotá: Eduardo Espinosa Guzmán.

Santa, Eduardo, 1961. *Arrieros y fundadores.* Bogotá: Editorial Cosmos.

Santa, Eduardo, 1962. *Rafael Uribe, un hombre y una época.* Bogotá: Ediciones Triángulo.

Santa, Eduardo, 1964. *Sociología política de Colombia.* Bogotá: Tercer Mundo.

Sarmiento, Domingo F., 1915. *Conflicto y armonías de las razas en América.* Buenos Aires: La Cultura Argentina.

Sauer, Carl O., 1952. *Agricultural Origins and Dispersals.* New York: American Geographical Society.

Scott, Robert E., 1967. "Political Elites and Political Modernization," in S. M. Lipset and A. Solari (eds.), *Elites in Latin America.* New York: Oxford University Press.

Shaull, Richard, 1966. "The Revolutionary Challenge to Church and Theology," Unpublished address at the World Conference on Church and Society, World Council of Churches, Geneva, C.A. No. 16.

Shaw, Jr., Carey, 1941. "Church and State in Colombia as Observed by American Diplomats, 1834–1906," *Hispanic American Historical Review,* 21.

Sheils, Howard Dean, 1964. "The Cross-Cultural Measurement of Value Orientations," M.A. Thesis. Madison: University of Wisconsin.

Shils, E., 1956. *The Torment of Secrecy.* Glencoe: The Free Press.

Silva Michelena, José A., 1967. Letter to the author (January 10th).

Silva Solar, Julio and Jacques Chonchol, 1965. *El desarrollo de la nueva sociedad en América Latina.* Santiago de Chile: Editorial Universitaria.

Simmel, Georg, 1955. *Conflict, the Web of Group-Affiliations.* Glencoe: The Free Press.

Simón, Pedro, 1953. *Noticias historiales de las conquistas de Tierra Firme en las Indias Occidentales.* Bogotá: Editorial Kelly.

Small, Albion W. and George E. Vincent, 1894. *Introduction to Sociology.* New York: American Book Company.

Smelser, Neil J., 1959. *Social Change in the Industrial Revolution: An Application of Theory to the Lancashire Cotton Industry, 1770–1840.* London: Routledge & Kegan Paul.

Smelser, Neil J., 1962. *Theory of Collective Behavior.* London: Routledge & Kegan Paul.

Smith, T. Lynn, 1948. *Land Tenure and Soil Erosion in Colombia.* Extract from the proceedings of the Inter-American Conference on the Conservation of Renewable Natural Resources. Denver, Colorado.

Smith, T. Lynn, 1953. *The Sociology of Rural Life.* New York: Harper and Brothers.

Solórzano, Juan de, 1647. *Encomienda indiana.* Madrid.

Sorokin, Pitirim A., 1957. *Social and Cultural Dynamics.* Boston: Porter Sargent.

Sorokin, Pitirim A., and Robert K. Merton, 1937. "Social Time: A

Methodological and Functional Analysis," *American Journal of Sociology*, 42, No. 5, pp. 615–29.

Soto, Foción, 1913. *Memorias sobre el movimiento de resistencia a la dictadura de Rafael Núñez, 1884–1885.* Bogotá: Arboleda y Valencia.

Spencer, Herbert, 1911. "Progress, its Law and Cause," *Westminster Review*, 1857, in Spencer, *Essays on Education, Etc.* London: J. M. Dent & Sons, pp. 153–97.

Spinden, Herbert J., 1930. *Maya Dates and What They Reveal.* New York: The Museum of the Brooklyn Institute of Arts and Sciences, Science Bulletin, IV.

Spiegel, John P., 1956. "A Model for Relationships Among Systems," in R. R. Grinker (ed.), *Toward a Unified Theory of Human Behavior.* New York: Basic Books, Inc., pp. 16–26.

Stouffer, Samuel A., 1949. "An Analysis of Conflicting Social Norms," *American Sociological Review*, 14, No. 6, pp. 707–17.

Strobel, Edward Henry, 1898. *The Spanish Revolution, 1868–1875.* Boston: Small, Maynard & Company.

Teggart, Frederick J. 1960. *Theory and Processes of History.* Berkeley: University of California Press.

Tiempo, El, 1965. May 12th.

Thompson, Laura, 1956. "The Societal System, Culture and the Community," in R. R. Grinker (ed.), *Toward a Unified Theory of Human Behavior.* New York: Basic Books, Inc., pp. 70–82.

Torres, Camilo, 1963. "La violencia y los cambios socio-culturales en las áreas rurales colombianas," in Asociación Colombiana de Sociología, *Memoria del Primer Congreso Nacional de Sociología.* Bogotá: Editorial Iqueima, pp. 94–142.

Torres, Camilo, 1966. *Biografía, plataforma, mensajes.* Medellín: Ediciones Carpel-Antorcha.

Torres, Carlos Arturo, 1935. *Idola fori.* Bogotá: Editorial Minerva, S.A.

Torres García, Guillermo, 1956. *Miguel Antonio Caro: su personalidad política.* Madrid: Ediciones Guadarrama S.L.

Touraine, Alain, 1965. *Sociologie de l'action,* Paris: Editions du Seuil.

Toynbee, Arnold J., 1947. *A Study of History.* London: Oxford University Press.

Toynbee, Arnold J., 1955. *México y el Occidente.* México: Antigua Librería Robledo.

Triana, Miguel, 1951. *La civilización Chibcha.* Bogotá: Editorial ABC. (Bogotá: Escuela Tipográfica Salesiana, 1922).

Umaña Luna, Eduardo, 1952. *Camilo Torres y el Memorial de Agravios.* Bogotá.

Umaña Luna, Eduardo, 1966. Speech in Colombia, *Anales del Congreso,* Cámara, Año IX, No. 86 (August 30th).

Umaña Luna, Eduardo, 1967. "Urgencia de un derecho social," letter to the author (February 8th).

Unamuno, Miguel de, 1922. *Andanzas y visiones españolas.* Madrid: Renacimiento.

Unamuno, Miguel de, 1945. *Mi religión y otros ensayos breves.* Buenos Aires: Espasa-Calpa, Argentina.

Urdaneta Arbeláez, Roberto, 1960. *El materialismo contra la dignidad del hombre.* Bogotá: Tall. de Editorial Lucrós.

Uribe Uribe, Rafael, 1904. "Discurso sobre el liberalismo," *Santo y Seña.* Bogotá, No. 22.

Uricoechea, Ezequiel, 1871. *Gramática, vocabulario, catecismo, etc., de la lengua Chibcha.* Paris: Maisonneuve.

Uricoechea, Fernando, 1966. "Una política para el desarrollo," *El Espectador.* Bogotá (September 23rd).

Van Leeuwen, Arend Th., 1966. "Cultural Unity and Pluralism," in E. de Vries (ed.), *Man in Community: Christian Concern for the Human in Changing Society.* New York, London: Association Press, S.C.M. Press, pp. 293–07.

Vasconcelos, José, 1930. *La raza cósmica: misión de la raza iberoamericana.* Paris: Agencia Mundial de Librería.

Vasconcelos, José, 1924. *Los últimos cincuenta años.* México.

Vega, José de la, 1913. *La Federación en Colombia (1810–1912).* Madrid: Editorial América.

Vergara y Vergara, José María, 1903. *El Precursor.* Bogotá: Imprenta Nacional.

Verghese, Paul, 1966. "Secular Society or Pluralistic Community?", in E. de Vries (ed.), *Man in Community: Christian Concern for the Human in Changing Society.* New York, London: Association Press, S. C. M. Press, pp. 359–82.

Visser't Hooft, W. A., 1966. Unpublished address delivered at the World Conference on Church and Society, World Council of Churches, Geneva, C.A. No. 5.

Von Schenck, Fr., 1953. *Viajes por Antioquia en el año de 1880.* Bogotá: Banco de la República.

Weber, Max, 1858. *The Protestant Ethic and the Spirit of Capitalism.* New York: Charles Scribner's Sons.

Weber, Max, 1922. *Wirtschaft und Gesellschaft.* Tübingen: J. C. B. Mohr.

Weber, Max, 1964. *Economía y Sociedad.* México: Fondo de Cultura Económica.

Weiss, Anita, 1968. *Tendenciás en la participación electoral en Colombia, 1935–1966.* Bogotá: Departamento de Sociología, Universidad Nacional.

Wendland, Heinz-Dietrich, 1966. "The Church and Revolution," Unpublished address at the World Conference on Church and Society, World Council of Churches, Geneva, C.A. No. 6.

White, Jr., Lynn, 1962. *Medieval Technology and Social Change.* Oxford: Clarendon Press.

Wilson, Godfrey and Monica Wilson, 1945. *The Analysis of Social Change.* Cambridge: Cambridge University Press.

Wirth, Louis, 1941. "Prefacio," in Karl Mannheim, *Ideología y Utopía.* México: Fondo de Cultura Económica, pp. xiii–xxxi.

Wood, Bryce, 1966. *The United States and Latin American Wars, 1932–1942.* New York and London: Columbia University Press.

Yinger, J. Milton, 1960. "Contraculture and Subculture," *American Sociological Review,* 25, No. 5, pp. 625–35.

Zalamea, Alberto, (ed.), 1957. *El diez de mayo.* (Documentos). Bogotá: Editorial Antares.

Zamora, Alonso de, 1945. *Historia de la provincia de San Antonino del Nuevo Reino de Granada.* Bogotá: Editorial ABC.

Zapata, Ramón, 1960. *Dámaso Zapata, o la reforma educacionista en Colombia.* Bogotá: El Gráfico Editores, Ltd.

Zavala, Silvio, 1935. *Encomienda indiana.* Madrid: Junta para Ampliación de Estudios e Investigaciones Científicas.

Zavala, Silvio, 1937. *La "Utopía" de Tomás Moro en la Nueva España.* México: Antigua Librería de Robledo, de J. Porrúa & Hijos.

Zavala, Silvio, 1947. "The American Utopia of the 16th Century," *The Huntington Library Quarterly,* 10, No. 4, pp. 337–47.

Zerda, Liborio, 1883. *El Dorado: estudio histórico, etnográfico y arqueológico de los Chibchas.* Bogotá: Silvestre y Cía.

Znaniecki, Florian, 1952. *Modern Nationalities: A Sociological Study.* Urbana: University of Illinois Press.

Index

Date Due

Date Loaned